At the Emperor's Pleasure

At The Emperor's Pleasure

Surviving Wartime Captivity in the Far East

Richard Graham

Pen & Sword
MILITARY
AN IMPRINT OF PEN & SWORD BOOKS LTD.
YORKSHIRE – PHILADELPHIA

First published in Great Britain in 2024 by
Pen & Sword Military
An imprint of
Pen & Sword Books Ltd
Yorkshire - Philadelphia

ISBN 978 1 03610 921 9

A CIP catalogue record for this book is available from the British Library

Typeset in INDIA by IMPEC eSolutions
Printed and bound in the UK by CPI Group (UK) Ltd, Croydon, CRO 4YY

Pen & Sword Books Limited incorporates the imprints of Archaeology, Atlas, Aviation, Battleground, Digital, Discovery, Family History, Fiction, History, Local, Local History, Maritime, Military, Military Classics, Politics, Select, Transport, True Crime, After the Battle, Air World, Claymore Press, Frontline Publishing, Leo Cooper, Remember When, Seaforth Publishing, The Praetorian Press, Wharncliffe Books, Wharncliffe Local History, Wharncliffe Transport, Wharncliffe True Crime and White Owl.

For a complete list of Pen & Sword titles please contact

PEN & SWORD BOOKS LIMITED
George House, Units 12 & 13, Beevor Street, Off Pontefract Road,
Barnsley, S71 1HN, UK
E-mail: enquiries@pen-and-sword.co.uk
Website: www.pen-and-sword.co.uk

or

PEN AND SWORD BOOKS
1950 Lawrence Rd, Havertown, PA 19083, USA
E-mail: Uspen-and-sword@casematepublishers.com
Website: www.penandswordbooks.com

MIX
Paper | Supporting responsible forestry
FSC® C013604

For those who did not come home

Contents

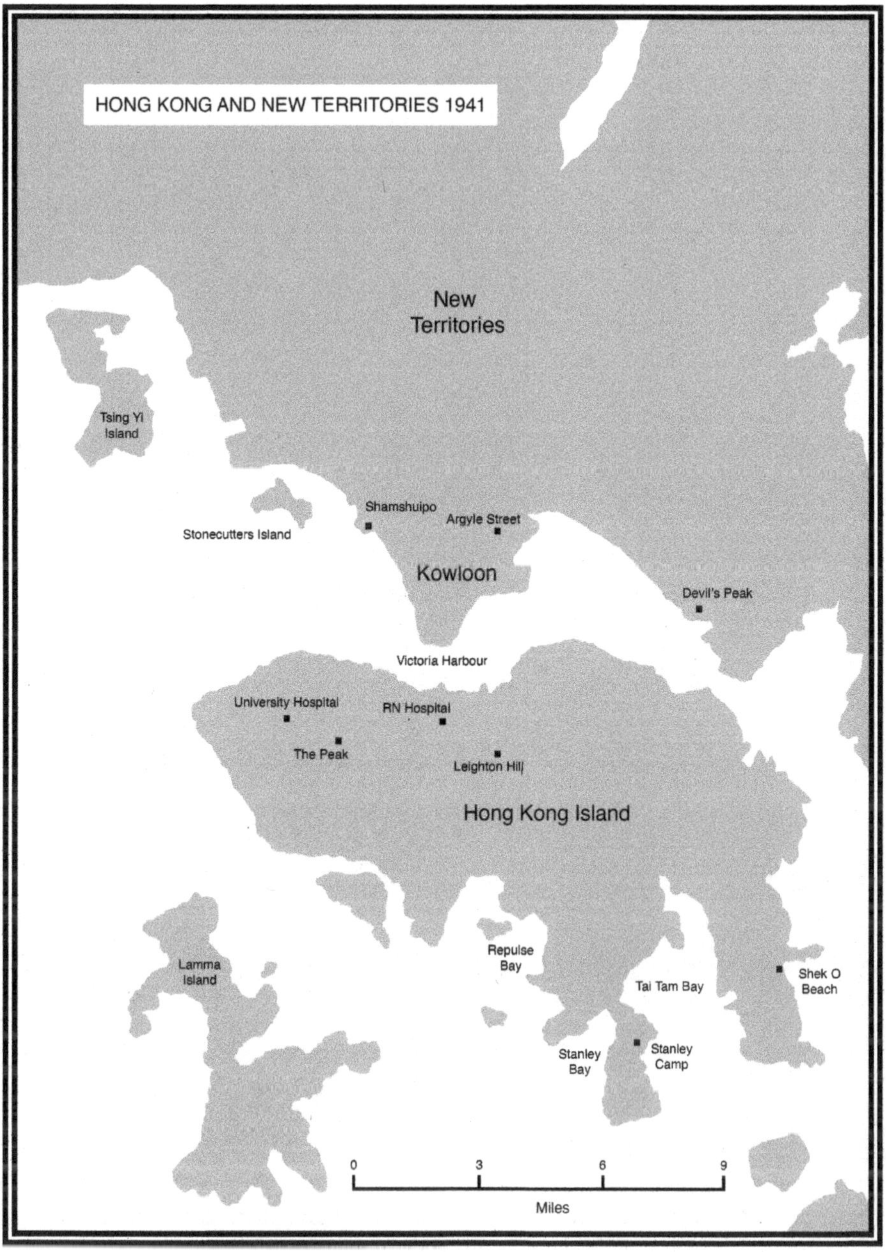

HONG KONG AND NEW TERRITORIES 1941
New Territories
Tsing Yi Island
Stonecutters Island
Shamshuipo
Argyle Street
Kowloon
Devil's Peak
Victoria Harbour
University Hospital
RN Hospital
The Peak
Leighton Hill
Hong Kong Island
Lamma Island
Repulse Bay
Tai Tam Bay
Shek O Beach
Stanley Bay
Stanley Camp
0
3
6
9
Miles

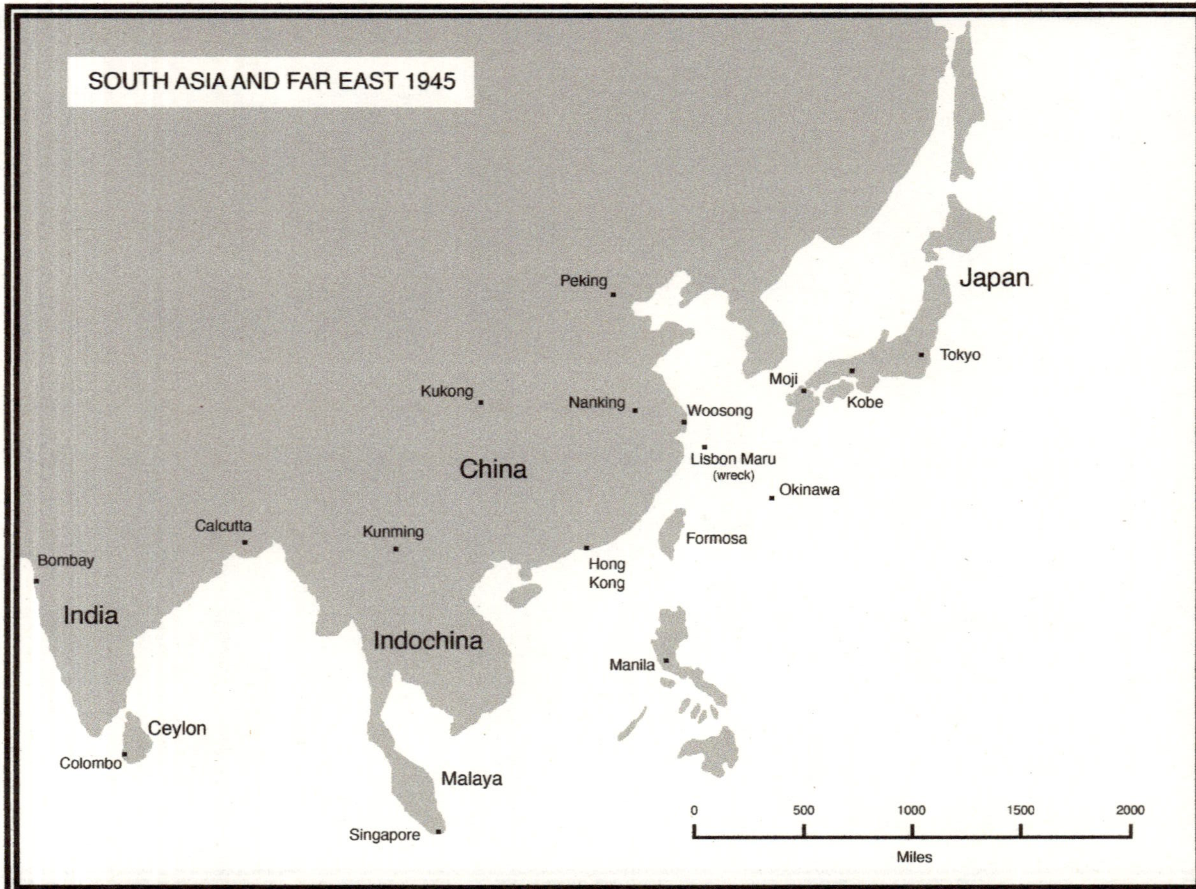
SOUTH ASIA AND FAR EAST 1945
Peking
Japan
Tokyo
Moji
Kobe
Kukong
Nanking
Woosong
Lisbon Maru
(wreck)
Okinawa
China
Calcutta
Kunming
Formosa
Bombay
Hong
Kong
India
Indochina
Manila
Ceylon
Colombo
Malaya
Singapore
0
500
1000
1500
2000
Miles

Prologue

An old man stands silent and still beside the grave they share, his eyes moist in the bitter north wind that carries the first flurries of snow across the Cairngorms and tugs mischievously at his white hair.

To get here, he has walked perhaps a mile from the station at Blair Atholl, first passing the gateway to the castle and then crossing the bridge over the Tilt. The river was running high, fast and agitated away to his right, fed by the rains of late autumn. A few minutes further, he followed the curve of a gap in the roadside stone wall where the narrow lane begins its long, straight course between the fields towards the far church that nestles against the lower slopes of a wooded hill. He paused there awhile to picture them both taking this path, hand in hand. Being that close, he felt a keen sense of walking in their footsteps. Step by step, the church came more sharply into view. It is guarded, and partly obscured, by a vast linden lime that long since surrendered the last of its leafage to the westerly gales that sweep across this wide gap between the hills. Beneath the towering tree, a wall in local stone, waist high, topped with neat, regular copings, wraps itself around the church and its cemetery. The church seems comfortable here where there has been a place of worship for more than four hundred years. It looks welcoming, too. It is the stone that gives it warmth. An artist would have to conjure up a palette of light grey with a hint of cream and the faintest blush of pink. The church is small, in keeping with the intimacy of its setting; just long enough to frame three tall, round-arched windows beneath a slated roof. An afterthought has been added to one gable in the form of a Gothic-style porch, complete with crenelated walls and a door beneath a pointed arch.

The pale grey headstone doesn't tell much of a story. It contains no epitaph, of course. 'Christopher would have insisted on that,' the old man thinks to himself. 'Modest to the end'.

The regimental badge dominates the top of the stone, and below it his military rank and decorations hint at how good a soldier Major General Christopher Man had been. It had been Christopher and not Chris; to all but his closest chums he had always made that clear. So had Topsy. She is there on the headstone as 'His wife Georgina Marr'. No more, no less. She died eleven months after him, so presumably that was how she wished to be remembered. No hint of the nickname by which everyone knew her. Come to think of it, hardly anyone would have known about the 'Georgina' at all, just as there were never many who knew even half of the story that lies behind those two engraved words 'his wife'.

The old man becomes aware of approaching footsteps. He turns to face the church and takes in a glimpse of a white clerical collar beneath a grey overcoat and matching scarf. The rector – tall, slim, middle-aged – holds out his hand in greeting.

'I hope I'm not intruding on something private. But I couldn't help being curious about what brings you here.'

The old man turns and points to the gravestone.

'They did.'

He feels the need to explain further.

'I knew them, you see. And I know their story. Not the complete story of course. They kept that to themselves. But enough to wonder at it. And to want to come and see their resting place.'

The rector shifts his gaze to the gravestone. 'I'm told they worshipped here regularly, but that was well before my time, so I never knew them. Those who did always speak of them with affection.' He gives the old man a smile of encouragement. 'So what's their story, then?'

The old man begins to speak and then pauses. 'If I hesitate, it's because the story takes some telling. It has so many strands. It is of course about Christopher and Topsy Man, but it's not only about them. To do the story justice will take a while.'

The rector places a hand on the old man's shoulder. 'Then let's take a while. We should get inside out of this wind.'

He leads the way to the porch. Once inside the church, they sit close to an electric fire and the old man begins his story.

Close to an hour has passed when they shake hands at the door.

'Are you sure I can't give you a lift to the station?'

'Thank you, but I still have an hour before the train to Perth leaves and I could do with the exercise.'

The rector, noticing the old man turn at the gate to cast one last look back towards the grave, calls after him.

'Thank you for the story. The grave will always remind me of it. And what a story! Someone should write a book about it.' The old man smiles and raises his hand in farewell. 'I did,' he replies. 'I just wanted to tell them I had.'

PART I: 1939–1940

Chapter 1

May 1940: Hong Kong

Christopher Man was in thoughtful mood as he looked around him in the Officers' Mess dining room in Nanking Barracks, Shamshuipo. Earlier that evening, he had taken his place for the silent toast, a regimental ritual which for more than a century had been repeated on 16 May in some form or other. Each year, whatever the place, successive generations of officers, warrant officers and sergeants had stood in a circle, side by side, to commemorate the fallen at Albuhera in 1811 when the regiment had earned its nickname 'The Diehards'. As was the custom, the commanding officer had addressed those present to remind them of the history of that day when Emperor Napoleon's designs on Spain and Portugal had met bloody-minded English infantrymen who refused to yield an inch of an unremarkable ridge in the undulating landscape of Extremadura.

Most of those gathered in the fading heat of a Hong Kong evening had heard the address before, but it never failed to refresh the sense of duty placed on them by their regimental inheritance. For Lanceray Newnham, this would be the last time that he would give this address and then hold the silver loving cup to his lips before inviting those present to follow him in drinking 'to the immortal memory'. It was said that the cup had been made from melting down the breastplates of those officers who had fallen during the battle all those years ago. Surviving brother officer were said to have gathered in a local inn at the end of battle and sworn that no year should pass without drinking to the memory of comrades lost on that day. Faithful to their pledge, they had met each year on Albuhera day until the time had come for them to hand the ritual on to the generations that were destined to follow them.

For those forming the solemn circle of brothers in arms, officer beside sergeant, silently drinking in their turn, the simple touch to their lips of that loving cup and the symbolic passing of it one to the other each year, was a privilege jealously guarded. More than that, it served to renew personal inner pledges to honour their forebears when the time came for them to be tested in their turn. And who knew when that time might come as, not that far to the north-east, another emperor contemplated his nation's design for more military conquest.

That evening, Christopher had handed the cup to Sergeant Frank Waldron. The regiment recruited its men from London but because much of the world was represented in that great city, the ranks of the first battalion echoed to accents from here, there and everywhere. Frank's accent placed him at the heart of the regiment; a south Londoner by birth and upbringing whose horizons prior to signing on had not extended far beyond the capital's streets. The Diehard soldiers may not all have been born within the sound of Bow Bells, but they were Cockney through and through, gifted with a distinctive spirit and spark that had served their predecessors well wherever they had been sent into battle.

Soldiers who spent their youth living off their wits amongst the stresses and temptations of city life were not the easiest to command in peacetime and if there was potential trouble near at hand, they were prone to find it. But they made fine warriors with sharply honed instincts for coping when the going got hard. 'Cockneys make the best Troopers' had been Wellington's tribute to them.

Frank Waldron was typical of them. Christopher, tall and lean, towered over him as he passed him the cup. Frank, by contrast, had the short, wiry build and alert look of a fierce scrapper who had had his tough moments during his early months in the ranks but had quickly earned the respect of his fellows since arriving in the battalion two years ago.

If Christopher was in thoughtful mood later that evening at dinner, it was because there was much for him to be thoughtful about. Three years previously, the battalion had been sent at short notice to reinforce Hong Kong in response to Japan's invasion of China followed by its rapid capture of Peking and Shanghai and its notorious rape of the southern capital, Nanking. No one could interpret what the Japanese intended once their armies reached the Chinese border with a British colony. A year later, Japanese troops had established themselves on Hong Kong's frontier along the northern edge of the New Territories, the hilly terrain that served as a buffer between China and the colony's Kowloon Peninsula and Hong Kong Island itself. The Diehards had promptly reinforced the frontier posts that were usually manned by police units.

Thinking back to those days, Christopher could recall the nervous excitement they had all felt as professional soldiers. Alarms had come and gone for a few weeks until the Japanese withdrew from the area of the frontier and it was deemed safe to hand back control of the border posts to the police. Much of the immediate tension had been eased, but the incidents had served a purpose. Looking back, it was easy to see that the initial surge of urgency which had driven the battalion on its arrival in Hong Kong to train hard for the likely battle ahead had begun to give way to thoughts that perhaps the battle would never come. The sight of their potential enemy, close up, had somehow brought the prospect of war much nearer, and in doing so had renewed motivation. It had also inspired confidence. Christopher was one of many who had taken a close look at the Japanese troops deployed along the colony's frontier and concluded that they were scruffy and poorly trained and equipped – an enemy that could be defeated in battle.

A further year had passed before this evening's Mess dinner which was being held to mark the battalion's commemoration of Albuhera and to 'dine out' Lance Newnham at the end of his two years in command. During that year, Christopher had begun to question his initial assessment of the Japanese as a potential enemy. He couldn't ignore the fact that during the first two years of the Sino-Japanese war they had inflicted defeat after defeat on the Chinese Nationalist army. Scruffy as their soldiers were, they knew how to fight and win battles. They needed to be taken seriously.

Christopher broke off his thoughts and turned to Tony Hewitt, the battalion's adjutant. Both wore the regiment's scarlet mess jackets with their distinctive, bold yellow cuffs. Over the years, red and yellow had come to symbolise the blood and sand image that Diehards had of themselves as soldiers. Both officers wore three embroidered Eversleigh Stars on each epaulette denoting their rank as captains, in Christopher's case the freshness of the third star indicating his recent promotion. They were both twenty-six years old, and had been at Sandhurst together, but Tony was the senior by a year or so. He had more dust on his boots – as colleagues would have it – having already served in Egypt and Singapore while Christopher was completing his three years at Cambridge. Christopher, conscious of his own lack of regimental experience, regarded him as a role model as well as a close friend.

'Lan will be a loss, but we should be fine,' observed Christopher, both expressing an opinion and seeking reassurance. They looked across to the centre of the table where today's and tomorrow's leadership of the battalion sat side by side. Lanceray Newnham – Lance to his wife but Lan to everyone else – was regarded with a degree of awe by his officers. It wasn't just his position as commanding officer which set him apart; there was an elusive something else about him. Perhaps his exotic parentage partly explained it. His father had met and married Ekaterina Yonova whilst serving as Military Attaché to the Russian court of Tsar Nicholas, and Lanceray had been born in India whilst the couple were accompanying the royal court on a tour there. He was a young captain in the regiment when it was deployed in 1915 to join the British Expeditionary Force in France. By 1917 he had fought at the Somme and at Arras and been awarded his Military Cross. As commanding officer, when he spoke about preparing for war, his men listened.

'We've been lucky,' replied Tony. 'Lan was the right man to get us this far, and Monkey is the right man to take us to the line.'

Their glance switched to the man at Newnham's side. Henry Moncreiff Stewart was the battalion's second-in-command and had been designated to take over command from Newnham. If war was coming, the battalion would be in good hands. 'Moncreiff' had long since given way to the nickname 'Monkey' which had been bestowed on him when a cadet at Sandhurst. At forty-six years of age he was older than most when taking command of a front-line infantry unit, but he had been an outstanding athlete and all-round sportsman in his younger days, and he could still give young officers a run for their money. He had been pitched into battle in France straight from his commissioning and by the end of the 1914–18 war he had been mentioned in dispatches three times and awarded the Military Cross. Along the way, he had been wounded but had recovered and returned to battle.

Like most of his generation of seasoned warriors, he rarely spoke of his personal experience of battle, and then only to pass on lessons learned so that mistakes could be avoided and soldiers' lives saved. But although he never paraded his proven credentials as a fighting soldier, to a man the battalion knew of them and looked up to him. And they did so with affection, too. Christopher and his fellow young officers had all taken note; in Monkey Stewart they had a natural leader with an innate ability to identify with the Cockney soldiers under his command. He wouldn't be in command of the Diehards until tomorrow, but he had already been accepted as a leader who would be 'one of us'. They would follow him wherever he led them.

There were to be no speeches at that evening's dinner, as was the regiment's strict custom. Those present would be left to reflect on their own silent tributes to their departing colonel.

The level of noise began to rise at one end of the table. Looking beyond the massive silver centrepiece and across the dense array of goblets and candelabra, Christopher noted that two of the youngest subalterns were getting especially boisterous. This was their first Albuhera Day in the regiment and, as had long been the custom, they had been initiated as Diehards in a ceremony conducted before the first call to dinner. The ritual of the ceremony was a secret strictly kept by those who had themselves undergone it. Only they would ever understand the strength with which it would bind them to their future identity as Diehards.

Christopher watched the Mess Sergeant place the port and Madeira decanters on the table. Soon the Loyal Toast would be proposed and the officers would move into the ante-room where the regimental band would play for them before the younger officers began the ritual of Mess rugby, watched with benevolent indulgence by their seniors who had seen it all before. Much later, Lance Newnham would be carried out of the Mess on the shoulders of his brother officers. He was to remain in Hong Kong on the staff of the military headquarters, but his regimental service was about to end.

Christopher gave Tony a questioning look. 'Did you know I had asked Lan for permission to get married?'

'Yes, I did. He thought I should know as adjutant. And he told me why he had refused to give it.'

Christopher thought back to what had been a tense interview only a few months back. Newnham had been forthright in his view of the matter. War was coming and Hong Kong would be no place for young brides. Come to that, the colony would be no place for any of the battalion's families. Already plans were made for them to be evacuated to Australia at short notice. Even Monkey Stewart's wife had been advised not to join him in Hong Kong.

Christopher had argued his case as forcibly as he could, but Newnham was not to be persuaded.

'Perhaps I'll have better luck with Monkey,' mused Christopher.

Tony smiled. 'I shouldn't count on it.'

Christopher found his thoughts drifting back to last autumn. It had been an eventful eight months in more ways than one.

Chapter 2

July 1939: Port Said, Egypt

Georgina Marr looked down from the upper deck of the P&O liner *Rajputana*. The scene below in Port Said harbour was alive with the colours and sounds of human activity. The narrow boats of several hawkers hugged the ship's side, their occupants calling out to passengers who lined the ship's rails far above them. A series of ropes and pulleys enabled baskets of local wares to be raised for the appraisal of would-be buyers. Deals were being negotiated in a clamour of offers and counteroffers conducted by shouts and gestures from one level to another. Immediately beyond the hawkers' boats, very young boys, near naked, splashed and waved and shouted for attention, inviting passengers to throw coins into the grey-green harbour water and then diving to retrieve them with nonchalant skill.

It was ten days since Georgina had embarked in London. Port Said was the first port of call. The ship and its passengers would spend two days in this port city before entering the Suez Canal. Beyond lay the searing heat of the Red Sea, the vastness of the Indian Ocean and a further three weeks at sea before they reached Hong Kong. For a young, newly qualified physiotherapist from Edinburgh, the pleasure of the moment and the promise of the future were almost too much.

It had all happened in a rush: a chance sight of the job advertisement in the newspaper; a week of 'shall I – shan't I'; a frantic gathering of references; an application submitted with a day to spare and then… silence for week after week. She had almost given up any hope of success when the envelope had arrived bearing an impressive On His Majesty's Service stamp. Would she please present herself for interview in ten days' time?

The letter informing her that she had been successful had left her scarcely daring to believe it could be true, and the full impact of the impending change to her life only came when weeks later a further buff envelope was opened and out fell a sailing ticket, first class no less, courtesy of the Crown Agents. 'Departure date: 14 July 1939. Port of Departure: London, England. Destination Port: Hong Kong, China. Ship name: *Rajputana*. Shipping Line: Peninsular and Oriental

Steam Navigation Company.' The excitement felt when holding that ticket for the first time had scarcely diminished and still left her breathless at times.

The voyage so far had been everything she had hoped for. The notorious Bay of Biscay had been in tranquil mood and the heat of a Mediterranean summer had been tempered by the breeze of the ship's passage.

Once through the Straits of Gibraltar via the legendary Pillars of Hercules, the journey had been set eastwards, the *Rajputana* easing her passengers from one region of the world to the next at a pace that allowed the mind and body to adjust gently, day by day.

As a young, single woman travelling unaccompanied at sea, she had embraced her freedom to choose when to have time to herself and when to accept offers of company. There had been plenty of these. It had been the same at medical college. She had a mature graciousness that other young students had soon come to recognize and admire in her. Blessed with one of those smiles that simply demanded one in return, and with a sense of fun that often bordered on the mischievous, she had been hugely popular amongst the sisterhood of trainee physiotherapists. Many a young male student had cast hopeful glances at her, drawn by those wide-set, deep brown eyes, fine, high cheekbones and a slim, athletic figure that belied the origin of her family nickname, 'Topsy', given her because she had grown like Topsy when very young.

There were several men travelling alone on the *Rajputana*. One of them had weighed her up and made his interest in her obvious, but she was well versed in the art of the firm but polite dismissal, and the message seemed to get around to others.

The mid-morning sun began to hint that the ship's top deck was no longer the place to be. The *Rajputana* was due to sail that evening and although Port Said lacked the glamour and excitement of Alexandria which they had passed in the night, there was plenty to do ashore, including lunch and a swim at the home of the British Consul. Not for the first time, Edinburgh seemed a long way away in time and distance.

*

Three weeks later, the *Rajputana* entered the long channel leading towards her berth in Hong Kong's Victoria Harbour. To the north, beyond the urban flatness of the Kowloon Peninsula, the distant hills of the New Territories hinted at the mystery and vastness of a China that was fighting for its life under the armed onslaught of imperialist Japan. To the south, the dense clutter of Hong Kong

Island's shoreline, framed by dark green hills, offered a newcomer the promise of a vibrant new life beyond what the eye could see. The scene was enough to drag the mind away from thoughts of war, whether close-by here in the Orient or far to the west where Hitler's Germany was casting eyes around for more *Lebensraum*.

Georgina was joined at the ship's rail by Margaret Lane. Married to a civil servant in the Hong Kong administration, she was returning to the colony, the death of her father having required her to travel to England to sort out his affairs. She and Georgina had provided each other with relaxed, unintrusive company during the long voyage. Margaret could see that, like most first-time arrivals in Hong Kong, Georgina seemed overwhelmed by the scene.

'It's gorgeous, isn't it? The harbour. It's one of Hong Kong's best treasures. They call it the Place of the Sweet Lagoons. This is the third time I've made the voyage here and the arrival in the harbour is just as striking as the first time.'

'It's truly breathtaking,' agreed Georgina. Looking towards Hong Kong Island, she pointed to a lush, green hill that towered above the western entrance to the harbour.

'That hill is so impressive; it must have a name.'

Margaret smiled. 'That's The Peak. You should see it at night when it is all lit up and sparkling. I've heard it described as being draped by the gods with a necklace of diamonds. Catch a rich husband and you could find yourself living up there.'

The *Rajputana* picked her cautious way between the buoys marking the approved channel, accompanied at a respectful distance by majestic, red-sailed junks which seemed to have assumed for themselves the role of serene outriders. By way of contrast, an ill-disciplined fleet of nimble sampans left it to the last moment before they scattered from the ship's path, as if resenting this intrusion into their routine passage between Kowloon and Hong Kong Island.

Watching the activity in the harbour, Georgina reflected on her still-fresh memories of a journey that had seldom strayed far from the reach of the British Empire. From Port Said, the *Rajputana* had headed south-east through the Red Sea to Aden, all dust and scorching Arabian sun, then north-east across the Arabian Sea until Bombay and its teeming millions had welcomed them to India. Then it had been south-east again to Colombo before heading east across the Andaman Sea to Singapore, the gateway to the Far East.

And here, at last, she was in Hong Kong. She scanned the quayside beyond the covered gangway that Chinese coolies had rushed to its place the moment the ship had come to rest. Last evening, she had been called to the purser's office to sign for a telegram. 'Welcome to Hong Kong. Meet you in arrival hall. Luggage will follow.'

For Georgina the past thirty days or so at sea had seemed a suspension of life, so much of normality having been abandoned or put on hold. She would not have missed the sea passage for the world, but she was ready for it to end and for life to resume.

She had been recruited to teach in the Central British School in Kowloon. It was a school for the children of expatriates and had been rebuilt three years ago on its new site in the hills of Ho Man Tin. The board had taken a liking to her at interview, sensing that she was an ideal fit for their school and the pastoral role it played in the colony.

She was collected from the harbour by Jane Greig, a young teacher at the school who had herself been a new arrival only a year before. Once their taxi was clear of the passenger terminal, she gave Georgina a reassuring look.

'I know what it's like to arrive here for the first time. Your head must be spinning. The last thing you need is to be swamped with a load of advice and Hong Kong gossip from me. There'll be plenty of time for that later.'

Georgina smiled. 'Thank you. You're right. It's all a bit overwhelming. So much to take in. Just tell me where we're going.'

'We're heading for your flat in Shamshuipo. It's not far. It's near the school. I think you'll love it.'

*

Georgina opened the door to the small balcony of the flat that had been rented for her on the third floor of a new block close to the western waterfront of Kowloon. She was in luck. She had been allocated an outside room facing west. There was no escaping the humidity that greeted her as she first stepped onto the balcony but the view that greeted her was compensation enough. There, rising in a green haze across ten miles or so of glistening sea, lay the mountains and forests of Lantau Island, by far the largest of the many islands that formed part of the New Territories. A knock on the door announced the arrival of her luggage. There was unpacking to do before Jane would return in the early evening to take her to meet some of her future colleagues over welcoming drinks. Her new life was about to begin.

Chapter 3

Autumn 1939: Qingbang Island, China

Lin Agen felt a great weight being lifted from his young shoulders as he secured the family sampan in the small harbour of his fishing village on Qingbang and began to sort through what was left of his catch. It was always a relief to make it back into the sheltered harbour on the rocky coast of the island, but today he had special cause to savour it. It had been another of those days when fishing in the coastal waters of the East China Sea near Shanghai had hardly been worth the trouble. For centuries his family, and countless families like his, had gained a living from harvesting these richly productive waters. The men had fished and the women had prepared the fish for market. At the best of times it was a perilous occupation because the weather and the seas were as unpredictable and violent as anywhere, and the shoreline of jagged rocks and powerful surf waited to punish moments of carelessness when returning to the harbour, tired out at the end of a long day at sea. The dangers were high and rewards low, but it was a living after all, with scarcely any alternative for islanders such as themselves.

But these were not the best of times. The lives of these simple, island communities in the Zhoushan Archipelago had changed for the worse since the Japanese army had captured Shanghai – only a hundred miles or so to the north – two years ago. The Japanese army was now thinly spread across the vast areas of China's countryside and long coastline, but war in one form or another still visited the villages of these small islands. Only last week a force of Japanese soldiers and armed collaborators had mounted a surprise raid on Qingbang in response to acts of sabotage by Nationalist guerrillas along the mainland coastal areas of neighbouring Zhejiang province where a railway bridge had been destroyed and a military convoy attacked. In reprisal, the villagers of Qingbang had been dragged out of their beds, and their homes and boats searched. Some of them had been beaten and interrogated under suspicion of running men and weapons from one coastal area to another under cover of their fishing activity. Three boats had been burned, seemingly chosen at random, and all fishing families had had their catches of fish seized.

More frequent had been the harassment at sea of the Zhoushan fishermen. Japanese coastal patrol boats were very active in these waters. Typically, the Japanese marines contented themselves with disrupting fishing activity by passing close to the sampans at speed and then watching with amusement as the fishermen struggled to stabilize their boats in the wash.

That day, as the sun had begun its descent over the distant hills of Hangzhou, Lin Agen had first been alerted to the fast approach of trouble by the sound of loud engines breaking the stillness of the late afternoon. His attention had been fixed on emptying and folding his net for the last time that day. His boat was one among a group of four that had been working the area since sunrise. He had been feeling pleased with himself. His catch for the day was good and would sell well enough to make up for the two days of forecast rough weather that would make leaving the shelter of the village harbour too hazardous, even for these skilled boatmen. The first target of the Japanese patrol vessel had been Weng Achuan who was fishing some three hundred yards distant. Even at that range, Lin Agen could see clearly that the Japanese marines meant trouble. They had boarded Weng Achuan's boat and were off-loading his catch. Lin Agen had been uncertain what to do. He was only sixteen years old and although he had been accompanying his father to sea for as long as he could remember, this was only the second time that he had fished alone. His father, Lin Shengtian, had been badly beaten by the Japanese raiding party last week and was not yet fit to go to sea. Lin Agen had quickly made up his mind. It was time to head for home, without obvious hurry, in the hope that they would not bother him.

He had not sailed far before a burst of machine gun fire disturbed the water immediately ahead of his sampan. He had turned his boat to face the patrol boat and sat and waited. It had not been long before the Japanese boat came alongside, allowing two marines to jump into the sampan. One of them, who looked barely out of his teens, carried a rifle with bayonet attached and was too excitable for Lin Agen's liking. But it was the other, much older, who had made him more nervous. Ill-shaven and smelling of alcohol, he had fixed Lin Agen with a cold, mean stare. Lin Agen had noticed with some relief that the man's pistol remained in its holster. The younger marine had shouted and gestured with his rifle that Lin Agen should move to the pointed prow of his boat. The two marines had then made a quick search of the shelter at the sampan's stern. Finding nothing of interest or value, they had forced him to pass the baskets containing most of his day's catch up to one of their fellow marines leaning down from the patrol boat's rail. Throughout, Lin Agen had remained silent and done his best to avoid eye contact.

They had left without so much as a word or gesture, giving Lin Agen scarcely a backward glance by way of acknowledging his existence. The patrol boat had already faded to a distant blur by the time he had stopped shaking.

Now, safely back in the harbour's early evening shadow, he prepared to unload the scraps that were all that remained of his day's work. Facing him was the long climb out of the harbour to his family home up there amongst the tight cluster of hutted dwellings that filled the steep terrace of the village. He steeled himself to break the news of a lost catch to his parents. It meant that the family would need to tighten its belt for that week.

Thinking about it, the rage at what had happened to him that day finally hit him.

Chapter 4

Autumn 1939, Hong Kong

Christopher took guard in one of the cricket nets at the Kowloon Cricket Club. He had kept wicket at school in Eastbourne and then for his college side at Cambridge, but he also took his batting seriously. He needed the practice. The start of the cricket season traditionally waited for the heat and humidity of the summer months to moderate, and the first match was next week. There was a lot of noise coming from the tennis courts on the other side of the pavilion. The two sports shared the ground, with cricket taking precedence on match days. He glanced across the field. Two courts were in use. A mixed doubles match was in progress on the nearest court; that was where most of the noise was coming from. Cheers and groans, as points were won and lost, drifted across to the cricket nets. Christopher could not recognize any of the players and shut them from his mind. He was out of practice and needed to concentrate, especially with Martin Weedon waiting to bowl at him.

Martin was quick and, knowing him, was likely to try him out with a bumper or two. Martin had been at Sandhurst with Christopher and Tony Hewitt. The three of them had had their fair share of scrapes there. Now in their mid-twenties, they were close friends as well as brother officers.

Half an hour later Christopher found himself taking his turn to field, retrieving the ball when attacking shots cleared the nets or eluded the bowler. He was being kept busy by the batsman who had replaced him in the net. They had met Jim Whitham soon after arriving in Hong Kong. He was a young banker who served as a volunteer officer in the Hong Kong Volunteer Defence Corps. Christopher had trained with him during an exercise up in the New Territories and they had got on well. Jim had won an athletics half-blue at Cambridge and was a gifted all-round sportsman. It certainly showed when he had a bat in his hand. He was giving the bowlers a hard time of it, even Martin.

Christopher heard Jim call 'Make it one more and that will be enough' and braced himself for a last ball slog that would probably send the ball way back over his head. Instead, Martin let fly with a bouncer that Jim could not resist hooking.

The ball flew off the edge of the bat, cleared the side netting and raced across the ground to finish in the middle of the mixed doubles tennis court.

Christopher ran after it. 'Sorry about that,' he called. 'I hope it didn't lose anybody a point.'

One of the young women flicked the ball up with the tip of her racket, caught it and held it high above her head in mock triumph. She gave him a broad smile. 'You're forgiven. Here. Catch.'

Christopher had half a mind to say something in response but he sensed that the woman's playing partner was keen to resume their game. A pity, he would have liked to know who she was. New to the colony, he guessed. He raised his hand in thanks and left them to their game.

*

Georgina looked around the classroom as she waited for her first Cantonese lesson to begin. She had just about found her bearings as a newcomer to the colony. It had taken some time, but she was beginning to adjust to colonial life and accept as normal some of its idiosyncrasies. Jane had accompanied her on a tour by taxi of a section of the New Territories to the north of Kowloon which had been sufficient to bring home to her how close the colony was to the reality of war. Kowloon leant itself to being explored on foot and she had set about it with enthusiasm. The thrill of waking each day in this exciting, vibrant place remained as strong as ever, but she already felt she belonged to it.

Hong Kong Island was a different matter. As yet, it remained a largely unexplored mystery to her. Everyone told her there would be plenty of time for that. She had made a start a few weeks ago by catching the ferry from Kowloon and walking to the university situated in the north-west of the island. She had wanted to enrol for her course in person. On the way, she had paused a while to take in the view of The Peak which towered high above this corner of the island. She smiled to herself as she recalled Margaret's advice on what it might take to enjoy the privilege of having a home up there on its slopes.

She had enrolled to learn some basic Cantonese. It was not that it was strictly necessary from a practical point of view because English was the second language of around half the colony's Chinese population, but Georgina had simply thought it a good thing to do.

There were eleven other students in the new term's evening class for beginners. She could not recognize anybody; not that she expected to. There was something vaguely familiar about one of them, but she could not place him beyond thinking that he had 'military' written all over him.

Dr Lau Ping-man watched from behind his desk at the front of the small classroom as his new class gathered and took their seats. This was the fourth year he had taught the beginners class and this latest group of students looked to be much as he had come to expect. Some would be from the business community or civil service, having been required to enrol by their employers. They could be relied upon to stay the course and earn their certificates of competence. Of the remainder, if past form was anything to go by, at least two or three would find it hard going and drop out at some stage. On the other hand, there would be two or three who would be back this time next year for the intermediate class. If there was one. He recalled the words of his young brother, Fung, who had warned him that everybody in Hong Kong would soon be speaking Japanese. Fung and his family lived in Guangdong. They had been under Japanese occupation for nearly a year now and their lives were a misery.

Dr Lau dragged his attention back to his new class. He introduced himself before asking the students to do the same. When it came to Georgina's turn, she declined to refer to her nickname. She was used to family and friends calling her Topsy, but she still thought of herself as Georgina and was choosy about who might be encouraged to use her nickname to her face. As soon as Christopher began to introduce himself to the class, the penny dropped. Of course, last week at the cricket club and an errant cricket ball.

'Impossibly good-looking,' she thought to herself, 'but at least he doesn't seem to be aware of it.'

Meanwhile, Christopher had not made the same connection, but he had registered an interest. There was something familiar about Georgina Marr that for a while drew his attention away from Dr Lau's explanation of how their studies would be structured for this first term. He made a note of her name.

By the end of the lesson, as much by design as by chance, he found himself holding the door open for her and feeling the need to say something.

'I should have done this course much earlier; I've been here almost two years.'

'In that case you ought to be impressed,' she replied, with just a faint hint of Edinburgh in her voice. 'I arrived only last month, and just thought I'd get stuck in.'

They took the stairs together. 'It's Georgina, isn't it?' he asked, knowing full well that it was.

'Yes,' she replied, and then, a few seconds later, heard herself adding 'but my friends call me Topsy.'

Later, back at her flat and watching the sun set over Lantau Island, she asked herself 'now why did I do that?'

*

It was a feature of county regiments in the British Army that officers' wives tended to bond together to form something akin to a matrimonial bureau. Each of the regiment's battalions was a family. A large family admittedly, but a family nonetheless. Within the family, side by side with the military chain of command, the officers' wives formed a mostly benevolent matriarchal society that came close to acting as a mother would. This included taking under their wing the love life of young officers when they first arrived in the battalion. There would be an understanding that girlfriends would come and go for a few years. They would be discreetly assessed and the progress of this and that romance would be monitored, sometimes with approval, sometimes without. In the main, the young officer would be unaware of this watch being exercised over him and it is also likely that the officers' wives would not themselves be wholly conscious of their role – but conscious or not, that was how it was. As the wives saw it, the aim was to protect these fledgling members of the regimental family from themselves and ensure that they avoided ill-advised romantic commitments. But in time a subtle change would set in. Where once the sisterhood's concern was to prevent a subaltern from losing his head, a captain heading for his thirtieth birthday without a future wife in sight became a candidate for help and encouragement. When Christopher had first joined the battalion he was just short of his twenty-fourth birthday, some three years later than most subalterns on first arrival due to his three years at university. It is not often that intelligence, sporting ability and striking good looks – all in one person – fail to arouse even the slightest trace of envy amongst colleagues, but in Christopher's case they attracted only respect and affection. Quite simply, he had everything going for him, but his justified self-confidence was of the modest kind and he was as straight as a die. Everybody liked him immensely. The officers' wives took due note and placed themselves on watch.

If anyone noticed that such scrutiny was going on, then it was those being scrutinized as potential regimental wives. Topsy was certainly aware of it. First there had been the invitation to partner Christopher in a session of mixed doubles tennis with the commanding officer and his wife. Lance Newnham was a keen player and his wife Phyllis had long since taken to the sport as a means of seeing more of her husband than she would otherwise have managed. The tennis evening had gone well, so much so that Topsy had played the last set as Lance's partner.

A week later, Phyllis had gone out of her way to invite Topsy to join her on a shopping walk through Mong Kok and its maze of colourful markets. They had been instantly at ease in each other's company.

At the ladies' guest night in the Officers' Mess just before Christmas, Topsy had felt very much on show but far from intimidated. All that scarlet and gold, all those elegant long dresses, the table almost invisible beneath all that silver and crystal, the unobtrusive playing of the regimental band's orchestra just audible about the noise of lively conversation amongst familiar friends – and she, the only non-wife present. It could so easily have been daunting. That it wasn't in the slightest was partly down to the man seated on her left. As was customary, places at table were set so that husbands and wives were separated. It was Tony Hewitt who had escorted Topsy to her place on his right and had then, throughout the dinner, banished any nervousness she might have felt. It helped enormously that he and Christopher had been at Sandhurst together. Listening to his account of the experiences they had shared – scrapes and all – Topsy learned more about the man she hoped to marry than he had previously cared to reveal of himself. But it went further than that; Tony was in his own right an interesting and entertaining dinner companion. It said much about him that he had been selected to serve as Lance Newnham's adjutant at the age of twenty-five, unusually young during peacetime.

Lance had taken the Mess president aside the week before the ladies' guest night. 'We must make sure Georgina Marr is well looked after at dinner. Tony Hewitt will be ideal. Have a word with him.'

Topsy's relaxed enjoyment of what could easily have been an unnerving gathering of the regimental family of officers was not due entirely to Tony Hewitt's company during the dinner. Both over drinks before the dinner call was sounded and when coffee was served after the loyal toast, the wives had gone out of their way to make her feel welcome as one of them. It was their way of acknowledging that Christopher, young as he was, no longer needed anyone watching over him.

Chapter 5

June 1940: Hong Kong

Christopher bided his time before asking for an interview with Monkey Stewart; after all, the new commanding officer had higher priorities than the marriage plans of one of his young officers. Not that there was much time if he was to marry Topsy before war overtook the Far East as it had already overtaken Europe. It wasn't a case of needing Stewart's approval of Topsy as his choice of wife, but there was a convention that a regimental officer intending to marry should first secure the consent of his commanding officer. The circumstances that had once given rise to that convention may have changed, but it remained one to be observed as a courtesy as much as anything else.

Besides, in the circumstances of mid-1940 Hong Kong, it was very much Stewart's responsibility as commanding officer to put the operational readiness of the battalion before all else. Each of his officers had a key role to play in preparing for war and needed to be focused on it.

And then there was the question of how fair it would be on any young bride, especially given that the order had just come through to evacuate the battalion's families within the next few weeks. The plans had been laid last year for implementation at short notice. Several thousand British civilians, including wives and children of servicemen, would be compulsorily evacuated, first to Manila in the Philippines, and thence to Australia. As the months had passed, it had become a matter of when and not if the order to evacuate would come, and now it had come, prompted by the Japanese army's move into more towns along the colony's frontier with China.

Monkey Stewart's view about Christopher's request to marry was the same as Lance Newnham's. Both men carried the memory of the heavy losses of the 1914–18 war and had seen too many hasty marriages cut brutally short by war. The prospect of any young officer's marriage did not sit comfortably with the knowledge that wives were about to be evacuated and their husbands deployed into battle positions. Stewart's wife, Dorothy, had not followed him to Hong Kong, partly because of the imminent evacuation of the families, and in her absence Lance's wife, Phyllis, had offered Stewart her opinion:

'Christopher is wise beyond his age; he knows what he's doing and he and Topsy will make it work. You should give them the nod when he asks you.'

*

When it came, the interview did not go well. As it happened, it coincided with the decision being made to evacuate dependents without delay. This meant that the Central British School was to close and its pupils and teachers were to be evacuated early next month. Topsy's future in Hong Kong hung in the balance.

Monkey Stewart was firm; he would not give Christopher a direct order not to marry, but nor would he give him his approval.

'How could I, Christopher, knowing as I do that the Japs are in strength along the border and I need to enforce the evacuation of our wives and children within days? I assure you, it's as much about looking out for Topsy as anything else – you know we've all taken to her.'

For the first and only time in the period that they served together, Christopher fell out with his commanding officer. He had bitten his lip, saluted and left Stewart's office without further comment. He determined to go ahead anyway. He hated the thought of doing anything behind the Colonel's back, but if necessary he and Topsy would marry quietly and to hell with the consequences.

Topsy took the news better than Christopher expected. She told herself that it was not as if they had thought of having a grand wedding. The closeness of war meant that Christopher would not be given leave for a wedding in Edinburgh or in his home village of Lydden in Kent, nor would any members of their respective families be able to attend a ceremony in Hong Kong. She admitted to herself that she was inwardly relieved at the prospect of a no-fuss wedding. If war was coming, she wanted somehow to be of use, whatever the changing circumstances, and nursing was an obvious option, given her medical training. It would mean that she, like Phyllis Newnham, would be permitted to stay in Hong Kong as an essential worker.

If she was worried about anything, it was that Christopher and Monkey Stewart had fallen out over the matter. She hated the idea of causing a problem and resolved to do something about it. She arranged to call on Phyllis and shared her sadness that at this of all times there should be a tension between the two men.

'Is there some way we can take the heat out of it?' she asked. 'If Dorothy were here, I'd ask for her help. You've known Monkey and Dorothy from way back, what do you think?'

Phyllis was instinctively sympathetic. She remembered that Monkey had been similarly impatient to marry as soon as possible after his return from the 1914–18 war, but his military duties had come first. She would remind him of that and ask him not to be influenced by his own experience. Times had changed.

She gave Topsy a smile of encouragement. 'I've already told Monkey that Christopher has his head screwed on. I can see he's not the only one. Leave it to me; I'll have another word with him.'

Whatever was said, Stewart took Christopher aside the following week on the rifle range.

'Look Christopher, I've been thinking things over. To be frank, I haven't changed my opinion about you getting married; I still think the timing is wrong, what with having to evacuate the families, getting the battalion ready for war and the bloody uncertainty of it all. But I will back your judgement that you and Topsy have thought it through.'

Christopher had not seen this coming. 'Thank you, Sir, I really do appreciate that.' Stewart held up his hand and cut him short.

'Before we get ahead of ourselves, it would help me if we could agree on how to play this. I'm asking you to wait until we've got the families away and settled before announcing anything. I'm worried about the whole evacuation business, not that I think it's wrong, just that it's likely to go down badly here.

What I'm asking is that you delay announcing your engagement here until quite close to the wedding.'

Christopher did not hesitate. 'That would be fine by me, but I ought to speak to Topsy.'

'Yes, you should,' agreed Stewart, before adding enigmatically 'but I think I know what she'll say.'

Christopher proposed to her the next day during an evening walk up The Peak.

They had stopped at a bend in the road to gather breath and take in the view. Far to the west, Lantau Island was lit up with reds and yellows as the sun dipped above it. They stood there a while, arm in arm, breathing in the soft scent of the nearby casuarinas, not needing to speak.

Christopher broke the silence.

'After all the hassle I've had, with Lance and Monkey, I suppose I'd better ask you to marry me.'

'And about time, too. I thought you'd never get round to it.'

Christopher did his best to look serious. 'Georgina Marr, otherwise known as Topsy, will you do me the honour of marrying me?'

She looked him in the eye with a straight face.

'Christopher Mark Morrice Man …' She couldn't resist breaking into a giggle. 'What a mouthful. I'd love to marry you, but there's a problem. I couldn't possibly marry a man who can't swim.'

'Don't worry, I couldn't possibly marry a woman who couldn't teach me.'

She held out her right hand. 'Then it's a deal.'

Later that evening, back in her apartment in Shamshuipo, Topsy reflected on how her life had been turned around in the space of only ten months. She had headed for Hong Kong without much regard for her long-term future. The colony had waited for her on the distant horizon and, once there, she had not expected to look far beyond it. Meeting Christopher had suddenly reset the horizon. It had all happened so fast after those two initial chance encounters. There had been no doubts, no hesitations; they just knew that they were made for each other, as simple as that.

But there was sadness and anxiety, too. She had come to love the Central British School and had been blissfully happy teaching there. When it had come, the enforced early closure of the school and the tearful scene on its last day had struck her as a symbol for the entire colony. The school as a community of many relationships was being ripped apart and the world as they knew it was coming to an end.

Their engagement was announced in The Times a few days before their wedding on 2 October. It was a quiet church ceremony in Kowloon with Christopher's fellow officers forming the traditional arch of drawn swords at the church door. Stewart had been right about the enforced evacuation of women and children proving controversial. Although the process went reasonably to plan during July and August it was not long before the evacuees themselves and their husbands and fathers left behind in Hong Kong had begun to question the entire project. Sensing that disquiet could spread to his own married men, Stewart ordered the entire battalion to parade and addressed them directly.

There is an art to speaking to 700 soldiers stood easy on a vast parade ground. Any leader can deliver the words but only the gifted few can make each soldier feel that the words are for him personally and that the speaker's eyes are on him. It was second nature to Monkey Stewart, and it showed as he stood before his battalion that still, autumn morning in Kowloon.

Stewart spoke without pause for fifteen minutes and when he took leave of the parade, he left his men in no doubt; as Diehards they would do as they always did, they would get on with it and so would their families. His words were not lost on Christopher. For the first time since his wedding two weeks ago, he was left wondering if Topsy ought to leave Hong Kong, too.

PART II: 1941

Chapter 6

Waiting for War

The clock of approaching war was ticking loudly in the Far East throughout 1941 and in Hong Kong the dwindling days of peace were being eked out in a mood of 'let's make the most of it while it lasts'.

There was to be no honeymoon trip for Christopher and Topsy, but they embraced what life in the colony had to offer newlyweds. They took an apartment on the lower slopes of The Peak from where they enjoyed some of the island's best views. Once spring had set in, late afternoons often saw them at Repulse Bay in the south of the island. There, in the bay's relatively calm water, Topsy set about teaching Christopher to swim. By the time the summer months arrived, he had become confident enough to join Topsy and friends in swimming out to the rafts anchored far from the beach. The pre-condition they had set for their marriage amused those who knew of it, but none of them, least of all Topsy and Christopher, could know just how significant that promise to each other would prove to be. Sometimes the couple were joined by Christopher's close friends, Tony Hewitt and Martin Weedon. Tony remained a highly eligible bachelor but Martin, like Christopher, had married young. He had met Elizabeth in Singapore and they had married despite Lance Newnham refusing his permission and insisting that Martin continued to live in the Officers' Mess. Elizabeth, remembering her own experience, had been one of the wives who had made Topsy feel especially welcome to the regimental family in those anxious early months of 1940. The two women had become close friends, so it had been a huge blow to Topsy when Elizabeth was reluctantly caught up in the compulsory evacuation of women and children. They were of contrasting personality, but they complemented each other well. Topsy missed Elizabeth's sometimes unconventional company and had chuckled to herself when she heard that, true to style, she had jumped ship in Manila to avoid being taken to Australia with the other wives. Instead, she had hitched a passage with another ship back to Singapore, just in time to give birth to her first child.

By the time Christopher's and Topsy's first wedding anniversary arrived, they knew that war was close, but Christopher was determined to celebrate. He booked a table at The Peninsula. They invited Martin and Tony to complete the trio from

Sandhurst days. The four of them gathered and reminisced, all thoughts and talk of war banished if only for a precious few hours.

*

'I'm bored,' Tony Hewitt declared to a group of brother officers who were sharing a mid-morning break for coffee in the Officers' Mess ante-room.

Martin Weedon broke off from studying the form for the coming weekend's racing at the Happy Valley course and peered over the top of his copy of the *South China Morning Post*. He waited for Tony to explain himself.

'Come to think of it, the whole battalion is bloody bored, too. Some of the men have been overseas now for the past nine years. Fine, Palestine was challenging and so was Egypt and I think we were at our peak after all that brilliant training we did there. But we went soft in Singapore; too many distractions and not enough soldiering.'

Martin nodded in agreement. 'It doesn't help that we've had so many cries of wolf here and then nothing's happened. Meanwhile, our second battalion and the TA have already taken on the Germans in France and have been through that mess at Dunkirk.'

Christopher had noticed the same frustrations amongst his men. It was easy to understand. Just over three years had passed since the successful Japanese invasion of China had caused the battalion to be hurriedly deployed from Singapore to meet the threat of an attack on the colony. That was a hell of a long time to keep professional soldiers in a constant state of readiness for war. Occasional incidents on the Chinese side of the frontier hadn't amounted to much and had done little to disturb the lassitude that had gradually crept in.

He kept his thoughts to himself. He was rather sensitive about his three years spent at Cambridge while his contemporaries had been serving overseas with the battalion. With some reason, he still thought of himself as something of a new boy.

Not that he didn't share their frustration. Their country was in a war that was passing them by, stuck out there in the Far East as they were. That was hard to take as a professional soldier. It was not that he felt a lust for war; it was more a matter of feeling you weren't doing your bit whilst others were.

'And another thing,' Tony added. 'I worry that we are underestimating the Jap soldier. I know what the C-in-C said last week: the usual stuff about the Japanese not fighting at night, their poor equipment, their sub-standard air force and so on. And the fact that they've enough on their hands dealing with the Chinese armies without taking us on here. I know we haven't been too impressed by what we've seen of the Japs on the frontier, but you can't get away from the fact that they've been giving the Chinese army a hiding for the past four years.

Martin raised a further issue that was on all their minds.

'It's the uncertainty that's hardest to deal with. If we knew for sure that the Japs intended to take Hong Kong, and that it was just a question of when they tried, we might receive the support we need to prepare for it.'

He paused to draw on his pipe. 'And there might be a recognition by the high command back in London that the garrison here is too small to hold out for long and needs to be reinforced.'

Later that evening, at home with Topsy, Christopher wrote to his elder brother Andrew who was also a Diehard officer. It was good to be able to confide in him.

'There are times,' he wrote, 'when I'm a bit down because there's so much we're lacking here as we prepare to face what seems to be the inevitable Japanese invasion of the colony. Having Topsy with me is a wonderful source of strength, of course, but I'm worried that she might be at risk. I'm genuinely encouraged by the battalion's tremendous team spirit. You will know from your own experience that our Cockney soldiers have all the courage and determination in the world and will do their bit. I just hope that will be enough.'

*

It was late one morning in mid-November that Christopher and Topsy watched as an elegant ocean liner came alongside Holt's wharf in Kowloon. The *Awatea* had been hurriedly converted from her usual role as a trans-Tasman steamship into a troopship. On board, two battalions of Canadian infantry were impatient to get ashore and join the military preparations for the defence of Hong Kong. That they had come so far from home to this part of the British Empire was the result of a much-delayed decision that the Hong Kong garrison had to be reinforced if the colony was to have any chance of being held. The Canadians' arrival was greeted noisily by a ceremonial fly-past of Royal Air Force planes and the shrill calls of Royal Navy ships' whistles. It was an occasion that Christopher and Topsy were determined not to miss. Christopher mingled with some of the Canadians as they gathered on the quayside before forming up to march off. He felt a huge sense of relief that at long last here were the reinforcements that the garrison sorely needed. He found himself casting his professional eye over them. They looked fit, very well equipped and full of confidence. 'I hope not too full,' he said quietly to himself.

Topsy joined him amongst the crowd just in time to overhear one of the Canadians asking, of nobody in particular, ‘When do we get to grips with the goddamned little yellow bastards?’

Topsy took in the fresh young face that was alight with the excitement of the moment. She wished she could take him aside and tell him what was on her mind. Instead, she whispered it to Christopher. ‘Bless him, he should be careful what he wishes for.’

Chapter 7

8 December: At War

Christopher and Topsy first became aware that something was up when the usual early-morning sound of the house boy's light tread on the stairs was replaced by the stomp of heavy boots. Instead of the customary cups of tea being placed by their bedside by Ah Yung, a loud knock on the bedroom door was followed by the appearance of Corporal Hughes, the Officers' Mess steward. 'Sorry to disturb you, Sir, but we are at war with Japan.'

Nearly everyone had seen it coming, not least the colony's Chinese population, many of whom had family in China. From there, an initial trickle of gossip and information had grown into a steady flow in recent days. The reaction of many had been to prepare for war rather than simply hope it would not arrive. Hoarding had become common, and some of life's routine commodities had become scarce. Shopkeepers, desperate to sell stock, stopped relying on customers coming through the doors and took themselves out onto the pavements to act as hawkers. For weeks, groups of refugees from China had been making their perilous way across the border, fleeing the terrors of military occupation in one place for an illusory sanctuary in another, only to find no places for them other than life on the already crowded streets of Hong Kong. There were of course those who were in denial and insisted that life should carry on as normal until the first bombs and shells fell.

That night, just after midnight, the Japanese invasion of Malaya had begun on the beaches of Kota Bharu and the first Japanese torpedo had struck the United States battleship *West Virginia* at anchor in Pearl Harbor. Just six hours later, as Christopher and Topsy prepared to make their way to their battle stations, Japanese warplanes bombed Hong Kong's airport at Kai Tak.

Topsy was headed for the Royal Naval Hospital, not far from their apartment and, by coincidence, close to the area where Christopher and his men were first to be deployed. They had both prepared for this day, but even so it came as a shock. They took time to stand together for a brief glance around what had been their home for just one year. They needed to take a memory of it with them.

Christopher turned the key in the door, trying to dismiss the premonition that they might never see their first home again. His driver was waiting for him outside to take him to the Z Company assembly point. They gave a lift to Topsy as far as the hospital where there was time for one last hug. Christopher stood watching as she hurried up the short drive to the main entrance. She reached the door and with a final turn of the head was gone from his view.

*

Christopher's Z Company was known, with much affection, as the 'Odds and Sods'. It was made up of soldiers who during the peacetime garrison life of the battalion were employed in roles that were not required by the conventional fighting companies on the field of battle. Christopher knew just how much the welding together of such disparate groups of men into an effective fighting force had tested his leadership during the last weeks of peace, but he was under no illusions, the real test was about to come.

The battalion's main armament was the Vickers machine gun. Deployed in favourable terrain, and operated by a well-trained team, it was a deadly weapon which had proved itself on the battlefields of World War 1. Z Company had twelve of them which were deployed to pillboxes constructed to cover the sites along Hong Kong Island's northern sea front where the Japanese were most likely to attack when seeking to force a crossing from Kowloon. Christopher's priority was to visit each position to check on his company's readiness. Approaching the first pillbox in the area of the Taikoo Docks, he was greeted by Frank Waldron, the sergeant with whom he had stood side by side during the Albuhera silent toast the previous year. Waldron was now responsible for two of the company's Vickers and their three-man crews, and for the riflemen assigned to give them local protection.

'Bleedin' eerie here Sir,' was his welcoming comment. Christopher had the same feeling as the two of them walked through the maze of workshops, cranes and sheds, all of them silent and empty of any life. He sensed that they were being watched by unseen eyes and recalled the warnings from the Intelligence Officer the week before that there was clear evidence of Kowloon and Hong Kong Island having been infiltrated by fifth columnists and saboteurs. Away to the north, they could hear the sounds of battle. The bridges on the frontier had been blown as the very first action to defend the colony, but Japanese engineers had quickly replaced them and hundreds of their infantry were already advancing south in contact with the garrison's forward defences. The sudden roar of aircraft sent Christopher and Waldron hurrying back to the cover of the pillboxes. As they ran, they could hear bombs exploding across the water in Kowloon followed by the grim chatter of machine guns as Japanese fighters, skimming the rooftops, strafed their targets. The Japanese air force, having heavily damaged the airport at Kai Tak, was now turning its firepower on the barracks at Shamshuipo which the Diehards had vacated to make room for the Canadians when they had arrived the previous month. Christopher could picture the scene at Shamshuipo. There was no cover from an air attack there. With a bit of luck, most of the Canadians would have deployed from the barracks to their battle positions hours ago. If they hadn't, it would be carnage.

By the end of that first day at war, Christopher had managed to visit all the positions manned by his company and had spoken to every single soldier. To a man they were ready for the fight. Any nerves were concealed beneath their natural Cockney talent for banter and dark humour. If anything, impatience was the dominant mood as they listened to the sound of distant battle on the mainland, their own sense of inaction being fed by thoughts of their fellow soldiers who were already taking the enemy on closer to the front line.

It was close to midnight before Christopher felt able to take a few moments for himself. His own spirits had been low in the immediate aftermath of leaving Topsy at the hospital, but they had been lifted by what he had seen and heard within Z Company that day. He was satisfied that the company was as ready for action as it would ever be, and he could now allow his thoughts to turn to Topsy.

*

Once Topsy closed the hospital door behind her that morning, she shut out the misery of her sudden separation from Christopher by immersing herself into the already busy routine of the Royal Naval Hospital. She had completed her training in the hospital and knew many of the nurses there. Most of them wore the pale blue uniform of the Queen Alexandra's Royal Naval Nursing Service but there were a handful in the light grey of the Auxiliary Nursing Service who, like Topsy, had enlisted with the approach of war. There was no time to dwell on personal circumstances because the first casualties of war were stretchered in before the morning had passed. The bombing of Shamshuipo Camp and the airport had been heard from within the hospital just inland from the Victoria Harbour waterfront. Some of the casualties from those two incidents had been diverted from the already crowded hospital emergency wards in Kowloon, many with shrapnel and burn wounds. They were amongst the first of the many victims of the day's air raids to be admitted to the hospital in the early hours of war. More casualties were to arrive before the day's end. Whilst Kowloon had been the first to feel the weight of Japanese bombing, Hong Kong Island was itself soon at the mercy of an enemy air force that had the freedom of the air. The garrison's air force had been destroyed on the ground by the air raid on Kai Tak airport, leaving the skies open for the Japanese to bomb the island almost at will.

It was mid-evening before Topsy was able to rest her feet in the quiet of the small room that she shared with two other nurses on her ward. Lying on her bunk bed, she allowed herself to confront the fears that had shadowed her that first day of war. She had shut them out but was now ready to face them. She had an inner confidence that Christopher would somehow be safe, but it had been a day of troubling rumours about what was happening on the battlefields north of Kowloon. The absence of hard news didn't help. Later that evening, she was woken by an on-duty colleague. There was a phone call for her. She headed for the ward office, trying not to run.

'I'll leave you to it,' the ward sister said. 'But don't be long.'

Topsy took the phone. It was Christopher.

Chapter 8

11–18 December: Enemy at the Gates

By the end of the fourth day of battle the Japanese army had advanced all the way from the colony's border with China through the hilly terrain of the New Territories and on down to Kowloon's southern waterfront. Kowloon was in a state of complete chaos. As the Japanese had fought their way south, edging ever closer to the peninsula, Kowloon's streets had been subjected to indiscriminate bombing and shelling, day after day. Streams of refugees, desperate to reach a makeshift refugee camp or the ferries that would take them across to Hong Kong Island, had to now pick their dangerous way through the debris of war accompanied by the stench of dead bodies lying where they had fallen. War had brought in equal measure both the nobility and the shame of humanity to the colony's streets. While the doctors and nurses who stayed at their posts in Kowloon were doing their best to save lives and limbs, all around them, greed and an instinct for self-preservation had led some of Kowloon's Chinese to turn on their own people and exploit their misfortunes. Many of Kowloon's shops had been damaged by bombs and shells, their doors and walls blown out, their goods and fittings abandoned as prey to hordes of looters and rioters. Fifth columnists had been activated and were stabbing and shooting victims, seemingly at random. The police were nowhere to be seen. The ferry site had long since abandoned any semblance of order. Many of the Chinese crew had simply disappeared, leaving the hard-pressed remnants of the military and civil authorities overwhelmed and having to bear the screams and curses of hordes of panic-stricken Chinese who were desperately seeking family members and fighting their way to the pier. Meanwhile, rumours were already rife that the Japanese army was meting out the brutal treatment known to have been inflicted on its occupied territories elsewhere.

Approaching midnight on that fourth day of war, the final ferry left Kowloon, chased on its way by fire from distant artillery and mortars and from the rifles and machine guns of Japanese soldiers who had rushed ahead to the waterfront. A fragile, wrinkle-faced Chinese woman, seemingly oblivious to the mayhem and danger around her, sat cross legged on the concrete floor beside two cardboard boxes that held her sole life possessions. Rocking from side to side, head in hands, she wept quietly, an unwitting symbol of the collective misery and despair that had invaded Kowloon and its quayside.

*

For Christopher and Topsy, the pattern set by the first day of war continued for the next three days. When possible, they kept in touch through phone calls. For Christopher and his brother officers, the challenge was to sustain the high morale of their men in the face of their impatience to engage the enemy. Their frustration was fuelled by the sounds and rumours of battle which reached them from the New Territories and Kowloon to the north whilst they had yet to see a single Japanese soldier. Their sole engagement with the enemy consisted of ducking to shelter from frequent bombing raids mounted by an air force that was unchallenged except for some ineffective anti-aircraft fire from the garrison's inadequate air defences. It was not in the genes of Cockney soldiers to remain patient, day after day, waiting for their turn to contribute to the fight in the knowledge that the Jocks of the Royal Scots and those Indian Army veterans in the Punjabi and Rajput battalions had taken on the enemy from day one.

In the Royal Naval Hospital on Mount Shadwell, Topsy and her colleagues waited for the full weight of casualties to make itself felt. They already knew the anguish of losing some of those in their care. The first death had come on the second day, followed by three more yesterday, and a further two today. By now, they knew with a dreadful certainty that there would be many more.

When Topsy went to bed at the end of the war's fourth day, Christopher was only a few streets distant, fighting fatigue inflicted by lack of sleep. Sleep for him was out of the question. The colony's mainland territory was now in enemy hands. The Japanese were in position on the Kowloon waterfront, separated from Z Company's forward positions only by the narrow sea channel that ran between them. Christopher knew that it was almost certain that enemy patrols were already being sent out under cover of darkness to reconnoitre possible landing points and test the garrison's ability to defend them. It had not taken the Japanese army long to demolish the myth that it could not move or fight at night.

*

Private Tom Stickley was cheesed off. Like the rest of the men of Z Company, he had been chased around Hong Kong by enemy bombs and shells without being able to do much about it. This was not what he had joined up for. He had celebrated his twenty-first birthday a few months ago and for a typical Cockney of that age it wasn't exactly his idea of a good fight to be harassed from one position to another, day after day, by an unseen enemy. He was on watch while the rest of the Vickers crew grabbed some sleep. None of them had had much since they had deployed from their barracks eight days ago. He peered out from the pillbox, scanning the near shoreline and beyond, across the narrow channel which was barely five hundred yards wide here. Looming over the far waterfront, Devil's Peak seemed to be close enough to touch, even though the moon was hidden in cloud. It was dead quiet out there. Too quiet for his liking. Christopher had needed to crawl across the final yards of open ground to reach Stickley's pillbox. The enemy was closest here. This would be the last Vickers crew to move out later that night to new positions and he wanted to brief them personally.

'How's it going Stickley?'

'No sign of the bastards yet, Sir. More's the pity. I was just thinking to myself; we've been at war for eight soddin' days, I've been bombed and shelled, I've changed positions three times and I haven't seen even one bleedin' Jap soldier yet.'

Christopher laughed. 'I've got a feeling you haven't long to wait.'

*

Monkey Stewart insisted on being where his presence as commanding officer was most needed, and if that meant being at the sharp end, that was where his instincts took him. He approached Christopher's new company command post on foot, using whatever cover from view was available. Any careless movement attracted accurate shelling and mortaring. He had lost too many men that way. His presence beside Christopher did not indicate a lack of confidence in the young, inexperienced company commander. Far from it. He had identified him as one of his most talented officers and had recognized an inner steel in him. But he remembered his own first taste of battle in Flanders when he was only a few years out of Sandhurst. Back then, his own self-confidence had been strengthened by the close presence and calming words of his first company commander who was already battle-hardened. Christopher's Z Company had been assigned the task of holding Leighton Hill, an isolated, partly built-up feature that guarded the approach to Victoria. If the Japanese fought their way ashore on Hong Kong's north-east corner and if they intended to capture the city area from there, Z Company stood in their way.

Stewart looked Christopher directly in the eye. 'Christopher, I'm going to put it to you bluntly. You're to stay here, hold this position and resist to the last man. Tony Hewitt will see that you get that order in writing, for the record, but I wanted to give it in person.'

When Stewart had left, Christopher prepared himself for passing on the order to his own men. He could not help wondering how they would react to their first battle face to face with the enemy. Come to that, how would he react as their leader? If he felt fear, it was of not coming up to scratch, letting others down, not being worthy to touch that Albuhera loving cup to his lips and drink from it. He had no fear of the Japanese enemy but had made his clinical appraisal of them as one soldier of another. Gone from his mind was the image of squat, grubby, seemingly ill-disciplined soldiers, one he had formed when watching them on the frontier on his arrival in the colony some three years ago. Gone, too, were some of the myths; that they were short-sighted, ill-equipped, robot-like and incapable of initiative. The evidence provided by the battle for the colony's territory on the mainland had dispelled such misconceptions. The Japanese soldiers who threatened Hong Kong Island were hardy, disciplined and well-trained. Many of them had recent experience of battle against the Chinese armies. And they were driven by a belief – verging on the fanatical and inculcated in them from the day of their enlistment – that it was an honour to fight to the death and a dishonour to surrender. It now fell on Christopher to prepare the men of Z company to meet an enemy they should respect but not fear.

*

In the Royal Naval Hospital not far from Christopher's new position on Leighton Hill, Topsy was beginning to feel the strain. She was changing the dressings on a casualty with severe burns and was having to do so whilst on her knees. The hospital was already full, and several patients lay on mattresses on the ward floors. If further casualties arrived, they would have to start using the corridors. All parts of the island were now vulnerable to bombing and shelling and the number of casualties was rising too fast for the various established hospitals to cope. With Kowloon now in Japanese hands, there was no access to the large military hospital there, and to make matters worse, the invasion had happened during a major outbreak of malaria in the colony with the result that many bed spaces were taken up by the sick. And then last night the hospital had been shelled for the first time. Five shells had landed in the hospital grounds, but a sixth had scored a direct hit on the hospital laundry, killing four Chinese workers and injuring two more. The windows in one of the wards had been blown out by the blast and one of the ambulances was riddled with shrapnel holes. It was too early to know if the hospital was being targeted but it had been an unnerving baptism by fire for Topsy and her colleagues.

Topsy struggled to focus tired eyes on the patient beside her; she could not remember when she had last had a good night's sleep. Matron was making her rounds and paused to brief her.

'Georgina, with all the permanent hospitals filling up, the authorities are setting up some makeshift hospitals where casualties with shell and gunshot wounds will be treated. I've been told that it's likely the auxiliary nurses will be redeployed. I'm sorry, but it looks like you need to be ready to move at short notice.'

'Any idea where to?' Topsy asked. 'It could be anywhere, but most probably at the university; they're converting the Great Hall there into three wards.'

Topsy knew the university well. It was close to her and Christopher's flat. She had fond memories of it; they had attended their Chinese language evening classes together there. She wasn't to know it, but the next few days were destined to leave her with an infinitely grimmer remembrance of the place.

Chapter 9

18–25 December: The Battle for Hong Kong Island

When they came, the Japanese infantry attacked in their thousands in the dark and the rain of the early evening. Their assault boats were halfway across the channel before they were caught in the beams of the searchlights that swept the surface, haphazardly this way and that. The defenders' machine guns began to take their deadly toll but still the boats headed remorselessly for the island's north-east coastline. Groups of enemy managed to gain the shore where they were reinforced by swimmers who had towed their equipment behind them on floats. Once ashore, they began to fight their way to the high ground.

On Leighton Hill, Christopher was enveloped by the fog of war. All around him seemed chaos. Mortar and shellfire from the mainland continued to hit his positions and inflict casualties. Fresh supplies of food and water had been unable to reach Z Company for days and stocks were now low. Information, when it came, was so vague that he didn't know who was to his left and right. He sent out patrols who reported that there was no sign of friendly troops. By day his men waited in buildings and trenches, ready to beat off the next enemy attack, then changing their positions at night under the cover of darkness. From time to time they were joined by stragglers from the battles to their front who had somehow found their way to Leighton Hill. They brought with them reports of heavy fighting against the odds and of merciless treatment of prisoners of war and the wounded by the Japanese. Everywhere, crowds of Chinese filled the streets of the built-up areas, heading anywhere and nowhere as long as it took them away from the fighting. In their panic, they neither knew nor cared that they blocked the lines of fire of Z Company's machine guns.

Christopher had felt relief when the Japanese infantry first attacked his positions. At last his men could see them. The company's Vickers machine guns repulsed wave after wave of the enemy, but still they kept coming, seemingly oblivious to casualties. A lull in the fighting allowed his thoughts to drift to Topsy.

He knew that she too was at enormous risk, because the Japanese had already shown in Kowloon that they would attack hospitals and butcher anyone found inside them, whether doctors and nurses or the wounded in their care. Last night he had managed to phone her at the hospital just to let her know that he was still in one piece, but within minutes the shelling had resumed. As one shell passed overhead and exploded close by, he found himself telling Topsy 'Hang on a second, that was a near miss.'

'That wasn't your near miss,' Topsy shouted down the line, 'it was mine.'

That was to be their last call to each other.

*

After five days of battle, it was clear to Christopher that Z Company's position on Leighton Hill was hopeless. They had begun the fight with over one hundred men and twelve Vickers and now no more than forty men and six guns remained to carry it on. The Japanese had infiltrated the surrounding streets and buildings, making it impossible to evacuate the wounded who had to remain under whatever cover could be found for them. Christopher was running out of ammunition. Without it, his orders to defend the position to the last man became pointless. He began to make plans for a withdrawal but kept them to himself. He knew that once the prospect of withdrawal was mentioned, it was inevitable that some men would start to look over their shoulders.

Christopher and Z Company were not alone in facing the prospect of being overwhelmed. Step by step, day by day, battle by battle, the defence of Hong Kong Island was being lost. Their own immense losses prompted the Japanese to offer the garrison the chance to surrender. It was refused, despite the seeming inevitability of further heavy casualties and ultimate defeat. Monkey Stewart managed to call Christopher when the damage to a field telephone line was repaired. He ordered Christopher to withdraw to the commercial area of Wanchai, close to Victoria Harbour, and to hold the Japanese for as long as possible. One by one they abandoned the buildings from which they had fought for the past five days and as they got out, the Japanese got in.

What was left of Z Company reached Wanchai just in time to beat off an attack by an enemy force that had fought its way from the east, along the waterfront. Christopher and his men were now all that stood in the way of a Japanese occupation of the island's entire northern coastal strip. The complex of buildings that offered Z Company the best prospects of defence against superior numbers happened to be a Chinese clinic for the treatment of venereal disease.

'First time in my life I've been in a clap shop.' observed Private Jim Baker to nobody in particular. An instant response came from under a camouflage net draped around a Vickers gun sited in the doorway.

'You must've been lucky then Jimmy, 'cos from what I've heard it wasn't for want of trying.' Not to be outdone, Baker insisted on having the last word.

'Not like you Smithy, eh. You probably know this place backwards.'

Christopher laughed with the rest of them, wondering how these Cockney soldiers could find humour in the most dire of circumstances. He took much strength from it as he braced himself to meet yet another attack.

*

Topsy tensed as yet another shell slammed into the hospital roof. That was the third in just a few minutes and there was bound to be another. They seemed to come in fives and sixes. One by one, the wards had suffered damage, some to the point where they had to be abandoned. And still the wounded arrived. For the lucky ones there was a camp bed or mattress on a corridor floor. The walking wounded sat on benches. An early bombardment had cut the water mains and a day later a shell had destroyed the hospital's water tank. The taps had long since run dry. The stench of unflushed lavatories seeped unchecked into the wards. The wounded could not be washed on arrival and even cleansing and treating their wounds had to be rationed as clean bandages became scarce.

Topsy was simply too tired, too focused on the patients, to be frightened. The time had long since passed when an exploding shell or nearby burst of machine gun fire had caused her to pause in her work. Like her colleagues, she just got on with it. But it couldn't last. The hospital was overwhelmed and the wards that remained serviceable could no longer cope.

As expected, the order came to evacuate some of the wounded to the makeshift hospital in the university buildings barely two miles to the west. Six of the auxiliary nurses, Topsy included, were to go with them. There was scarcely time for her to grab a bag holding her few personal possessions. She checked; yes, Christopher's photograph was there. A small convoy of Red Cross ambulances took them to the university. Nerves were on edge because the Red Cross symbols were no guarantee that they would not be attacked. News had spread that four days ago at Wong Nai Chung, Japanese soldiers had murdered ten stretcher bearers wearing Red Cross armbands, bayoneting them to death in cold blood.

The three university halls that had been converted into hospital wards were already nearly full of casualties but had so far remained untouched by bombing or gunfire. The university had its own water supply and adequate stocks of critical drugs and dressings; to Topsy it was a whole new world compared to the Royal Naval Hospital which by now was well and truly on the front line of battle. Her thoughts turned to Christopher. Would he know she had moved to here?

Unknown to her, the hospital she had just been forced to leave was only a couple of streets away from where Christopher and Z Company were fighting for their lives.

*

Christmas Day. The sun was about to throw its early light on the Red Cross flag flying prominently above the auxiliary hospital in St Stephen's College on the Stanley Peninsula when Lieutenant Colonel George Black began his first round of the wards. He had around one hundred military casualties under his care, many of them Diehards who had been wounded in the heavy fighting in the south of the island. Black was in his late sixties and, being a resident of Hong Kong, had been mobilized when war came. Accompanying him as he went from bed to bed was an English nursing sister. Both were tired after a night's sleep constantly broken by the close noise of battle and the inevitable arrival of yet more wounded. Helping them to run the makeshift hospital were ten voluntary nurses – some Chinese and some English – and three medical orderlies.

Without warning two doors burst open and several Japanese soldiers forced their way past Black and the nursing sister and began driving their bayonets into the wounded who lay helpless in their beds. In the space of seconds, a place of care had become a scene of merciless butchery. Black tried to grab the nearest attacker but was promptly shot and then bayoneted to death where he had fallen. Captain John Whitney of the Royal Army Medical Corps was Black's deputy and was on duty in a neighbouring ward when the frenzy of killing began. He rushed to intervene but was shot and bayoneted as soon as he entered the ward. Two Japanese soldiers forced the walking wounded at bayonet point into one room and locked them in. One by one they were taken out, hands tied behind them and bayoneted to death. Other soldiers dragged the eleven nurses outside the hospital. One was forced to lie on dead bodies while she was repeatedly raped; others were raped amongst the bushes before being shot. Four escaped with their lives by feigning death.

*

Less than a quarter of a mile from the slaughter at St Stephen's College, Martin Weedon steeled himself for the action to come. At first light that morning, the Japanese had fought their way onto a piece of high ground that overlooked two of B Company's pillboxes. From there the enemy were now directing fire onto these posts and the company was taking casualties. If the Japanese were given time to reinforce their position, the pillboxes could not survive for long. Martin assessed three options: abandon the pillboxes, defend them till he ran out of men and ammunition, or counterattack – now. He didn't hesitate. They would counterattack. There was no time for an elaborate plan. He gathered as many men as he could, split them into two forces and waited for the company's light mortars to lay down a local smoke screen. The first of the smoke rounds began to hit the ground just up-wind of the enemy positions. The screen they provided would not last long. It was time to go. He and his men had trained for close, hand-to-hand combat but no peace-time training could have fully prepared them for what was to come. One group right, the other left, they moved at pace on the flanks of the open ground between them and the unsighted enemy who were firing randomly into the smoke screen in front of them. Martin saw two of his men hit and fall before the rest of them were amongst the Japanese in a frenzied, screaming, man-to-man melee of bayonets, rifle butts and close-range shooting. Within minutes the Japanese were in retreat, under covering fire from another position. A bullet slammed into Martin's right shoulder, spinning him round and dropping him to the ground. He dragged himself to his feet. There was no time to lose. It would not take the Japanese long to bring up reinforcements and mount a counterattack themselves. Martin watched as his company's casualties were stretchered down to the cover of the pillboxes. He had felt no pain when he was hit and had lost all feeling in his shoulder, but he knew it was only a matter of time before he would need treatment himself. A shot of morphine from the company medic would help. Right now, the priority was to prepare to defend the ground they had regained. The Japanese would come again.

*

General Christopher Maltby faced the most crucial decision of his life. Fight on or surrender? From London, Churchill signalled: 'The order of the day is hold fast.' From Government House in Hong Kong, the Governor, Sir Mark Young, sent out an equally defiant message: 'Fight on. Hold fast for King and Empire.' But Maltby knew, as did his senior commanders, that further resistance was both futile and unjustifiable. Everywhere the military situation was dire. The Japanese had suffered a massive number of casualties but still far outnumbered the garrison's forces which by now consisted of little more than isolated groups of survivors holding out where they could. The enemy had complete control of the air and sea and his artillery continued to pound the island with undiminished savagery. With few exceptions, the Japanese occupied all the key military terrain and Maltby no longer had sufficient forces capable of retaking any of it. Hopes that Chinese Nationalist forces on the mainland would get close enough to attack the Japanese from the rear had vanished. The Chinese population throughout Hong Kong was in despair: their streets were piled high with heaps of rubble and littered with the decaying bodies of the dead; the island's hospitals were under attack and overwhelmed by casualties; water supplies, drains and power lines were in ruins and law and order had broken down with gangs of criminals and fifth columnists looting and murdering at will.

Whatever decision Maltby made, it would be his alone, but he needed to hear personally from his commanders on the ground. Which is why he had summoned Monkey Stewart.

Stewart's report was grim. All his battalion's positions were close to being overwhelmed by sheer numbers. Twelve of his officers were dead, a further four wounded. Casualties amongst the other ranks were in their hundreds and still more would die if their wounds remained untreated much longer. The dead lay where they had fallen. Those who survived were critically short of ammunition.

When he had finished, Stewart looked Maltby straight in the eye. 'General, for the first time since the battle began, I find myself thinking the unthinkable.'

Chapter 10

25 December: Surrender

By mid-afternoon on Christmas Day, General Maltby had learned enough. He informed the Governor: further military resistance being impossible, he was ordering his commanders to cease fighting and surrender to the nearest Japanese commander. Monkey Stewart knew in his heart that it was the right thing to do, but that didn't make it any easier. He took hold of a white flag and with Tony Hewitt at his side headed through the battle-scarred streets of Wanchai district towards the nearest enemy headquarters.

Close by, Christopher gathered his men around him. There were only thirty of them. He had come to expect a surrender but had refused to allow himself to anticipate it. Till the end, he had led his men in the belief that they would stay where they were until they ran out of ammunition or were overrun. They had resisted thoughts of capture, having heard enough of how those of their comrades who had fallen into enemy hands had been mistreated.

Now that the end had come, it felt like an anti-climax to the men of Z Company as they were ordered to return to barracks.

'I can't believe it,' protested Frank Waldron. 'It's just like it's the end of a bleedin' exercise and we're all going back to barracks to have a shower.'

Christopher knew just what he meant; it all seemed so weirdly unreal. There was one order that he intended to disobey. They had been told to hand in their weapons undamaged. It was an order too far, and by the end of that day all Z Company's arms had been rendered unserviceable and dumped in Victoria harbour.

The terms of the surrender required the Diehards to assemble in Murray Barracks, close to the waterfront. They were to make their way there as best they could, in formed, disciplined groups. Desperately tired as they were, and deeply dispirited that the battle for the colony had been lost, their instincts as soldiers remained strong. The survivors of Z Company marched out of battle in column, backs stubbornly straightened, heads defiantly held high, Christopher leading them. The streets were beginning to fill as word of the surrender spread. Most buildings were pock-marked by shell and bullet; some had white sheets hanging from windows in a desperate plea to be spared retribution, while others already displayed the Rising Sun flag. Looters were quickly about their business, sensing that it would not be long before the Japanese invader became the Japanese occupier. As Christopher and his men approached Murray Barracks, he caught sight of a group of Japanese soldiers manning the gates, bayonets fixed to rifles. He sensed potential trouble. He knew his men well enough to know that some would be finding the rawness of defeat close to unbearable and could react with hot heads if provoked. He halted the small column and spoke to them. They remained Diehards even as prisoners of war and they would show it to the end. And with that, he led them into captivity.

*

At work in their new surroundings at the auxiliary hospital, Topsy and her colleagues struggled to separate rumour from fact as stories of Japanese atrocities reached them. The university was only one of several auxiliary and relief hospitals set up to treat the casualties of war in Hong Kong. Others had been established in schools and convents, and the grandstand of the Jockey Club had been rapidly converted to serve as a relief hospital for the treatment of civilians. The rumours reaching the nurses at the university painted a grim picture. The story emerging was one of hospitals being overrun by Japanese soldiers with the fate of patients and medical staff being determined by luck alone. At the Jockey Club on Christmas Eve, the Japanese soldiers had dragged terrified nurses away and subjected them to hours of rape and beatings before dumping them back at the makeshift hospital. Not far away, those manning the auxiliary hospital at St Albert's Priory had been lucky. Although threatened and held at gun point, they had escaped harm because they were given credit for having treated a dying Japanese officer brought in that morning.

As daylight began to fade, Topsy was busy changing the dressings of the latest wounded arrivals when news of the surrender reached her. The hospital had escaped the shelling and none of those working there had seen any Japanese soldiers, but by now they knew it was only a matter of time before they did. Topsy struggled to shut from her mind anything that lay beyond the tasks facing her. There was no end to them. The ceasefire had enabled several casualties to be evacuated to the hospital after having been beyond reach of the stretcher bearers during the fighting. All three of the halls converted to wards were bursting at the seams, the air loud with the cries of the wounded.

*

The victorious Japanese commanders were wise enough to leave the garrison troops to sort themselves out within Murray Barracks. The barracks had already been looted and were in a bad state. The Japanese could see that if some semblance of order was to be established until an effective prisoner of war camp could be established, the British chain of command was best placed to do it. Contained within the barracks, their weapons discarded, those who had surrendered were safely out of the way. For the time being, all the victors needed to do was guard and control the barrack entrance.

As soon as he was satisfied that Z Company was accounted for, Christopher allowed himself to think of Topsy. He had no idea if she had survived. He knew that some of the hospitals had been shelled and he had heard the reports of atrocities having been committed by the Japanese against non-combatants. If she had survived, he needed to find her before they became separated in captivity. An idea came to him. He would get himself designated as a casualty and hitch a Red Cross ride to the hospital, but first he needed the Colonel's blessing. He set out to find him. Stewart listened to Christopher's request. He had much on his plate but was very much aware that Christopher was the only officer whose wife had not been evacuated.

'Go ahead, and good luck. Just get back here as soon as you can.'

Christopher found the battalion's Medical Officer in the barracks medical centre. He agreed to help. As darkness fell, the Red Cross ambulance negotiated its way out of the barracks after a cursory look into the back of it by the Japanese guards at the gate. The Royal Naval Hospital was still in use, despite having been hit by around one hundred shells. Christopher feared the worst as his glance took in the hospital walls scarred by shrapnel and machine gun bullets. There were no Japanese in sight, so he walked straight through the main door. He stopped the first nursing sister he could find and asked after Topsy. She had left two days ago. Where to? The auxiliary hospital at the university. The ambulance that had brought him was loading a casualty who had been treated at the hospital and was now fit to join those in captivity at Murray Barracks. Christopher jumped in and explained they needed to divert to the university.

Once there, Christopher asked after Topsy and was pointed towards one of the halls. From the doorway he spotted her straight away, a small figure in light grey uniform and white hat, sitting on the side of a bed, chatting away to a casualty.

At first, Topsy didn't recognize him when he waved from the far door to the hall. Two weeks of fighting had left their mark. It wasn't just the shrunken eyes, the much-thinned face and the tattered uniform; even that upright, athletic walk so familiar to her had gone. But it was him, even though she scarcely dared to allow herself to believe it.

There was time only for one lingering hug and a few precious words and tears shared amidst the bustle of the over-crowded ward. She had work to do and his place was with his men.

Four hours later, as Christopher grabbed his first sleep in three days, a party of Japanese soldiers, wild-eyed and flush with the excitement of victory, made their way through the university grounds towards the hospital wards where doctors, nurses and casualties awaited whatever fate had in store for them.

At the same time, some twelve miles to the south on the Stanley Peninsula, the final macabre and gruesome rites of that morning's atrocity were being enacted in the grounds of St Stephen's College. Those who had survived were now making a funeral pyre designed to destroy evidence of what had happened there that day. Still under the threat of execution themselves, they made a pile of the hospital furniture, topping it with blood-soaked blankets and sheets. Next, they would have to collect the bodies of those who only hours ago had been their colleagues and their patients, and then consign them to the flames.

They didn't know it, but the war had ended. A few hundred yards from them, Martin Weedon didn't know it either. The order to surrender had not reached him.

He knew the enemy counterattack would come soon, and when it did, he and the remnants of B Company would resist the irresistible. It would be their last act of war.

PART III: 1942

Chapter 11

Captivity

It was only when Christopher looked about him on the day of his return to Shamshuipo Camp in Kowloon that the full impact of captivity hit him. The three days following the surrender had not been the best time for introspection. For one thing, he was at the extreme limits of exhaustion – as they all were. The unremitting stress of fighting and the lack of sleep, day after day, had left them drained of energy. And there had simply been too much to do. The barracks were a shambles, the looters having stripped the buildings of anything of conceivable use or value. Nothing worked, so the priority had been to get on with restoring some sort of order as hundreds of surrendered servicemen were crammed into their temporary, ramshackle home. Christopher's first concern was for the welfare of those in Z Company who had survived, not that he could do much about what was most important to them all, the recovery of their dead and their wounded. Christopher knew exactly where they had left them but was powerless to do anything about it. Requests had been made to the Japanese for unarmed search parties, under Red Cross supervision, to be sent out to find and recover the wounded into the care of the hospitals. These had been refused. Christopher knew, and his men knew, too, that the refusal amounted to a death sentence for some of their wounded. As for the dead, the Japanese were content that the bodies of their enemy and of Chinese civilians should be allowed to rot where they lay, some among the streets and alleyways of the towns, others out on the fields and hills, still others fated to remain hidden in gulleys and ravines until a chance discovery – all of them abandoned as human detritus from the eighteen days when war had come to Hong Kong.

The prisoners had marched under guard from Murray Barracks to the ferry point, carrying what they could of their possessions. Monkey Stewart had insisted on leading his men into captivity. Close behind him, Christopher had marched at the head of the survivors of Z Company, perhaps for the last time. They had been through a lot together and deserved to share the aftermath of battle all the way into long-term captivity.

Many of the Chinese lining the routes to watch them march into captivity had been quick to recognize that their immediate best interests lay in adopting new loyalties. The Rising Sun flag was everywhere. Some onlookers stood impassively, as if still stunned at being confronted by such a sudden change in the colonial order, as yet unsure what to make of it. Others though had been in the mood to add insult to humiliation. For them, the trudge of defeated British soldiers towards captivity was a welcome symbol of an end to British colonial rule. So they had jeered and hurled taunts and anything they could lay their hands on at the passing column and had laughed and cheered whenever the Japanese guards felt like adding the prod of a bayonet or the slap of a face to the indignities being inflicted on the defeated soldiers. Weary and dispirited as he was, Christopher had seethed inwardly and, in his anger, had found a new source of strength and resolve. He had muttered to himself. 'We'll show them, we'll bloody-well show them.'

The ferry had taken them across to Kowloon. They had then marched through streets which used to be so familiar to them as noisy, bustling routes to and from their barracks, but were now a shambles of shattered glass, heaped rubble and rotting bodies. Once-busy shops now stood shuttered against roaming mobs of looters and scavengers. In their place, hundreds of Chinese squatters, as if offering a human metaphor for the spoils of war, had set up street stalls selling looted goods.

At the entrance to their old barracks, the march had halted to allow Monkey Stewart to go on ahead. He had then stood alone inside the gate to return the salute as those who remained of his beloved battalion marched passed him, back to their former home, arms swinging and strides lengthened one last defiant time as a tribute to the man who had led them in a battle lost with honour.

Once back in Shamshuipo Camp, it was being confronted with the brutal contrast between the vibrant battalion home it had been in peacetime and the bleak prisoner of war camp it had become that had shaken Christopher into accepting that life as he knew it had changed, perhaps forever.

The Japanese had bombed Shamshuipo on the first day of the battle and the damage inflicted on the barrack structures was all too apparent. Some of the blocks had been reduced to mere shells and those huts which had survived the bombs had been stripped bare with an efficiency and thoroughness that was the hallmark of the Chinese looter. As he passed the guardroom, the bare walls and open roof mocked his warm memories of those night-time moments when, as Orderly Officer making his rounds, he had shared comradely chats with the regimental policemen and guard commanders. Then, the building had been a shrine – all polished brass and gleaming tiles – now it was a scene of squalor. Next, his glance took in the Officers' Mess where last May, during the Albuhera silent toast ceremony, he had received the Loving Cup from Sergeant Tom Baker and handed it to Sergeant John Burgess. They both lay dead on the battlefield. The scavengers had left their mark here, too, in this corner of the barrack square now scarred by bomb craters. Doors and window frames had all been removed, and those elegant, long tables that had once groaned with the weight of silver goblets, statuettes and candelabra had long since disappeared into Kowloon's black economy.

'Bloody sad and hard to take, eh.' It was Tony Hewitt.

Christopher grimaced in agreement. 'It's a good job Monkey did what he did about the silver.' He was thinking back to the previous year when the families had been evacuated and Monkey Stewart had ordered the regimental silver to be packed up and shipped away from Hong Kong into bank vaults in Singapore.

'I couldn't bear the thought of it all being in the hands of the Japs, or being flogged off by the scum who looted the barracks.'

Tony had something else on his mind.

'I ought to share with you what we did with the Colours. We have boxed them and buried them in the grounds of Government House. Monkey knows where and so does Lan Newnham. The Governor is also in the know, but I don't know who else. I'm telling you just in case we don't all survive.'

Christopher reflected a while on this news.

It was a relief to know that the precious Colours might escape becoming a trophy of war for the Japanese, but that did not disguise the fact that this battle had been lost. The evidence of that loss met his eyes wherever he looked. Yes, they had fought as well as they possibly could; yes, the odds were against them from the start; and yes, it was a defeat with honour. But it was a battle lost, and to have fought the enemy for eighteen days only to have been defeated was hard to take for professional soldiers. And it had left a dreadful question: could they look in the eye the dead and wounded who lay untended on the battlefield and tell them it had been worth it?

*

Four days after Christopher and Tony Hewitt had marched into Shamshuipo Camp in Kowloon, some twelve miles to the south, on the Stanley Peninsula, Martin Weedon was setting out on what for too many fellow prisoners of war had already proved to be a death march. His wounded shoulder had been patched up as best as the depleted resources at the Stanley prison hospital could manage, but he had been left in poor shape. Ahead of him and several hundred fellow prisoners of war lay a forced march across the high hills of Hong Kong Island's spine. Most of them were headed for eventual captivity in Shamshuipo, but first they had to make it to the island's northern waterfront. Halfway along their journey they would pick up the route already followed by those men captured during the battle for the key strategic ground in the centre of the island. They had included the walking wounded, some of whom had struggled to keep pace with the march. Some had made it to the end only because others had simply refused to let them drop out and had dragged out of them their last reserves of stamina – already overspent – drawing on the fast-fading glimmer of their will to live. But some had been beyond support. They had fallen time after time until finally they could make it to their feet no longer, despite blows from the rifle butts of their guards and the desperate pleas of their comrades. As if enacting a macabre ritual, the Japanese guards had first severed the wire which bound them to their march companions and then, with their victims cut loose, had bayoneted them to death. Their bodies still lay beside the way, waiting to serve as a dark warning to those who had yet to follow that same path into captivity.

*

At the university hospital, Topsy took her place in the group of nursing staff waiting in the forecourt to climb into the truck that would take them down to the waterfront where they had been told to wait until boats would ferry them round the coast to an internment camp on the Stanley Peninsula. Three weeks had passed since the surrender on Christmas Day and the ordeal to which they had been subjected late that night and into the early hours of the next day. Each of them would have to find their own way to deal with what they had gone through, but Topsy was clear that she would cope best if she shut it away and drew a line under it. If she shared any of it with anyone, it would be with Christopher, when the time was right. She sensed that if she allowed herself to dwell on it, it would eat away at her determination to rise above what she suspected lay ahead. That determination was fragile and rested hugely on her hope to be reunited with Christopher. Without that hope, she doubted she had the will to do anything more than go through the motions of living from one day to the next. She clung to the knowledge that Christopher had survived the fighting, but scarcely dared to think of what might have happened to him after her last sight of him at the makeshift hospital. There were conflicting rumours doing the rounds about the Japanese treatment of prisoners of war, but she had an instinctive faith that if anyone could survive the privations of captivity, it was Christopher.

A Japanese army officer emerged from the hospital doorway and addressed them through an interpreter. He told them they were fortunate; a special camp had been prepared for them. Their life there would be good. The Imperial Japanese Army would provide them with plentiful supplies of food and would ensure that conditions would be pleasant there. They should be grateful that the soldiers of Nippon are always kind to women, and they should repay that kindness by being respectful and by obeying the rules of the camp. There would be many women and children in the camp where they would be expected to continue to work as nurses.

Topsy and her colleagues had been left to their own devices once the Japanese soldiers who had first invaded the university hospital had been withdrawn. The medical and nursing staff had been ordered to stay where they were until a camp had been prepared for them. Three days after the surrender, Topsy had risked a walk to the apartment she and Christopher had shared for only a year. She knew how dangerous it would be to stray outside the grounds of the university, but after all she had been through, she was almost beyond caring. She wanted to rescue what she could reasonably hope to keep with her during the captivity that awaited her.

One sight of her former home was enough to make her regret having returned to it. It had been stripped bare. Nothing remained; no furniture, none of their personal possessions, no fittings, not even the window frames and doors had been spared by the looters. There in the corner had stood Christopher's golf bag. In it had been his pride and joy, an Edward VIII engraved sword which no doubt was already being touted for sale on the city streets. The elegant ball gown she had worn for her first appearance at the Officers' Mess two Christmases ago had hung in the wardrobe which had stood over there, along the wall where now a pile of broken tiles littered the concrete floor. Their favourite wedding photograph had gone, along with its ivory frame. She had lingered a while at the empty space that had once been the window where they had so often stood, side by side, sharing the view it offered across the harbour towards Kowloon and beyond. Below the window, in its accustomed place at the edge of the lawn in the communal garden, a lone casuarina provided a painful reminder of how things had been. She and Christopher had often sat in its shade of an early evening, accompanied by the gentle sigh of the wind through its branches and the familiar, heavy scent of its leaves, as they talked and watched the sun lower itself over an expanse of shimmering sea.

She had drawn a deep breath and headed for the stairs; the time had come to draw a line under life as it had been and face whatever fate had in store for her.

Now, at the waterfront, they were joined by several women and children. They had been detained and confined elsewhere, some in former brothels, others in overcrowded, improvised hostels without proper sanitation or other basic facilities. Topsy noted that there were some children who appeared to be unaccompanied by an adult. One, a young boy, struggled to carry a tiny suitcase. He wore a rope belt from which hung items that someone – perhaps a despairing mother – had thought he would need: a penknife, a fork and spoon, an enamel mug, a torch and a toothbrush. Topsy took his hand.

They were crammed into a scruffy cargo launch which spluttered into life and chugged its way out from the pier before heading down the inshore waters of Hong Kong Island's west coast. A cold wind blew rain showers in from the north-east and had roughed up the open sea, so the launch hugged the coastline as close as it dared. There to the left Topsy caught sight of the streak of white sand that formed the beach at Repulse Bay. She allowed her thoughts to stray to those happy hours spent teaching Christopher to swim there. Could it really have been only a few months ago that they had last swum there? Often they had lingered over a drink at the hotel above the beach. She smiled to herself as she remembered once feeling self-conscious about being under-dressed for such a smart, ultra-colonial place. The poor light now dimmed her view of the hotel's battle-scarred walls above which the Rising Sun, straining in the wind, announced the island's changed order.

It was close to dusk when the launch pulled alongside the jetty in Stanley Bay. With a wave of his rifle, the Japanese guard motioned everyone to step ashore and pointed them towards a track that led away from the beach. Cold and wet, Topsy and the others trudged their way into captivity in the last of the day's light. They were met by three Japanese soldiers at a makeshift gate that offered access through a gap in a barbed-wire fence. One of the soldiers gestured to the group to follow him as he headed towards a group of tall buildings. He directed those with children to a door in the first building where a woman in Red Cross uniform waited to welcome them. He then led the remaining women to the next block and, without a word, turned on his heels and left them all to it.

Topsy looked around her. There was nobody there to allocate them to rooms; they would have to pack themselves in as best they could. All the rooms on the ground floor were already occupied so Topsy headed for the stairs, closely followed by two nurses she knew from the relief hospital. They kept climbing until at last, on the second floor, they found an empty room. It was small, but by now they were beyond caring.

Topsy did not sleep that night, nor did the other two nurses. Soon after midnight, they were joined in their cold, grey cell by a young woman. She was close to collapse, so they made room for her. Towards dawn, in the light of the single light bulb that hung from the ceiling, Topsy reached into her bag and took out the pocket diary for the year just gone. The dates and the days wouldn't match for the new year just begun, but the pages were relatively clear because she had never used a diary to record the daily narrative of her life. Now she just knew it; the time had come for her to start doing just that. Sitting cross-legged on the room's stone floor, she prised the small pencil from the diary's spine and made the first of her entries as an internee of Stanley Camp.

'My first night in Stanley will always be a nightmare,' she wrote. 'There are four of us in this tiny cell. We have no beds, no furniture. We couldn't sleep, so we huddled together for warmth and company. We talked and talked, about our husbands, our wedding days, how wonderful it will be when we are released. Anything to keep our spirits up. But we can't live like this – we will die.'

*

Christopher concentrated on hammering home the last slat of his improvised bed. January 1942 was proving to be unusually cold and wet by Hong Kong standards; or that was what it felt like to the prisoners of war trying to come to terms with the harsh regime in Shamshuipo Camp. The Japanese had separated the officers from their men and ordered them into Jubilee Buildings, a four-storey block that had served as the married soldiers' quarters at the southern, waterside edge of the camp. After several nights spent trying to sleep on the bare, concrete floor, Christopher had resolved that enough was enough. He had scavenged and scrounged until he had enough scraps to improvise a sleeping platform of sorts. Scavenging, scrounging and improvising had quickly become a necessary way of life in Shamshuipo; you either adapted to it or settled for utter misery. His new bed might still be uncomfortably hard, but at least it would enable him to lie an inch or two above the slab of concrete that had chilled every bone in his body throughout those first few sleepless nights.

His attention was drawn to a large group of new arrivals who had marched in and were now standing in line at the far side of the barrack square, as if waiting for someone to tell them where to go. The Korean guards seemed to be giving them a rough time, yelling at them and slapping a few faces. Christopher and his fellow early arrivals in the camp had come to regard the Koreans as no better than the Japanese. They seemed to lack any sense that their captives were fellow human beings. Easily provoked, they were quick to deploy brutality and humiliation as a standard method of enforcing discipline. The new prisoners were led towards a group of huts, and as they crossed the square Christopher recognized Martin Weedon among them. His right arm was in a rough sling and he seemed to be struggling to keep up with the others. Christopher made a note of which hut Martin was led to; he would make contact with him that evening.

The queue for a meal shivered and cursed in the chill wind as it shuffled towards the two serving points at a frustratingly slow pace. Christopher and Martin queued side by side. Martin had barely survived the forced march from Stanley, and it had taken a lot out of him. His shoulder wound was still raw, leaving his right arm useless.

The meal they were queuing for consisted of rice and nothing else but a few leaves. Most days, when the rice ration was spread over crude tables before cooking, it was so heavily infested with weevils and maggots that the surface was in constant movement. The queue was slow moving because the rice was being boiled in huge metal drums that had once held fuel and had been washed out to serve a new purpose. The cooks had to constantly stir the rice, otherwise the contents at the bottom of the drums burned whilst the top remained raw. The resultant tasteless sludge took an age to dish out.

Christopher held out his mess tin and watched curiously as his meal was ladled into it by Corporal Les Hughes. It seemed a lifetime ago that Hughes had woken him and Topsy to the news that they were at war with Japan. Later that day, Hughes had taken his place as a fighting soldier in Christopher's Z Company. Having been pursued across Hong Kong by bomb and bullet for two weeks, he was now back in something like his usual role

Christopher picked a leaf out of his rice stew and examined it.

'As a matter of interest, chef, what are the leaves?'

'Chrysanthemums, Sir,' came the reply. 'I'm told they're good for the digestion. They dumped a truckload of them inside the camp gates this morning.'

Christopher smiled ruefully. He knew that Monkey Stewart had complained the previous day to the Japanese camp commander that his men were falling sick through lack of vegetables in their diet. This was the apparent response.

Christopher took Martin aside. 'Get your kit together this evening and come and set yourself up in our block. There are ten of us sharing a couple of rooms, including Monkey and Lan Newnham. It's crowded, but we'll make room. We'll need to keep together if we're going to survive in this place.'

Chapter 12

January: Stanley Camp

Far to the south on the Stanley Peninsula, the dawn of Topsy's first day of captivity within the internment camp brought with it a partial lifting of her spirits. The damp, chill gloom of their arrival into an unknown place, the utter bleakness of that bare room which was to be their home for God knew how long, and the sudden, brutal separation from all that was familiar, had dragged her down to the depths of despair. Now, as the first hint of light seeped into the room through a solitary window, Topsy resolved that there could be no more feeling sorry for herself. No matter how grim life was about to become, it needed to be lived to the full. She reminded herself that she had always been the one to encourage others; in the family, at school, at medical college and at work, she had been there with a cry of 'come on, let's do it.'

She took stock. She was just about in one piece, unlike some who, like her, had stepped forward to serve at a time of the colony's need. Although she had received no news of Christopher since their hurried farewell late on Christmas Day, at least she knew that he had survived the fighting. The word was out that most of the prisoners of war had been taken to Shamshuipo. Fate had been kind to her in its random selection of her room companions. To pass the sleepless hours of the previous night, they had talked and talked.

Joyce, the late arrival in their room, had been employed as a secretary at Government House and had been taken into captivity with the Governor of Hong Kong. She had spent the last hours before the surrender in helping to burn all the codes and ciphers. News had reached her that her widowed mother had also been interned in the camp at Stanley, but she did not know where and was desperately worried about her. She had spent the previous evening looking for her but had given up, with barely enough energy left to find a space for herself to spend the night.

Daisy had been the nursing supervisor at the University Relief Hospital and had shared with Topsy the terror of those final days of the fighting and all that had followed the surrender. Her husband had been a solicitor serving in the volunteer forces and had been commissioned into the garrison's artillery regiment as invasion was threatened.

Her daughter Beryl was the fourth member of the room. Two years younger than Topsy, Beryl had also been one of the nurses deployed to the university when the Japanese had invaded. She had married a young army officer less than a year ago. Neither mother nor daughter knew if their husbands had survived the battle.

But if all four of them began the new day with some of their thoughts straying to others elsewhere, the immediate priority was to focus on their own survival. Topsy went to the window. They were on the top floor of a three-storey, concrete block. As far as she could see, theirs was one of several similar blocks, all of them showing the outward scars of battle. During the fighting, their own small room appeared to have been cleared by the Japanese by simply tossing a grenade through the door, the evidence being a shallow, charred crater in the stone floor and walls peppered with shrapnel marks. She stepped outside their door into the corridor. The number 33 had been chalked onto the door. Other rooms were showing signs of life as the new arrivals began to explore their immediate surroundings. Topsy reached one end of the corridor where a foul stench indicated what had once been a communal toilet and washroom serving that floor of the accommodation block. She tried a tap in one of the basins. There was no water. She opened a door to one of the cubicles and instantly closed it again; the sight and the smell were too much even for a nurse who had long since lost any previous squeamishness. She made her way down the flight of stairs and stepped out into the large open area of hard standing between the accommodation blocks. No doubt it had once been well maintained but it was now a sorry sight. Each block had been fought over and the debris of war was everywhere. There were no Japanese to be seen; in fact, there was no sight of anyone in a uniform of any sort, just individuals and small groups of internees who, like her, were finding their bearings. She caught sight of a group gathered round a middle-aged man who was addressing them, occasionally turning to point here and there. As she approached them, the group dispersed. She caught up with the man and introduced herself as one of last evening's new arrivals. She was in luck.

He extended his hand. 'I'm Charles Roberts. 'I was interned a week ago and have been delegated to act as the camp's billeting officer. There are a few of us in a team, trying to bring some form of organization to the chaos here.'

He explained to her that the camp had effectively no sanitation. They were working to restore damaged pipes and drains, but for the time being the only running water came from improvised standpipes. He pointed in the direction of the nearest one where a queue had already formed. Temporary latrines had been dug.

He gave Topsy a smile. 'They're desperately unhygienic and lack any privacy, but don't worry, we all soon lose our shyness here.'

The news about food was equally depressing. The only kitchen in the camp to have survived the fighting was in the sector allocated to American internees. The British, who far outnumbered any other nationals, were having to make do with a crude, emergency cookhouse. There were three meals a day. At eight in the morning there was a camp version of *congee*, a sort of rice porridge. Roberts cautioned her. The rice was poor in quality, was often contaminated and there was nothing to give it any flavour. At eleven o'clock another bowl of boiled rice was served. If they were lucky it came with a spoonful of meat gravy. A further bowl of boiled rice was served at five o'clock, often with very little else to make it more nutritional or appetizing. There were precious few vegetables coming into the camp, and no fruit. In time, they would grow their own, but in the meantime internees were already falling ill from malnutrition.

Roberts gave Topsy a stern look. 'The food is disgusting, but I advise you to take on board one of the first lessons about life here: we have to eat to stay alive. Pleasure doesn't come into it.'

'By the way,' he added, 'if you have your own knife, fork, spoon and mug, hang on to them for dear life. We're short of everything, including plates and dishes.'

He turned away as if to leave, and then paused.

'I tell you what, meet me here in an hour with your roommates and I'll show you round the camp. You can then do the same for others. I've got my hands full and just can't do everything I need to. It will help if we can spread knowledge in that way.'

When Topsy returned to their room she found that Joyce had already left to look for her mother. Topsy passed on what she had learnt to Daisy and Beryl. Having heard what Roberts had to say about the camp food, none of them was in a hurry to visit the temporary kitchen. Besides, their immediate needs were for water and a dreaded first visit to those latrines.

Charles Roberts was true to his word and was there when the three of them went looking for him. He began by explaining the general camp set-up.

'The good news is that the Japanese military have handed responsibility for the camp over to the Japanese Foreign Affairs Department. Apart from some Japanese army guards, the only Japanese you'll come across here will be officials. They've set up a camp headquarters in those buildings there.'

He pointed to two houses grouped close to each other on high ground some four hundred yards from where they were standing. That news brought sighs of relief from Topsy and her two companions; they had good cause to fear the unpredictability of the Japanese soldiery, and the less they had to deal with them the better.

Roberts continued. 'The bad news is that the Japanese seem to have made no plans at all to deal with British and allied civilians once they occupied the colony. That's why everything is so chaotic here. We're doing our best to sort things out, but we're short of just about everything we need.'

'Who do you mean by "we"?' asked Daisy.

Roberts smiled. 'Good point. The Japanese have delegated two senior Hong Kong government officials to assist them in running the camp. One of them is Dr Selwyn-Clarke; I guess you will know him. He's been the Director of Medical Services for the past four years. The other is Franklin Gimson, the Colonial Secretary. You won't know him; poor bloke, he arrived in Hong Kong only days before the invasion.'

Topsy shook her head. 'Bad timing.'

Roberts nodded. 'Bad timing indeed. Gimson is an internee like us. The only reason the Japs haven't interned Selwyn-Clarke is because they fear an epidemic in Hong Kong, so they need him to carry on working outside the camp. They've realized that if they want this camp to work, they need help. Gimson and Selwyn-Clarke have set up a camp council and co-opted internees like me to serve on it. They asked me because I've been in business in Hong Kong for twenty years and know what makes the place tick.'

Roberts looked at his watch. 'Look, I can only spare an hour. Let me show you round your new home. We might all be here a long time.'

The part of the peninsula occupied by the camp was about a mile long at its longest and just over half a mile at its widest. The camp perimeter was defined by a barbed wire fence that prevented access on its western edge to the shoreline of Stanley Bay where they had landed the previous evening, and in the east to the beach of Tai Pan Bay. Much of the irregular terrain of scrub, rock and low hills had been built upon. In the northern sector of the camp, Roberts pointed out St Stephen's College. Nobody yet knew the complete story of the massacre that had taken place there on Christmas Day, but dark rumours and a troubled sense of tragedy lingered there. They paused a while in silence beside the scorched ground where the wretched survivors of that grim episode had been forced to burn the evidence of what had taken place there. Close to where they stood, but unknown to them, was the pillbox from where Martin Weedon had led his counter-attack and been wounded.

The prison dominated the southern sector of the camp. It had been built only four years before the invasion and the Japanese intended to keep it as a prison for Hong Kong's criminal classes, but completely separate from the internment camp. Close to the prison's north-east corner, a busy complex of assorted buildings had once accommodated all those who worked in support of the prison, some of them with families. These were now to be the over-crowded home for all but a few of the camp's internees. The block where Topsy had found her room was one of several that had previously housed the prison warders and guards and their families. Roberts told them that they were in Block 15 and that the number 33 hastily chalked on their room's door would be their room number. If these gaunt, concrete structures had ever offered a hint of architectural merit or provided a decent home, the ravages of war had erased the evidence. The Americans and Dutch each had their own blocks but most of the buildings – whether bungalows, houses, the college or these huge utilitarian blocks – were occupied by British internees who already numbered more than two thousand. Around eight hundred of these were women and a further two hundred or so were children, not all of them accompanied by an adult. Roberts explained, almost by way of an apology, that he and his team had not been able to cope with the sudden influx of internees. They had been swamped by the sheer number of them and had not been helped by the confused information coming from the Japanese authorities who themselves had been overwhelmed.

Topsy mentioned that Joyce was still looking for her mother. 'I'll do my best to help her,' said Roberts, 'but I can't promise to find her. In time, we'll have a proper register of who's here and where they've found a room for themselves. We'll then be able to move people around. Till then, I'm afraid the priority is on survival, sorting out the sanitation and water supply, getting food in and making sure the sick are looked after.'

That reminded him. 'As nurses, you will want to help. We are well off for doctors amongst the internees and there seem to be several of you who are nurses. I'll show you what we've managed to set up by way of medical facilities.'

They passed through gardens that Roberts indicated were earmarked for the growing of vegetables and fruit. Just beyond the gardens, a two-story building had been roughly converted to serve as a medical centre. It was already in heavy use.

'We refer to this place as the camp sanatorium,' Roberts explained. 'It's not suitable to serve as a hospital but we intend to convert that large block there.

He pointed towards a large building close to the shoreline of Tweed Bay. The three women followed his gaze, sensing that they would be spending much of their time there in future.

'It used to house the single Indian warders. We've already christened it the Tweed Bay Hospital.'

On the way back to their block, they skirted the eastern perimeter of the camp. A young woman stood close to the barbed wire, her back towards them, her eyes fixed on the beach beyond. Roberts felt the need to explain.

'She's an English girl and her brother's body is there on the beach. He was killed on Christmas Day and the Japanese won't allow him to be recovered. Since she arrived three days ago, she's come each morning and evening and just stood there, watching over him, so close but cruelly beyond her reach.'

Chapter 13

January: Shamshuipo Camp

At Shamshuipo, Monkey Stewart called a meeting of all Diehard officers to discuss how they would confront their new lives as prisoners of war. Twelve of them had survived the battle. All but two of them had already spent three weeks in Shamshuipo. Jim Whitham, like Martin Weedon, had been a late arrival. Last autumn, with war fast approaching, he had been offered an emergency commission and had grabbed the chance to join his cricketing friends in the Diehards. Of the six officers in D Company who had fought the Japanese at Stanley, he was the sole survivor, but had been wounded in both legs. He had made it to Shamshuipo in a Red Cross ambulance, along with two other wounded members of the company.

Tony Hewitt was sporting a bruised face. That morning he had failed to bow to a passing Japanese officer and for his pains had been set upon by two guards. The previous week, Stewart had been slapped in the face when he had informed another Japanese officer that his men would not bow to any Japanese. He had added that in England, only butlers and waiters bowed. That had earned him another blow.

They sat on the concrete floor of a small room bare of furniture of any kind. The door and windows had been ripped from their frames and there were large gaps in the ceiling, so the chill of the north-east wind filled the room. They still wore the shirts, shorts and boots they had been wearing when they had fought themselves to a standstill back on Christmas Day. They had had to ditch any of the kit which they couldn't wear or carry with them on the march to the camp. Christopher had lost his greatcoat but had managed to keep hold of a pullover and a blanket which he now wrapped round his shoulders.

Monkey Stewart scanned the faces of the young officers gathered around him, looking for signs. They weren't the same men they had been in the peacetime garrison. Eighteen days of fighting and more than three weeks as prisoners of war had changed them, perhaps forever. He knew that applied to himself, too. The battle, and above all the losses and final defeat, had taken a toll on his health. God, he was tired. He was going to need them to step up yet again. They all knew the time had come to think beyond the aim of individual survival from one day to another; they needed to rebuild the battalion and restore its morale.

It had fallen on them and the surviving core of experienced senior ranks to provide the rock on which the battalion's fortunes in captivity would be built. They simply couldn't allow themselves or their men to just drift along, apathetic and satisfied with supine submission to life as prisoners of war on terms dictated by the Japanese. That was why he had called this meeting.

*

The problems they faced were daunting. They began with Colonel Tokunaga Isao who was in command of all Hong Kong prisoner of war camps. The Diehard soldiers had quickly given him the nickname of the White Pig. Pasty-faced, squat and overweight, he was an out and out sadist for whom the holding of power over several thousand allied prisoners was a dream come true. He had set himself up in a comfortable town house in Kowloon, complete with house staff and a Chinese mistress. He set the harshest of tones for the regime within the camps under his command. Even minor infringements of camp discipline were met with beatings which could easily escalate to torture. Most acts of punishment were spontaneous and random, but others were performed as a ritual, with fellow prisoners forced to watch. Tokunaga's signature form of humiliation was to order the entire camp to parade and then keep them waiting for hours, at attention, until he deigned to arrive and inspect them. He would waddle along the front of each rank of soldiers, now and then pausing on a whim to either slap a face or kick a shin, always with a guard in close attention, bayonet fixed to rifle, in case anyone on the receiving end was intimidated into retaliating. He was notoriously foul-smelling.

Frank Waldron had once observed to Christopher, 'I'd rather take a slap or a kick in the shins than have him breathing his bleedin' fumes into my face.'

Where Tokunaga led, his underlings followed, some of them with zeal. The daily parade for roll call, *tenko*, provided the most sadistic of the guards with ample opportunities to inflict pain and humiliation on their prisoners. When his turn came, each prisoner had to call out his prison number in Japanese. Any lateness on parade, any stumble, any slowness in answering, any call made too quictly, was liable to attract a punch or kick. Even the simple act of being ill could be enough to be singled out for rough treatment. Whilst the purpose of *tenko* parades was to keep track of the prisoners, the Japanese used them to inflict collective punishment. Whenever they thought that infringement of camp rules by individuals was getting out of hand, they would hold several parades at unpredictable times during the day and night. The aim was not only to punish; it was meant to drive a wedge of resentment between offenders and the rest.

These parades soon became part of the grotesque theatre of camp life at Shamshuipo, but they had their lighter moments, too. The battalion's Cockney soldiers were born mimics, and *tenko* parades provided them with temptations that some of them just could not resist, even if the inevitable outcome was a beating forcibly watched by the entire parade. The mere sight and sound of Japanese soldiers on the parade ground was enough to bring a smile to British soldiers' lips. They thought the Japanese looked ridiculous and far too comical to ignore. What they saw were ill-fitting uniforms, short, bandy legs tightly swathed in puttees from ankle to knee and a strange, jerky form of drill, all accompanied by shrill, squeaky words of command that sounded more suited to the music hall than a parade ground. It made the Japanese easy targets for mimicry. Stewart had taken one repeat offender aside and advised him to keep out of trouble for his own safety's sake.

'I know it's going to get me hurt, Sir,' was the reply. 'But honestly, it's worth it just to take the piss out of them and give the boys something to laugh about.'

This epitomized the dilemma facing Stewart and his leadership team. If the Japanese intention was to humiliate and brutalise them, what was the best response? If the policy was to stay out of trouble and avoid antagonizing the Japanese – literally, by bowing to them – many prisoners' spirits would break. For some individuals, that could make the difference between surviving and dying when things got really tough. But out and out resistance and obstruction also carried risks. The Japanese had signed the Geneva Convention but had refused to ratify it. During the battle for Hong Kong and the immediate aftermath of the surrender, they had ignored the convention and now, in those early weeks of life in the prisoner of war camps, they had already shown their contempt for it. Minor infringements of camp rules were regularly being punished with brutality and ritual humiliation, while breaches considered as serious invoked systematic torture, in some cases followed by execution.

Stewart was clear in his own mind: when it came to confronting their Japanese captors head on, he would do it himself. That would be his role. The rest had to find a balance between the two extremes of abject submission and outright defiance. If they were to confront the Japanese, it should be on issues that really mattered, issues like medical care for the wounded and sick, proper sanitation, and the provision of sufficient food and clothing. Defiance on issues that didn't matter much weren't worth the pain of the inevitable Japanese retaliation.

One such case was still fresh in his mind. On the day following the surrender, the Japanese had demanded that all prisoners sign a declaration that they would not attempt to escape. This contravened King's Regulations which were clear; if taken prisoner, it was the duty of every soldier to attempt to escape. This had posed a difficult question for Monkey Stewart: should he order his men how to react to the Japanese demand? On the one hand, signing the declaration made no difference; if a prisoner of war was going to attempt escape, he wouldn't allow his signature on a piece of paper to stop him. But it wasn't that simple; there was a principle at stake. And it was a principle shared by Company Sergeant Major Ed Soden and around twenty of his men – all that survived from C Company. They had defied the Japanese and refused to sign. They might have been defeated, but they were in no mood to comply with whatever the Japanese demanded of them. They had been tied up and left all day on the square in Murray Barracks without food or water. Every hour, a Japanese officer had approached them and ordered them to sign; each time they had refused. Early in the evening they had been taken to a courtyard in the barracks and lined up against a wall. A machine gun had been set up and aimed at them, and the officer in charge had stepped forward to offer them a last chance to sign. They had replied in the defiant vernacular of Cockney soldiers whereupon the machine gun had fired a prolonged burst aimed above their heads. A tense silence had descended on the entire barracks until, one by one, the men of C Company had limped and staggered into view, no longer tied and with their declarations still unsigned. It had been a symbolic victory, but one achieved by a dangerous gamble over a matter of little practical significance.

Three weeks later, looking back, Stewart was in no doubt; only the fear of provoking a mass riot of prisoners had prevented a mock execution from becoming a real one. His message to his young officers was clear; Tokunaga's regime of brutality and humiliation would be answered by the battalion's own regime of discipline and order. There was no time to lose. Before the men's morale sunk irretrievably low, before their collective discipline broke down and before quarrelsome and maverick groups emerged and began to undermine one of the Diehards' strengths – their collective spirit – they would re-establish a chain of command that was recognized and respected, together with a clearly understood structure to the life of the battalion that was as close as possible in captivity to what it had been in a peace-time garrison. There would be a battalion routine to each day. The officers and senior ranks would be seen and heard everywhere from reveille to lights-out. Signs of apathy, self-pity and selfishness would be met full-face. They would encourage, persuade, cajole, sympathise, criticise, rebuke, shame – whatever it took. Every last man should understand and accept that their best chance of survival as individuals lay in preserving and deploying their strength as a disciplined battalion.

Then there was the food; or the lack of it. Countless small kitchens had been improvised around the camp. One of them was cooking its meals in a bath. Each one was a miracle of the prisoners' ingenuity, but they could only cook what was given to them, and that was rice, rice and rice. And not nearly enough of it. The camp menu had quickly come to be labelled 'boiled rice with leaves for breakfast, leaves with boiled rice for supper.' The ration they were allowed by the Japanese in those first few days was barely a third of the amount needed if they were to stay healthy. Unless the ration was increased and the diet improved, widespread malnutrition and disease were inevitable. Stewart had demanded to speak to Tokunaga but had been refused. Tokunaga's message was that food was in short supply in Hong Kong and the prisoners should be grateful for the generosity of the Imperial Japanese Army. As soldiers who had surrendered rather than die, they were fortunate to receive what they were given.

Faced with Tokunaga's refusal to improve the food ration, the prisoners had looked to their own ingenuity. Many of the battalion's soldiers had grown up in an environment in which scrounging was a way of life; it was as if living on their wits was in their Cockney genes. Several had contacts amongst the Chinese community and, however tight camp security might be, ways and means could be found to smuggle extra rations in. The camp was bordered on two sides by the sea, but along the other two sides all that separated it from Kowloon's streets was an eight-feet-high fence reinforced with barbed wire. Some Chinese were prepared to run the risks of smuggling food and tobacco into the camp, either for money or simply out of friendship. Guards were being bribed to turn a blind eye or even to participate in bartering, and ways were already being found to outwit and swindle the Japanese supply staff. It was not just more rice that was needed. Commodities normally taken for granted such as salt, sugar, cooking oil and flour, had overnight become highly prized luxuries. The question for Monkey Stewart and his leadership team was just how far this nascent black market should be allowed to become a free for all. They were all agreed; there would always be an element of collecting and hoarding items by individual soldiers for their own enjoyment, but that would have to exist alongside a structured arrangement designed for the benefit of the battalion as a whole.

Stewart turned to Tony Hewitt. 'It's time to deploy one of our best assets. I need you to arrange for our friend Albert to come and see me. The battalion has need of him.'

In the battalion there were a select few amongst the ranks who had earned instant recognition by their first name alone. Every Diehard, from the commanding officer down, knew who Albert was. Before joining the army, Albert Poole had spent his whole life scrapping for survival amongst the poverty of an underprivileged East End community and he hadn't allowed the instincts and skills developed in his youth to wither on the vine once he had enlisted in the regiment. Unsurprisingly, this had led to his rise to the status of 'a battalion character'. It was typical of Lance Corporal Poole that on Christmas Day, on hearing that the garrison had surrendered, and in the absence of clear orders what to do now that the fighting had stopped, he had ordered his section to disable their Vickers machine gun and rifles, throw them into the sea and then head for the nearest bar. There they had been captured by the Japanese, but not before they had celebrated Christmas lunch by consuming a jarful of pickled onions washed down with a bottle of cognac, all that they had been able to find in the bar that had been heavily looted. They all agreed that the rough treatment they then received had been worth it. Already in those first three weeks at Shamshuipo, Poole had assembled a small team of hunter gatherers whose mission was to improve the prisoners' rations, by hook or by crook. He had made a good start by compromising a Japanese NCO, Sergeant Sako, who worked in the camp's ration store. Sako had been effectively 'bought' when Poole had persuaded him to trade some rations in exchange for a cigarette lighter and a wristwatch. Once snared, Sako lived in terror of being reported to Colonel Tokunaga and had thus become a useful source of extra rations.

'When I talk to Albert,' Stewart added, 'I'll make it clear that any racketeering is directed towards the common benefit of the battalion.'

'That will be an interesting conversation,' commented Christopher. 'Any chance of being a fly on the wall?'

Those first three weeks of captivity in Shamshuipo had identified a further problem that was certain to worsen in time – disease. The battle for Hong Kong had left most prisoners in a poor shape to resist disease. Even those with the strongest will had been worn down by day after day of savage contact with the enemy. Quite simply, they had spent too much of the resilience in their account and had no reserves of physical strength left. More than that, the rawness of defeat and humiliating surrender had left them psychologically drained, too.

A dangerous cocktail of conditions confronted them in the camp. Even in those early days of their captivity there, the combination of poor sanitation, severe overcrowding and hopelessly inadequate diet was producing casualties in unmanageable numbers. They were overwhelming the camp's crude medical facilities which were already short of drugs, medicines, dressings and beds. Many of the wounded should have been receiving treatment in the military hospital on Hong Kong Island, but instead had to make do with what had been improvised at Shamshuipo.

They were victims of Lieutenant Saito Shunkichi who was responsible for medical matters in all the colony's prisoner of war camps. He rivalled Tokunaga in his inhumanity towards the prisoners. He held the sole authority to send patients from Shamshuipo to receive the treatment they needed in the military hospital, but it was an authority that he shamelessly neglected, rarely bothering to see patients himself before deciding their fate. Already, prisoners were dying who might survive if only Saito would select them for treatment in hospital. Infections were rife as neglect of the wounded led to many cases of wound sepsis. An outbreak of dysentery had hit the camp and was seeping its insidious way from overcrowded hut to overcrowded hut, its progress propelled by the lack of sanitation and hygiene. And then, to make matters far worse, diphtheria began to take its toll and went unchecked because the Japanese withheld the medicines that could have treated it. Christopher had been shocked when he visited one of his men from Z Company in the camp's crude hospital, a leaking hut with no windows. It was only the third week of captivity, but all rooms in the hut were already full to overflowing. The air was filled with the noise of patients in various degrees of pain and discomfort while a foul stench testified to the lack of basic hygiene measures. The dysentery cases were kept as isolated as possible from other patients. A large room had been set aside to serve as their latrine. A dozen wooden seats – each set above a bucket – were in constant use.

Christopher had turned to one of the RAMC doctors. 'It's hard to believe that we've descended this low. We simply can't go on like this.'

'We just have to,' came the weary reply. 'The worst dysentery cases spend most of their days and nights squatting there, poor sods. I'm a doctor, but I might as well be a bloody mechanic for all the good I can do here. We're short of everything I need: clean dressings, medicines, drugs. Half the patients here should be in hospital, but that bloody man Saito has been to Shamshuipo only once and never made it past the gate.'

Almost as bad was the utter boredom. The two thousand prisoners confined in Shamshuipo camp were mostly in the prime of life but had simply nothing to do. They couldn't repair the camp because they had no tools or material. There were no books to read, no board games to play. They had become so desperate for something to do and talk about that they volunteered in their droves to go out on working parties to recover and dispose of the dead. It had taken two weeks for the Japanese to get round to this gruesome task and when they did, it was not out of any moral conscience; it was no more than a necessary process of beginning to clean up Hong Kong.

Christopher was suffocated by ennui and a feeling close to despair at not being able to do much about it. As each day began, there was scarcely anything to look forward to in the tedious hours ahead. There were two meals a day, but meals had long since ceased to be a pleasure; they were no more than a necessary function to fuel the body – inadequately at that – as part of staying alive for another day. The Japanese had failed to confiscate his officer's field notebook which he began to use for writing a diary of sorts. But what to write? How did one record boredom? He had an inner faith that – somehow, somewhere, sometime – this nightmare would end and there would come a time for retribution. He made an early resolution to prepare for that day. He began to make a written record of evidence that might one day bring Tokunaga and Saito and their like to some form of justice.

There was no relief from boredom in any form of outdoor recreation. The Japanese simply had no concept of it as part of their prisoners' lives.

They refused to allow groups of prisoners to gather outside their barrack blocks unless it was for one of their own parades, such as for roll call or being forced to watch a prisoner being punished. Individual prisoners were free to leave their huts unless a curfew was imposed, but in practice it was dangerous to roam far. The more a prisoner strayed from the door to his hut, the greater the risk of encountering camp guards or sentries who would humiliate their captives on a whim whenever the opportunity presented itself. Christopher had discovered this at the cost of sore ribs in his first week in the camp when he had stepped outside to stretch his legs. Rounding the corner of the hut he had caused two passing Japanese soldiers to swerve round him. He had stood his ground when they screamed in his face a volley of words he did not understand, only to be felled by a blow to the body from a rifle butt.

But for Christopher, there was a part of his new existence that was every bit as hard to deal with as the constant threat of brutality, the lack of food, the incipience of widespread disease, and the insufferable tedium to which he awoke every morning and took with him to his uncomfortable bed each night, and that was the total absence of news of Topsy. He was left with speculation about what might have happened to her, and the speculation tortured him every waking hour. There had been nothing but rumours to go on, and there was no shortage of those.

Monkey Stewart was clear about the need to fix the absence of news from outside the camp. They needed to establish a network of contacts with the world beyond the barbed wire perimeter of Shamshuipo. The risks for those involved would be high but it was unthinkable to continue months and probably years of confinement without knowledge of what was happening out there. Information needed to replace rumour and part of the answer lay within the battalion. Most of the Diehard prisoners had served in the colony for more than three years before the Japanese invasion. Many had made friends with members of the Chinese community, some of whom were in positions of influence and might still enjoy access to useful knowledge. Then there were the contacts made at an altogether different level. For many a soldier the word 'friendship' would not accurately describe their personal relationships with their own regular 'downhomers', as certain young women had come to be known. In time, ways would be found to smuggle messages in and out of the camp.

It was close to midnight when Monkey Stewart brought the meeting to a close.

As the group broke up, Tony Hewitt waited until he and the Colonel were alone. He had something to ask him. 'I plan to escape this place and would welcome your permission, Sir.'

Chapter 14

February: Escape

Tony Hewitt flattened himself against the concrete floor by the edge of the waterfront at Bamboo Pier. He had used the pier many times to board a ferry when the battalion had been based in the barracks, but this was altogether different. They had waited until the full moon was covered in thin cloud. At three o'clock in the morning, Shamshuipo Camp was silent, so silent that Tony's stretched nerves heard each scrape and stifled grunt of their hurried breach of the perimeter fence as if it were magnified a hundredfold. There were no Japanese guards deployed along this western side of the camp's perimeter, but the whole length was covered by fire from each end. One careless sound would be enough to leave them as sitting ducks. He peered into the half-light, anxious for a first sight of the sampan. Nothing; just the slush of a calm sea against the jetty wall. Tony began to have his doubts. This wasn't the original plan. It was only at the last moment that they had heard that a small group of prisoners had used a contact on the outside to persuade a sampan coolie to bring supplies to the edge of the camp under cover of darkness. Their new plan was to get away on the sampan as soon as it had offloaded the packages onto the jetty. Lying there now, with the moon threatening to reappear at any moment, Tony began to question whether they had made the right decision.

*

Two days as a prisoner of war in Shamshuipo had been enough for Tony to commit himself to escape. The sooner the better because the camp was not yet tightly guarded. Japanese sentries patrolled the two sides of the camp that were bounded by land, but the two sides that bordered the water were left unguarded. The perimeter fence was not yet electrified or covered by lights, but it was only a matter of time before some prisoners escaped and prompted the Japanese to make the camp more secure. An early decision had been whether to escape alone or form a small team. Straightaway he had taken Christopher into his confidence. Christopher's every instinct was to join him but he took only seconds to rule himself out.

'As far as I know, Topsy is alive and in Hong Kong, so there's no question of me leaving here. But you should find someone to go with you.'

Tony had been thinking the same. 'I came close to making a bolt for it in the confusion straight after the surrender. Monkey feared the worst about what the Japs would do to us and he urged me to have a go. But I'm glad I didn't. I don't think I could have made it. My only hope is to get to the Chinese Nationalist Army in Kukong and that's around two hundred miles. There'll be Japs everywhere for the first one hundred and fifty miles, and Chinese bandits will be a serious threat just about the whole way. I think two or three of us will stand a better chance, especially if one of us could speak a bit of Cantonese.'

'Do you have anyone in mind?' Christopher asked.

'As a matter of fact I do. Duggie Scriven. But we need to be careful,' Tony warned. 'I don't want it to get around. The fewer who know the better.'

*

Dr Douglas Scriven was an officer in the Indian Medical Service who had been drafted in to serve as the Diehards' Regimental Medical Officer only a few weeks before the Japanese had invaded the colony. In his early thirties, he was a fluent Cantonese speaker and a determined individual to have on one's side. Douglas had quickly gained a reputation as a bon viveur with an expensive taste in champagne, but Tony Hewitt had seen him in action and had been impressed.

During the fighting, Douglas had set up his regimental aid post close to battalion headquarters from where Tony had been able to observe how well he reacted to stress when the going got tough. And then, during those final desperate days of street combat when every soldier – whether cook, clerk, signaller or medical orderly – had taken part in the fighting, Tony and Douglas had fought side by side, so close that a shell blast that blew Tony off his feet on the morning of Christmas Day had struck Douglas with one of its splinters, wounding him just above the eyes.

Picking himself up, Tony had joked 'It could have been worse Duggie, it could have damaged your precious monocle.'

Christopher, too, had been impressed by Scriven, and now that Tony had taken him into his confidence about escaping, he was quick to tell him so.

'I don't think you could ask for a better bloke to escape with you. I have a hunch he will bring you good luck. Mind you, he'll need to shed some weight first.'

Tony had smiled. 'That's settled then. I'll ask him. As for his puppy fat, I've plans to get rid of that.'

Two days later, Tony and Douglas had met and shaken hands on a promise to escape together. Their plan was to smuggle their way in a junk as far north as possible on the Chinese coast. That way, they would reduce the journey on foot through Japanese-occupied territory and avoid some of the worst of what was known as Chinese bandit territory.

The next day, Martin Weedon had arrived in the camp after his arduous march from Stanley. Tony had not immediately mentioned his escape plan to him, but after two days sensed that it was time he did so. An escape team of three would be ideal, and a fit Martin Weedon would be a strong asset.

Martin had forced back tears of frustration when he had to concede that he was not yet strong enough to escape. The march north to Shamshuipo had left him in no doubt about his condition – his wounded shoulder meant he would be a handicap to an escape team.

So they had left it at that. As soon as Tony had mentioned his planned escape to him, Monkey Stewart indicated his support and went to discuss it with General Maltby. Escape bids invariably resulted in reprisals being taken against those left behind, and there was the further risk that one escape bid could easily jeopardise the success of another. With that in mind, there was an understanding, generally accepted, that escape bids needed to be approved by Maltby.

Maltby gave his approval to Tony's escape bid and undertook to provide money for it from a fund available to him. He asked one favour in return. Would they accept a third member of the team?

*

Pilot Officer Eddy Crossley was a New Zealander who had been attached to the Royal Air Force at Kai Tak. When the Japanese destroyed the garrison's aircraft on the ground on the first day of their invasion, Crossley had immediately been attached to one of the Canadian battalions and had fought as a machine gunner with them before being taken prisoner. As a young pilot in his early twenties, he would be a clear asset to the allied war effort elsewhere if he escaped. It was just the sort of escape bid that justified the risks. So when Crossley had approached Maltby, the general had offered his support, but on one condition; Crossley had to find someone to go with him.

Tony had already met Eddy Crossley by chance. He had shared his assessment of him with Christopher. 'A typical Kiwi; tough as nails and a good sort to have on your side in a scrap.'

Douglas had not been so easily convinced that they needed a third member of the team. He had dug his heels in for two days but had changed his mind once he had met Eddy. Tony had let out a long sigh of relief when Douglas gave him the go-ahead. That was it. That clinched the matter. There was now no stopping them.

If any team stood a good chance, it was theirs, but the hazards facing them were undeniable. The war in China had reached stalemate, with the Japanese still in control of a belt of territory up to 150 miles deep along the South China Sea coast. Rumour had it that they had ruined all the crops and driven the Chinese rural workers out of the countryside. Westerners on the run could not be sure that any Chinese peasants left would be friendly and, even if they were, that they would be willing to risk being helpful. What was more, large tracts of China were effectively lawless and at the mercy of organized, armed bandit gangs. Tony and his team had to plan on the assumption that every step of the way to making contact with the Chinese Nationalists would be made through hostile territory.

First though, there was the little matter of escaping from the camp in one piece.

*

Tony heard the sampan before he saw it nose its way round the corner of the pier and onto the slipway. He raised himself to a crouch. The boat was being paddled by a coolie and a second man was standing in the prow. Tony spotted the two prisoners who had arranged the delivery of food edge their way down the slipway and secure the sampan to the side wall. They quickly unloaded the packages and then engaged the sampan's two occupants in a whispered conversation accompanied by much arm waving from the second man in the sampan.

Watching this and unable to hear what was being said, Tony found the tension unbearable. The conversation had now risen above a whisper. Surely the guards would hear them. What the hell was going on? He signalled to Douglas and Eddy to follow him as he moved down the slipway. Turning to Douglas, he whispered 'Find out what the problem is.' Douglas quickly established what was causing the hold-up. The man waving his arms about was the middleman in the arrangement. He was demanding three hundred Hong Kong dollars to take them. Take it or leave it.

'For God's sake, give him the money,' Tony muttered, as Eddy took the lead by jumping into the sampan, dragging Douglas after him. Once aboard, the three of them pushed like mad against the slipway wall until they were clear of the pier. They were on their way.

They had been lucky. Throughout their breaching of the wire and getting aboard the sampan, the moon had remained behind cloud. No sooner were they clear of Bamboo Pier than their luck began to run out. The moon broke clear with a suddenness that ended their brief exhilaration at being free. The sampan was now sharply silhouetted against a calm sea bathed in moonlight. To make matters worse, the middleman began to tell them his life story in loud pidgin English. He wanted them to tell the Chinese Nationalists that he had helped them to escape. Douglas urged him to keep quiet. At that moment, the coolie stopped rowing and started to shout at Douglas and the middleman. Douglas translated for them. The coolie wanted more money, otherwise he wouldn't go any further. Before they could shut him up, the first shot rang out. Three more followed as sighters before the machine gun at the nearest corner of the camp opened up on them. The bullets were striking the sea behind them, some ricocheting closely overhead. The coolie now lost all thought of bargaining for more money and began working the oar as if his life depended on it. Which it did. If he and the middleman escaped the bullets, they still risked capture, and capture meant certain torture followed by execution. They rounded the edge of a breakwater which gave them cover as machine gun bullets crashed into the concrete wall above them. Between them and the far shore lay some four hundred yards of open water. They couldn't afford to wait. Their intended landing place close to Lai Chi Kok village was dangerously predictable because it was the nearest point to the camp. If the Japanese had been alerted to their escape, they were likely to deploy a patrol to intercept them. At that moment the moon went behind cloud again, leaving the machine gunners unsighted. The firing became wild and sporadic. It was time to go.

The few minutes of frantic rowing towards the shore seemed an eternity to the three escapees. Surely the Japanese would be there waiting for them. They urged the coolie to speed up. He needed no encouragement. He was a typical Chinese boatman, slim and wiry in build and very strong. The sampan sped on until it ran itself to a stop on the sand and pebbles of the beach. There was no time for the rituals of a farewell to their reluctant helpers. Without a backward glance, Tony leapt ashore and led the dash up the beach towards a gap in the houses, closely followed by Eddy and less athletically by Douglas.

Immediately ahead lay a road they had to cross. They had rehearsed how they would do it. Tony would check that the road was clear of Japanese patrols and then signal the other two to follow. Once across, Tony would lead followed by Douglas. Eddy was to act as rear man, tasked with making sure they weren't being followed. Tony had insisted that they practise this way of moving at night in the camp until it became second nature. Doug and Eddy had thought it ridiculous to get up in the middle of the night to prowl around camp like boy scouts, but they had gone along with it. They were about to demonstrate that it had all been in vain. As Tony approached the road, the silence of the night was brutally shattered. First came the loud barking of a lone dog, rapidly followed by the appearance of a Chinaman shrieking at the top of his voice. Within seconds, the barking dog had been joined by others. All discipline and previous training now deserted the escapees. Eddy let out a yell and dashed headlong across the road and up a narrow lane. Douglas followed him, head down, elbows pumping as he tried to keep up. Tony kept as calm as he could, checking to see if the rumpus had drawn anyone else to the scene, before heading after them. He caught up with them some two hundred yards up the lane where they were desperately trying to recover their breath.

'What the hell was that all about?' Tony asked of Douglas. 'Did you understand what the old man was yelling about?'

'From what I could hear, he thought we were thieves.'

They paused only long enough for Tony to deliver a lecture. His message was clear. If their movement discipline was to break down the moment they encountered trouble, they had little hope of making it through the days ahead. So far, they had done the easy bit; the real test started now.

They pushed on, intent on putting distance and height between them and the waterfront. They made good progress. Tony was familiar with the area, having conducted military training exercises in the hills there. He had even brought a girlfriend there for a picnic overlooking the reservoir that now reflected the moonlight as they skirted its edges. Step by step, their elation at being free was joined by a growing self-confidence. They had their second wind. They no longer flinched at each shadow cast by a waving branch or each flutter of wings from a bird disturbed by their presence.

This had all the makings of a careless mistake, and they duly made one. They found themselves crossing the skyline, their black, sharp-edged silhouettes moving across the bright moonlight. Loud, questioning shouts reached them from a track only a few yards below them. They ran, this time in their agreed formation, Tony leading the way, Eddy at the rear watching for signs of pursuit and a breathless Douglas scurrying along between them. Tony cursed himself. As an infantry officer, he had committed the cardinal sin of night patrolling. Despite the real scare, he chuckled to himself; they had got away with it, but if Monkey Stewart had been there, there would have been hell to pay.

At the first sign that dawn was about to break, they left the track and headed into the nearest undergrowth. There, they camouflaged for themselves a space where they could hide out for the day ahead. They were high up on the southern slopes of a ridge overlooking Hong Kong Island. Below them in the gathering light, The Peak and parts of the harbour came into view.

Tony knew exactly where they were, but an exhausted Douglas was downcast. Had they really only come that far? And then, as if to confirm their new-found freedom, the faint sound of a bugle call reached them. It was reveille being sounded in Shamshuipo Camp. The camp was hidden from their view, but as they lay huddled against the cold wind from the north, they could picture the scene unfolding far below them. For the first time since the surrender, the morning *tenko* would not involve them.

*

Christopher had been woken during the night by the sound of shooting and feared the worst. He half-expected to see three dead bodies on display at the morning roll call and was relieved to note that there were no obvious signs of trouble when they all formed up. That morning's *tenko* was under the command of Lieutenant Wada Hideo. Nothing unusual in that. The Diehards in the camp had been quick to bestow the nickname 'Ratface' on him; they thought he looked like a rat and behaved like one. Monkey Stewart took up his customary place centre-front of the Diehard contingent, his officers one pace to his rear, spread out one pace ahead of the front rank of their companies.

It took only minutes for the absence of the three escapees to be revealed and a few more to check that they were neither in their huts nor in the sick bay. Wada's face contorted with rage. He confronted Stewart, launching a volley of screams and spittle into his face. Stewart did not flinch and just stared ahead with those light blue eyes that had intimidated many a young Diehard officer.

The interpreter thrust his face close to Stewart's. 'There are three officers missing. Where are they?'

'If they're not in the sick bay, I don't know where they are,' Stewart answered, truthfully.

Wada was now beside himself with a fury that was partly driven by panic. Three officers might have escaped whilst the camp was on his watch. Colonel Tokunaga would take the news badly. Even at the best of times, he was a man to be feared. Almost as bad, he, Wada, was at risk of losing face in front of his men. He needed to assert his authority. He slapped Stewart as hard as he could with his open hand. Stewart had seen it coming and was braced against it. He didn't move. Wada slapped him a second time.

Christopher could feel the tension rising amongst the Diehard ranks. They didn't take kindly to seeing their commanding officer knocked about. Sensing trouble, the Japanese soldiers escorting Wada brought their rifles from the shoulder to the alert and held them so that their long bayonets pointed threateningly towards the ranks of prisoners.

Stewart again held steady. He shouted a warning over his shoulder.

'Don't do anything stupid, any of you. That's an order.'

Wada squealed an order and two Japanese soldiers rushed forward and dragged Stewart away towards the guardroom.

They interrogated him throughout the day. Tokunaga arrived mid-morning. The situation was clear to him. Two of Stewart's own officers had escaped. He must have known about it and given his permission. What were their plans? How did they get away from the camp? Who helped them? Where were they heading for? Stewart pleaded ignorance. They forced him to stand holding a fire bucket filled with sand above his head. Every time he dropped to the floor with exhaustion, they dragged him to his feet and hit him.

Late that evening, the guards dumped him at the bottom of the stairs of Jubilee Building. Christopher and Martin helped him up the stairs to his room. All day, he had been denied food and water and was having to dig deep into his reserves of strength, but those fierce blue eyes were undimmed.

'I must admit it bloody hurts,' he mumbled through swollen lips, 'but it was worth it, just to know they got away.'

Chapter 15

April: Stanley Camp

In the gathering warmth of a mid-April morning, Topsy sat on a rocky knoll in Stanley Camp and took in the view to the east across Tai Tam Bay. The blue-green wooded hills of the D'Aguilar Peninsula seemed tantalizingly close. They might just as well have been a hundred miles distant, such was the complete separation of her life in the camp from the world outside. Whatever the weather, she came here as often as she could when not on duty in the hospital or the school. So much of her life was spent in the close company of other internees, whether in the crowded room in Block 15 or the busy wards of the hospital or the crush in the canteen at mealtimes, that she needed regular time and space to herself. Already the overcrowding in the accommodation blocks was beginning to tell on morale, and the new experience of living cheek by jowl with people who had previously been strangers was testing new relationships beyond breaking point. Even close friends had begun to find each other irritating.

She glanced down towards the beach beyond the wire. The young English girl still came to stand at the wire for a few moments each day, no longer to watch over her dead brother but simply to hold onto the memory of him. Week by week his remains had succumbed to the elements and become nothing more than carrion for the rats and birds until the only visible trace of him were the rags of his uniform. And then they too had been picked up and taken by the winds and tides of late winter and early spring.

After three months in the camp, Topsy had much to reflect on in these precious moments of solitude. She was as certain as she could be that Christopher was alive. Women whose husbands were prisoners of war in Hong Kong had begun to receive a small allotment of money from time to time. Topsy had just received the first of these payments which had been accompanied by a chit bearing Christopher's familiar signature. She had breathed a sigh of relief. Christopher must know she had survived and was being held at Stanley. The odds were that he was at Shamshuipo but a rumour was doing the rounds that the Japanese were going to move the officers to a different camp. She inwardly cursed that there was still no system which would enable news of individuals to reach the internees, let alone allow any direct exchange of letters, or even messages, between next of kin. For now, she had to be content with seeing that precious signature on a chit.

She shifted her position. Looking back towards the built-up area of the camp, she was prompted to reflect on what had been achieved since those first days when spirits had been so low. She smiled to herself; the British had done what they always do when a community is in a tight spot – they had formed committees. There was a committee for education, another for medical matters and still others for supplies, accommodation, sanitation and work party rosters. One squad had soon got going on scrubbing amenity areas, walkways, pavements and hallways, while another cut and scavenged wood to fire the crude kitchen ovens. A group of maintenance volunteers was quickly busy repairing everything from damaged drains and pipes to lavatory cisterns, while still others improvised madly to make tools and utensils and build window frames, doors and beds.

The allocation of accommodation was a sore point. An advance party of internees had been sent into the camp in early January to do what they could to clear up the area which had been the scene of heavy fighting only days before. The worst of the detritus of war had been removed but some of the workforce had taken the opportunity to grab the best of the accommodation by setting themselves up in bungalows and cottages that had been earmarked for families and the elderly.

For the rest of the internees, as Topsy had experienced herself, finding a room had been a free for all. There was a general view amongst the British internees that the worst places to live were the blocks that had previously served the prison as quarters for some of the warders. Topsy's room 33 was in one of them. The Japanese had crammed 780 British internees into these blocks which had been built to house 260 Indian warders and administrators. The larger rooms in Block 15 now held four internees. The room into which Topsy and her room mates had groped their way in the poor evening light of their arrival in the camp was one of the smaller ones. Joyce had since been reunited with her mother and had opted to move out to share a room with her, it must be said with some misgivings. Room 33 was scarcely big enough to provide space for the three of them who remained, but at least it now felt more like a home. Towards the end of February, the billeting and supplies committees had managed to procure some camp beds. When made up, these beds covered the floor space of Topsy's room, leaving just enough space to step between them. This had led to a daily ritual whereby the beds were assembled at bedtime and dismantled first thing in the morning. Similarly, a small table and matching canvas chair were folded away at night and unfolded each morning. Daisy had one day returned with them in triumph from a foraging expedition but had refused to say from where she had rescued them.

The three of them shared a washroom with the four occupants of the larger room next door to theirs. The washroom had a basin, a cold water tap and a hole-in-the-floor lavatory which had been restored into use. Although primitive, it was a cherished bonus after two undignified weeks spent dashing to the communal latrines. Block 15 had a balcony which overlooked the eastern side of the camp area and the bays beyond, but Topsy rarely spent time taking in the views from there, much preferring to escape the claustrophobic embrace of life in the block whenever possible. The spot she had found for herself had quickly become 'her spot', a retreat untroubled by the presence of others. She had become jealous of it.

Her life in the camp had received a boost in her second week there. She had been returning to her block one morning from a walk round the northern edge of the camp area when she spotted, at a distance, a familiar figure that she could not at first place. As they drew closer, both women felt a dawning recognition which grew step by step until they fell into a long, tearful hug of reunion. It was Phyllis Newnham. Phyllis explained that she had been allocated a small room of her own in one of the buildings close to St Stephen's College. As far as they both knew, they were the only Diehard wives who had not been evacuated and now found themselves as internees at Stanley. They had something else in common; they both knew that their husbands had survived the battle but had been left guessing about their whereabouts. Topsy had felt a special bond with Phyllis ever since they had colluded to persuade Monkey Stewart to give Christopher permission to marry. Now, she had further cause to feel grateful; in Phyllis she had found a kindred spirit with whom to share the tough times that lay ahead of them.

And there continued to be tough times. The food was scarcely fit to eat and there wasn't enough of it anyway. The rations comprised inferior grade rice that was accompanied sometimes by minute quantities of meat of dubious origin, at other times by rotting fish. If the internees ever saw vegetables, they were invariably the dried out remains of tasteless Chinese cabbage or pumpkin. The problem was compounded by the odious Cheng Kwok-leung, a Chinese collaborator who had ingratiated himself with the Japanese authorities. Having secured the post of camp supervisor, he intended to make as much money out of it as he could. Fat, corrupt and greedy, he operated a regime of bribery and theft. He took bribes from the wealthiest internees in return for favours and he hived off for himself a percentage of the rations provided to the camp by the Japanese and recycled it on the Hong Kong black market.

Topsy had been quick to notice that camp life brought out the worst in some internees. A few had subsided into a pit of apathy. Others, a minority, had simply turned their backs on any concept of community effort and focused ruthlessly on their own welfare.

But for the most part, the internees strove to make the most of their lives under captivity. Kitchen ovens were constructed out of the rubble of war-damaged walls and crude bricks made from the peninsula's yellow clay. Dustbins were cleaned and used as saucepans for cooking the rice. Improvised millstones were used to grind rice into flour which was then mixed with water and sugar to produce yeast. The bread that resulted was tasteless, but it had a prime virtue – it was not soggy rice. One of the first adjustments they had all had to make was how to swallow mouthfuls of bug-infested rice without bringing it all up moments later. Topsy grimaced at the thought of it. Things were improving though. Recently, the rice ladled onto her tin plate had contained fewer weevils. Somehow, those in charge of the kitchens had managed to make some fine-gauged sieves and routinely spent hours patiently shaking the daily rice ration through them until most of the unwanted creatures had been separated.

To the internees, all versions of rice meals became known as 'slum rice'. One unreliable relief from it lay in finding ways to smuggle in items that in the world outside were regarded as everyday and basic but within the life of the camp assumed the status of luxuries. Sugar and salt, tea and coffee were available to be bought at extortionate cost through the bribing of camp guards. Somewhat cheaper were loaves of bread already shrouded in mould.

But it was improvisation and resourcefulness that were the internees' principal weapons against the wretchedly poor diet inflicted on them. If the internees were to avoid severe malnutrition and the diseases that would surely follow, it was up to them to find ways. And they had already begun to find them. Near the top of the list for usefulness were soya beans. They mixed them with water to make an acceptable form of milk, or they ground them down and roasted them to act as a passable substitute for coffee powder. Once used, the grounds could then be retained to form the ingredient for a cake.

Some internees were born scavengers. A team of them routinely picked through the dustbins outside the camp headquarters, and it was the banana skins retrieved from one of these rummages that had helped make the banana-flavoured soya cake that Topsy had tasted at a party to celebrate a friend's birthday. Others experimented with varying degrees of success. Peanut oil was relatively easy to have smuggled in and was discovered to be edible when mixed with rice and a bit of sugar. It was not long before it established itself as a regular feature on the camp menu and became known, affectionately, as Stanley Pudding.

Scavenging and ingenuity did not end with the provision of food. Many staple items taken for granted in their previous lives were now unobtainable. There was no toothpaste, but trial and error revealed that dipping a wet finger into wood ash or the powder from ground cuttlefish bones, and then rubbing one's teeth with it was an effective substitute. There was no soap either, but wood ash again came to the rescue. Mixed carefully with warm water it helped wash away the worst of the day's grime, but they had yet to find a way of adding a decent scent to it. Peanut oil was not only used as cooking fat and in the making of Stanley Pudding but was also kept to act as a substitute for paraffin whenever the Japanese cut the camp's electricity supply and small lamps were needed to provide light.

Topsy had learned to treat meals as no more than the taking of fuel to sustain life. She neither expected pleasure from what she ate, nor felt any. But coming to terms with permanent hunger and malnutrition on a personal level was one thing, the constant sight of so many children going hungry was altogether more challenging. She had a regular shift at the camp hospital and already was accustomed to caring for children showing early signs of a poor diet. Invariably, mothers went even hungrier, often going without their full ration so that their children could have a little extra here and there. The results were to be seen everywhere, both in the number of cases presenting themselves in the hospital and in the obvious loss of weight for everyone. A sewing group of more than fifty women had been formed. They were kept busy taking in the waists of baggy shorts and dresses, and improvising tops and shirts out of pieces of material of all sorts.

Topsy thought back to last week. There had been rumours of Red Cross parcels about to reach the camp. Most of the anticipation had been of luxuries such as meat, sugar, chocolate, dried fruits, coffee and tea; anything that would relieve them from the monotony of rice and yet more rice. When the boxes came, they were opened to cries of disappointment. Topsy had welcomed a new pair of shorts, a shirt, some underwear and rubber shoes that she desperately needed since the soles of her shoes had worn thin and the canvas uppers were starting to rot away. As for the new pair of socks, she could have done with those when the weather had been at its coldest, but she would keep them safe till winter came again. She would make the two bars of soap last for months and the cigarettes would be bartered for something she really needed. But where was the food? Where were the tins of bully beef and stew, the packets of sugar and tea, the cocoa powder, the tinned milk and the chocolate bars? Didn't the Red Cross know that each day she awoke hungry, each evening went to bed hungry and most nights lay waiting for sleep hungry?

Topsy pulled herself up onto her feet, aware of the ache as her stiff joints adjusted. Already she was feeling the effects of three months of malnutrition. She was down to do a four-hour shift in the hospital that afternoon. Not that there was much that could be done of a medical nature. Medicines and dressings were in short supply and were hopelessly overwhelmed by the demand for them. Already the deficiency of key vitamins had brought the onset of disease and scarcely any internees were free of some sickness or other. Pellagra, dysentery and beriberi had already taken hold. Topsy was having to watch helplessly as the first signs of rickets amongst the children were making themselves felt and both of her room-mates, Daisy and Beryl, were showing the effects of scurvy and septic sores. It was only a matter of time before some internees went down with malaria and typhus, and if typhoid fever or diphtheria ever hit the camp, Topsy could not see how they would be able to isolate and contain them, such was the overcrowding and poor sanitation in the camp.

The sun was high now and she could feel the humidity closing in for its daily confrontation with the cooling breeze that wafted in from the South China Sea beyond the bay and its far hills. The distant sound of the school bell reached her as a reminder that it was time to collect her plate, spoon and mug from her room and head for the camp kitchen and her second meal of boiled rice that day.

The school held classes for more than two hundred children of all ages. Topsy had instantly volunteered to join a teaching staff of all the talents and backgrounds, and now spent three mornings each week taking classes.

Block 15 and its neighbours stood gaunt and uninviting down the slope. A slow walk would take her there in five minutes. She was in no hurry. She hated that building. No matter they had made what they could of their room, it would always be the place where boredom was at its height, sleep at its most elusive and nightmares ever present. It didn't even offer the feeling of security that she and most women craved. The terrors of the December battle's final hours and its immediate aftermath were never far away. Only two weeks ago they had threatened to return.

It had been late in the night when she first became aware of his presence. She had heard nothing. It had been his smell that first alerted her. Daisy and Beryl could be heard breathing heavily in sleep. She forced herself to open her eyes. At first, nothing. Then, as her eyes became used to the dark, the faintest of shadowy outlines stood, framed in the open doorway, motionless, close to the end of her camp bed. The smell of sweat and drink was all too familiar to her. The silhouette gathered detail: a short, stocky figure; the distinctive shape of a Japanese soldier's peaked cap; the rifle with its long bayonet prominent above his shoulder. Topsy froze, unable to move or scream. And then he was gone, with only the slightest scuff of his rubber shoes on the concrete floor of the corridor. The next morning, she had alerted other residents of block 15. She had heard stories of camp guards at night peering through the windows of rooms on the ground floor but had thought herself relatively safe in her room on the second floor. No longer.

Chapter 16

September: Argyle Street Camp, Kowloon

For several weeks there had been rumours that the Japanese intended to transport their prisoners of war from Hong Kong to Japan where they were needed as slave labour. Japan's resources being dangerously stretched, it made sense to put thousands of prisoners of war to productive work in Japan instead of letting them idle their days away in prison camps in Hong Kong.

The prospect of being transported to Japan to work for the enemy's war effort was viewed with mixed feelings by the prisoners themselves. Most found the concept of aiding the enemy in any way repugnant and against all their instincts as soldiers. What was more, they lived in the hope that somehow the Japanese would be ejected from Hong Kong, perhaps by the Chinese Nationalists, in which case it would be far better to stay where they were. And then there were the other rumours about being released and repatriated as part of an agreement to swap prisoners.

But there was a contrary view that life might be better as a prisoner of war in Japan. The conditions could hardly be worse and perhaps being forced to work might be marginally better than the suffocating boredom and futility of life in Shamshuipo.

Christopher was in no doubt about his preference. As long as he believed that Topsy was still in Hong Kong, he wanted to stay. Not that it mattered much in practical terms. There were no means of communicating with her, and he assumed that she was kept similarly ignorant of his fate.

Towards the end of August, rumour gave way to fact. Monkey Stewart and other commanders were ordered by the Japanese to provide the names of those men in Shamshuipo who were classed as troublemakers. Those nominated were to be shipped to Japan. For Stewart this was a task he did not welcome. He knew that it had less to do with getting rid of difficult prisoners than with recruiting forced labour for Japan's mines, foundries and docks. He would be selecting men to work in support of the enemy's war effort and he wanted no part in it.

Not that the candidates weren't obvious. They were known as the 'hard men'. They were the sort who in peacetime had the longest conduct sheets and had spent most time in the cells of the guard room. But they had been amongst the best when it had come to fighting the Japanese. To a man, they resented authority in any form, and in captivity they continued to give their captors a hard time, even if the pleasure it gave them meant taking a beating as punishment.

Stewart, reluctantly, began to give thought to which of his men would be in line for transportation. Private 'Mickey' Head would have to be the first name on the list. He was one of those who had survived the mock execution for refusing to sign away his right to escape. He had then taken a severe beating for giving a Japanese officer the two-fingered salute instead of a bow. He was a marked man in Shamshuipo and it might save him from himself if he were transported to Japan. Then there was Private John Middleton. If his memory served him well, Stewart reckoned that this Diehard's conduct sheet was at least four pages long. He was a constant thorn in the side of the Japanese, and just couldn't resist making a mockery of the *tenko* parades by answering his name and number in cockney rhyming slang. Whilst Middleton himself was prepared to take his punishment, the Japanese often made those on parade suffer for his disruption, so it might be in everyone's best interests if he took his talent for mimicry with him to Japan. Another who came to mind was Private 'The Major' Cullen. He owed his nickname to his habit of addressing everyone, no matter what their rank, as 'old boy'. It was a measure of the man that he not only got away with it but also made himself popular amongst his fellow Cockneys who did not normally take kindly to being 'old-boyed' by anyone. He was another Diehard soldier unable to resist the temptation to make fun of the Japanese. They didn't know what to make of 'the Major'. Improbably, they found themselves as captors being patronized by one of their captives, but it was only a matter of time before he would go too far for his and everyone's good.

Such names came readily to Stewart's mind, as did those of the officers best suited to command them. Captain Harry Badger and Lieutenant Graham Hill would be ideal. They were known and respected as tough men themselves who would stand no nonsense.

So it was that on 3 September 1942, 127 Diehards paraded for the last time at Shamshuipo. They were among more than five hundred fellow 'hard men' from other units in the camp. They were made to parade at four in the morning and were then held there for two hours as their Japanese captors inflicted one final frustration on them. Harry Badger and Graham Hill led the Diehards as they marched out of the gates towards the ferry that would take them out to the *Shi Maru*, a battered old coastal freighter. Spirits were high and defiant. They sang 'Why don't they send for the old Diehards' and gave the thumbs up sign to anyone who cared to look their way. They were cheered and whistled on their way by the Diehards they left behind, some of whom were thinking that life in Shamshuipo would not be the same without them, for good or bad. Barely a mile distant in Argyle Street, Christopher joined Monkey Stewart and fellow officers to stand together a while and share a bitter regret that they could not be there to see them off on their journey to a life of hard labour which they knew many would not survive. It was especially hard for Stewart who had rarely been anywhere but with his men wherever the battle had been most fierce and imprisonment most tough. He had pushed as hard as he could to remain at Shamshuipo when the officers had been forcibly transferred to Argyle Street back in April, but Tokunaga would have none of it. The whole point of separating the officers from their men was to make life easier for the Japanese, and the last thing that Tokunaga needed were strong characters like Stewart leading from the front in the largest of his prison camps.

*

Christopher had known it was coming, but when it came a few days later the news hit him hard. All the officers in Argyle Street Camp were ordered to parade. They were to be addressed by Colonel Tokunaga himself who had good news for them. Once on parade, they were kept waiting, as they knew they would be, before Tokunaga swept into the camp in a black Mercedes that had been requisitioned from one of Hong Kong's principal banks. Tokunaga was accompanied as usual by his civilian interpreter, Niimori Genichiro.

Niimori's education in Canada seemed to have fuelled his hatred of Westerners. He had already shown himself to be a pathological sadist who took especial pleasure in inflicting pain on any prisoner who did not bow to him with sufficient lowering of the head. He was loathed and mocked in equal measure by all prisoners. Now he stood beside Tokunaga, all arrogance and ridiculous self-importance, as he translated his master's message, relishing every word that reminded the British officer class of just how far they had fallen.

They would soon be leaving Hong Kong for Japan where they and their men would be privileged to work for the wonderful people of that land. Only those fit to work hard would be selected to enjoy the benefits of being transported to a place where conditions and the climate would be so much better. Lieutenant Colonel Stewart was to command the draft of two thousand fit men, and he had a week to submit a list of those selected.

'He'll be lucky to find one hundred,' whispered Christopher to Martin Weedon beside him.

He had a point. Already weakened by malnutrition and dysentery, the prisoners in Shamshuipo's overcrowded camp were now succumbing in alarming numbers to an outbreak of diphtheria and other related diseases. The daily death rate was rising pitilessly. To demand the selection of two thousand fit men from among those at Shamshuipo and Argyle Street was a cynical farce, but Stewart had no choice but to make it. His message delivered, Tokunaga waddled to his car, the odious Niimori in his wake, watched with ill-concealed amusement by the assembled officers. Once dismissed, they gathered for a briefing from Stewart.

'This is a difficult one, gentlemen. We all know there aren't even five hundred men in Shamshuipo who are fit to travel, let alone be subjected to hard labour at the end of it. But it's clear, Tokunaga wants his two thousand. Our list will have to include many who shouldn't be on it. I see one consolation in all this: there's a fair chance that conditions will be better in Japan than here in Hong Kong. Shamshuipo is hopelessly overcrowded and ridden with disease, so it's possible that both the two thousand who go and those they leave behind will be better off. The only exceptions from the list should be those unfit to travel. I want us, together, to select men fit enough to board a ship, with or without help. Let's see how many we can find.'

Christopher knew that Stewart was right. Shamshuipo was in desperate need of being thinned out, and many of the prisoners might be better off in Japan. But what of the likes of Martin Weedon and Jim Whitham? Martin was still greatly troubled by his wounded shoulder and Jim, wounded in both legs, could walk only with the aid of an improvised crutch. As for himself, Christopher knew he had to be on the list. He dreaded the prospect of leaving Topsy in Hong Kong. It had kept him awake ever since the rumours about transportation had begun. No matter that their separation was already complete in practical terms; every instinct cried out against adding to the distance between them.

After five days, Stewart and his officers had found no more than fifteen hundred men who met his criteria for selection. Tokunaga's response was uncompromising: he had given Stewart the opportunity to make the selection and he had failed. In that case, Lieutenants Wada and Saito would select the remaining five hundred men. And they did. Except that by the end of the two weeks which followed the closing of the list, deaths and cases of incapacity from diphtheria, beriberi and dysentery had reduced the number to just over eighteen hundred. Despite their wounds, Martin Weedon and Jim Whitham made it onto the final list which included all but a few of the Diehards held in Shamshuipo.

*

Those officers in Argyle Street Camp who had been selected for transportation were ordered at short notice to gather their few possessions and prepare to move to Shamshuipo. They would be there for just a few days; no longer than was necessary to process them before they embarked for Japan.

Finding himself back in Shamshuipo Camp for the last time, Christopher took in the scene. It was five months since they had been separated from the battalion's other ranks and force-marched to Argyle Street, and in that short time Shamshuipo had become even more of an overcrowded shamble.

As the mid-September days drifted by, tension in the camp grew. Ever since the departure of the 'hard men' at the beginning of the month, the prisoners had allowed speculation about their own future to stray beyond the horizon of life in Kowloon. They had no idea of what imprisonment in Japan would be like and what difference it would make to their lives, so a mixture of excitement and unease was in the air.

In the course of processing those waiting to be transported, Tokunaga spotted a further opportunity to humiliate his prisoners. Saito insisted that each prisoner bound for Japan should undergo a medical check-up. This turned out to be nothing more than each prisoner having to strip naked and bend over for an anal examination conducted painstakingly with a glass tube. If the Japanese thought that such an indignity would humiliate Cockney prisoners, they were mistaken. If anyone was humiliated it was the holders of the glass tube who had to concentrate solemnly on the task in hand whilst listening, uncomprehendingly, to ribald comments addressed to them by the upside-down faces that peered backwards and upwards at them from between the knees of prisoners who were beside themselves with laughter.

Private William Beningfield couldn't resist temptation. 'I don't know what you're looking for up there, mate,' he quipped to a bemused Japanese medical orderly, 'but whatever it is, I bet I've got it.'

Monkey Stewart and Christopher were in earshot, awaiting their turn.

'He would have said the same thing if it was Duggie examining his backside,' observed Stewart, referring to Douglas Scriven who had escaped with Tony Hewitt back in February.

'Mind you, Duggie might have objected to being called "mate", but he would have laughed as loud as anybody.'

Christopher nodded. 'The Japs just don't know how to cope with it. If they have a sense of humour, it's on another planet to ours.'

One by one they were vaccinated with blunted needles, photographed, given a number and directed towards a long shed at the water's edge. Entering the shed,

Christopher was taken aback. The Japanese were issuing each departing prisoner with new kit. He was handed a mess tin, spoon and water bottle. Next, he tried on a pair of boots and canvas shoes – not a great fit but they would do. Two shirts and pairs of shorts and some underwear were clearly too baggy for his skinny body but who cared, they were new and clean. A haversack and two blankets were thrust into his arms and finally an overcoat – he could have done with those back during those cold winter days and nights spent on the concrete floor of his first room in Shamshuipo.

As he and Monkey Stewart headed towards their room, carrying their new possessions, he shared his thoughts aloud.

'I know this is bloody ridiculous, but I can't stop myself feeling grateful to the bastards.'

Monkey Stewart gave him a wry smile. 'Don't let it worry you, Christopher. It won't last.'

*

September 25th dawned warm and humid as they all gathered on the Shamshuipo parade ground in groups of fifty, for the last time. They made a pitiful sight. Dysentery had reduced many of them to wrecks of men. Constant victims of an incontinence that embarrassed both themselves and their fellow soldiers, they had lost not only their fitness but also much of their dignity. If it wasn't dysentery, it was invariably something else. Some with beriberi barely had the strength to walk, while others fought the constant pain of legs and crutches left raw by pellagra, a disease from hell nicknamed without affection by the soldiers as 'rice balls'. Many were losing their hair or their sight through malnutrition, and some were still afflicted by the malaria they had caught before the battle for Hong Kong had begun. And perhaps most sinister of all, the diphtheria which had already reduced the size of the draft for Japan had not yet finished with them.

Christopher could hardly bear to look at the scene. He turned to Martin. 'I can't see them all making it onto the ship. Just look at them. This pretence by Tokunaga that we're sending men fit to work in Japan is a grotesque mockery of the truth. Half of them can hardly stand.'

'I'm afraid you're right,' replied Martin. 'I feel bad about taking some of these poor buggers with us. Left here, they might stand a chance, but I don't think the Colonel had any choice.'

Christopher glanced across to Monkey Stewart who stood in front of all the assembled groups, waiting for Tokunaga to appear. Tokunaga had known what he was doing when he appointed Stewart to command such a large contingent of men drawn from several different units. If all these prisoners were to be successfully transported to work in Japan for the war effort, it was in the Japanese interest that the draft retained some discipline. They couldn't be allowed to descend into a rabble. Stewart was the right man to lead them. All the Diehard soldiers knew him as the seemingly indestructible man who had led them from the front through the toughest of times. They knew the quality of the man and they made sure that all the men in Shamshuipo knew it, too. Not that they needed to. Those who had been in the camp before Stewart had been moved to Argyle Street had seen for themselves how Monkey – as he was known to everyone by now – had not spared himself in confronting the Japanese prison regime. He had fought for the welfare of all of them, no matter what cap badge they wore. Even the Japanese had themselves come to respect him and were wary of him. Even more so now that things had changed. The prisoners were now a valuable source of labour for the benefit of the imperial war effort. Japan had need of them and Tokunaga needed Stewart to establish some sort of chain of command amongst them.

'Monkey looks dreadfully tired,' observed Christopher. 'All this has been a huge personal blow to him, and it's taken a lot out of him.'

Martin was thinking the same. He had reached his own personal low point when his wounded shoulder had prevented him from joining Tony Hewitt on his escape back in February. They'd had no news of him but presumed they would have heard if any of the three had been recaptured. Martin couldn't help but speculate that he might have made it to freedom but for his unhealed wound.

He nodded in Stewart's direction. 'I'll always be grateful to Monkey for letting me come with you all. Despite the shoulder, I'm in much better shape than many of us. I couldn't have coped with being left behind here.'

*

They waited, and then waited still longer. It was as Tokunaga had intended: one last demonstration of who had won and who had lost; one last reminder that in allowing themselves to be taken prisoner they had sunk beneath any living thing. One tedious, uncomfortable hour followed another. At last Tokunaga made his grand entrance onto the parade ground, his attentive minion Niimori close on his heels, their arrival greeted with an ill-concealed ripple of amused comments from the assembled draft. These prisoners may have been damaged, but they were not broken. If there was a last laugh to be had, they would have it.

Tokunaga offered the parade a repeat of the speech he had made to the officers a couple of weeks ago. The same generous emperor who had granted them life after their ignoble surrender would now offer them the opportunity to redeem themselves in a place far better than this corrupt corner of the degenerate British empire. If they worked hard and behaved well in Japan, they would be treated far better than they deserved.

And with that he turned his back on them, relieved that he was soon to be rid of their pestilent presence in one of his camps. He left them as the unwilling captive audience of Lieutenant Wada Hideo. Wada was now in a state close to nirvana. He was not only destined to return to his homeland but would have the additional pleasure of exercising power over this pathetic rabble during the voyage home. Immensely pleased with himself, he addressed the parade through Niimori. Most of what he had to say was carried away by the breeze, far above the attention of his restless audience. For them, it was the usual ritual reminder – tiresomely repeated – of how fortunate they were to be alive and well treated and how doubly fortunate they were to be heading for Japan under his watchful eye. But ears did prick up at one welcome item of news. They were not going to march to the ferry point in the harbour; instead, they would board their ferries at the Bamboo Pier, which was where Tony Hewitt and his fellow escapees had jumped aboard the sampan that had taken them towards freedom. Christopher uttered a sigh of relief. He had been worried that so many men would not survive even the short march to the usual ferry point. He had been especially concerned for Jim Whitham. This latest news meant that they had to negotiate only a few hundred yards across the camp. For most of them, that could not come a moment too soon.

Chapter 17

25 September: Embarkation

Christopher stepped from the edge of Bamboo Pier onto the flat-bottomed barge that was to take him and his group of fifty Diehards out to the ship. Like the others, he had just been compelled to stand on the pier and turn himself around twice while two grinning Japanese soldiers sprayed him from head to toe with disinfectant. This was intended to be one last indignity imposed with some relish by Colonel Tokunaga, but instead it served only to demonstrate the clash between Japanese and British culture. For the Diehard soldiers it was too good an opportunity to miss. They were quick to turn it into a pantomime. Some performed an exaggerated pirouette; others gave the sprayers a coy wink and raised their arms as if their armpits were being sprayed with deodorant. Many finished the performance with the flourish of a bow. The Japanese guards simply didn't know what to make of it and reacted in the only way they knew, by lashing out and screaming orders.

For Christopher, there was no nostalgia in leaving a camp where he had enjoyed good times before the war. His best memories of the place had gone, and the sooner he could turn his back on the place the better. But he felt bad about leaving behind so many of his fellow Diehards, some of whom had fought side by side with him in Z Company and were now so weakened by sickness and mistreatment that they couldn't hope to withstand the passage to Japan, let alone what awaited them as forced labourers in the land of the emperor. Others had survived the battle and made it to the camp only to succumb to the inhumanity of their Japanese captors. Some had embraced death as a blessed release from a wretched existence that had stripped them of every shred of dignity. And there were those who still haunted Christopher. They had been left wherever the battle had taken their lives, whether in the streets of the city or on the hills behind, and had lain there for days, even weeks, out of reach of their comrades, war's garbage at the mercy of the sun and assorted scavengers. For the lucky ones, oblivion had been delivered suddenly by an unexpected bullet or shell, but others had fallen victim to an orgy of Japanese brutality and been left, mutilated and alone, to pray that death might come quickly.

The boat chugged its way towards Stonecutters Island which lay a short way offshore in the harbour. His first sight of their ship failed to lift his spirits. She was an old, rust-covered freighter that had clearly seen better days. The best that could be said of her was that she looked sturdy. As they drew closer, he looked up to the ship's bow. There, painted in white, was the name *Lisbon Maru*.

He looked back over his left shoulder towards Hong Kong Island. There was The Peak, caught in the rays of the mid-morning sun. There on its lower slopes, he and Topsy had set up their first home together. They had known that they were on borrowed time there, but those had been blissfully happy days that now seemed an age in the past. To the left of The Peak, Leighton Hill rose high above the Hong Kong waterfront. Christopher had lost several of his Z Company men up there. And far beyond those hills, in the Stanley Peninsula, an internment camp had been set up. He had heard the rumours of Japanese atrocities at the makeshift hospital at the racecourse and in St Stephen's College and there had been dark times when he couldn't help but fear the worst. If Topsy had survived, she was sure to be in Stanley Camp, but he had had no news of her at all. Every three months he had signed a piece of paper that authorised money to be paid to his next of kin, but he had no idea if it had been paid. He had to believe she was down there in Stanley, not far from that beach where she had taught him to swim. He knew it was nonsense, but somehow he felt he was about to abandon her. He turned away and made his way abord the *Lisbon Maru*, not once looking back.

*

Captain Kyoda Shigeru was a worried man as he watched the latest boatload of British prisoners climb aboard his ship. He had served for twenty years in the Japanese Merchant Marine and the *Lisbon Maru* was his third command. His first two ships had both been sunk, one by a sea mine, the other by an American submarine, so he needed no reminder of how dangerous the passage of vessels in the South China Sea could be. Which was one reason why he was worried. The *Lisbon Maru* had been fitted with two four-inch guns, one mounted on the ship's bow, another at the stern, and to all intents and purposes she was now an armed merchantman which enjoyed no immunity and could be sunk on sight. Only yesterday he'd received a warning that American submarines were active in the seas around Japan. To minimise the risk to his ship, he intended to sail as close as he could to the Chinese coastline but the four days at sea would be full of danger.

He had other worries, too. It was bad enough that nearly two thousand prisoners were to be crammed into the ship's three holds which had been crudely fitted out to accommodate a human cargo, but even worse was the news he had just been given. Most of the men were sick. His ship was simply not equipped to cope with either the numbers or wholesale sickness.

It wouldn't help that he would be carrying around eight hundred Japanese soldiers who had fought in the battle of Hong Kong and were now heading home after enjoying nine months as part of an occupying army. Not long ago, he had served on a troopship and he knew the problems. In his mind he pictured a worrying scene: several hundred Japanese soldiers, still flush with their victory, occupying the ship's open decks for four or five days whilst beneath them, in the suffocating heat of the overcrowded holds, hundreds of disease-ridden enemy prisoners were expected to survive without causing trouble. It was not the sort of passenger manifest that any sea captain would welcome.

*

As Christopher climbed abord the *Lisbon Maru* he spotted Monkey Stewart standing where he could be seen by every prisoner as they first stepped onto the ship's deck. He had insisted on being first to board the ship and had positioned himself for all to take note that they still had a leader who expected much of them. Cruelly weakened in body by dysentery, a physical shadow of the man he had been, those eyes were as fiercely challenging as ever. He looked every inch the commanding officer and made sure he had a word for each one of them before they lowered themselves through the open hatches and down the ladders into the stifling gloom of the ship's holds.

Christopher eased himself down the wooden ladder leading from the hatch opening. The Diehards were all being directed into Number 2 hold, the ship's main hold amidships. The Navy prisoners had already filled all the spaces allocated to them in the forward Number 1 hold, while Number 3 hold in the stern awaited the arrival of the Royal Artillery who would be the last to board.

It took Christopher a few minutes before his eyes adjusted to the semi-darkness. It was noisy down there as hundreds of bodies jostled and pushed in a scramble to find personal space. The Diehards had been joined in Number 2 hold by men of the Royal Scots, which meant that a mixture of Cockney and Scottish accents rang round the rapidly filling space. Christopher peered around him. As far as he could see the hold had been fitted out with two levels. He was crouched on the top level, close to where a second wooden ladder led down to the lower level. A familiar voice reached him over his shoulder.

'Welcome to the Savoy, Sir.' Christopher turned his head. It was Sergeant Frank Waldron.

'Funny you should say that; it was always an ambition of mine to have tea at the Savoy. When do they serve it here?'

Frank Waldron had been in the first group to board the ship and had had time to explore the hold that was to be their home for the next few days.

'If you think it's bad here, the Royal Scots have got it worse.'

He pointed to the ladder leading further down. 'Poor buggers, they're down on the next level. Some of them are even further down, lying on the ship's ballast below the waterline. They say the Japs dumped a whole lot of stinking sandbags down in the bilge and there are rats everywhere.'

Christopher had to agree; the Diehards were indeed lucky. At least they were nearer the hatch openings which were the only sources of light and fresh air. He looked for a space for himself. Each level in the hold had been fitted with two tiers of wooden platforms fixed to the sides of the hold and bulkheads, one above the other. On these platforms the Japanese had allowed no more than two feet of space for each prisoner. Christopher slid onto one of the lower platforms. Lying on his back, the upper platform was no more than three feet above him. The sense of claustrophobia was instant. He couldn't possibly sleep like that. He climbed onto the platform above. This was better. He could see one of the two hatches from here.

Up on the deck, the interpreter Niimori strutted his self-importance here and there, cane in hand, prodding prisoners on their way, barking out instructions. Having spent much of his life in Canada, his English wore a heavy North American accent and was full of colloquialisms that were totally out of context. That only made him even more of a joke figure in the eyes of the British prisoners, and some of the battalion's Cockneys just couldn't resist showing it as they passed, judging it well worth any retribution it might earn them. Watching over the embarkation was Lieutenant Wada. He was in his element. This was his dream command. Kyoda might be the ship's captain, but this was a slave ship and he was its slave master. He grinned as he watched prisoner after prisoner struggle to climb through the hatches and then disappear into the squalor of the holds below. For the next few days he had free rein to inflict humiliation after humiliation upon these British prisoners, all the time enjoying a free passage home.

Hour by hour the holds filled with still more prisoners. By mid-afternoon it had become close to impossible for each one of them to lie down on the platforms at the same time. All but a few were suffering from dysentery to some degree or other, but there were no latrines in the holds, only buckets and urinal pipes. The only latrines available to the prisoners were in the form of wooden contraptions slung over the side of the ship. To use them, a prisoner had to clamber over the ship's rail and sit over a hole in the wooden box, facing inwards to the ship. Those suffering from beriberi were too weak to climb the ladders from the hold to the deck and had to use the buckets which soon overflowed.

By early evening all prisoners were on board. Christopher had been in the hold for only six hours, but already the stench was unbearable. In Number 2 hold the sick were now crammed together cheek by jowl, their living space for the days ahead offering a fertile breeding ground for the further spread of disease. Already, two Diehards had shown the first sinister signs of diphtheria and had been banished to lie in the open in a segregated area on deck. They were destined to be ferried back to Shamshuipo Camp. For them, the journey to Japan was over before it had begun.

Christopher felt the need to wash away the sweat and grime of the day. With luck they might be under way soon and now might be the best time. There was no running water in the hold and only one tap, located on the foredeck, to serve all eighteen hundred of them. Christopher hauled himself up the hold ladder and out of the hatch opening onto the deck. He was suffering from mild dysentery himself and was not looking forward to his first use of the facilities. Several prisoners had been declared too sick to remain in the holds and they had been laid out on deck in spaces between the hatches. Christopher picked his way between them. The improvised latrine device presented a challenge. Nine months of captivity in Shamshuipo had been more than enough to banish all traces of modesty from every single prisoner; even so, it was difficult to negotiate this new contraption without feeling self-conscious. In the event, it proved to be a less precarious experience than he expected but it left him with the thought that repeating it at sea in rough weather would be an entirely different matter. He made his way onto the foredeck. As promised, there was a tap but it was running at a tediously slow rate. He joined the queue. Waiting stoically in queues was part of everyday life as a prisoner of the Japanese and it seemed that life on board the *Lisbon Maru* would be no different.

*

What Christopher didn't know was that the ship would not sail that evening. Other than the Japanese, nobody knew. What was worse, the ship wouldn't be sailing the next day or night either. It was late in the afternoon the next day when the Japanese troops began to board the ship. They came on board in high spirits, singing loudly, laden with the spoils of war, showing off the watches, cameras and jewellery they had looted. Many were clutching bottles of *sake*. Some paused on their way across the deck to launch taunts through the open hatchways down into the squalor of the holds below. A few tossed down a cigarette or two for the fun of watching desperate prisoners scramble for them.

Christopher stood on the upper level of Number 2 hold, alert for the signs of trouble. If there was tension in the air, he couldn't sense it. All he could hear were muttered comments exchanged amongst the Diehards themselves. They simply couldn't be bothered to allow themselves to be provoked. They had spent the best part of two days and a night in the stinking, stifling air of the hold and just didn't have the energy to react to the jeers and insults being thrown at them. One comment reached Christopher which he thought probably summed up what all of them felt.

'I'm hungry, thirsty, bored and I've got the shits. I'm buggered if I'm going to drag myself up that bleedin' ladder to give that soddin' rabble up there the satisfaction of mixing it with them. Goodnight everybody.'

Christopher decided he could relax.

*

Sunday 27 September dawned clear and still. The hatches had been closed overnight, shutting off the prisoners' sole access to fresh air. Few of them had been able to sleep and tempers were short. To a man they were desperate to hear the sound of the ship's engines being fired up and to feel the movement of the open sea. They were all of one mind: 'the sooner this trip is over the better, so for God's sake let's get moving.'

The *Lisbon Maru* pulled away from Stonecutters Island at eight o'clock. To mark the occasion, the prisoners were permitted on deck for one hour. This surprised Christopher. Perhaps Wada intended them to witness their humiliating expulsion from a Hong Kong that was no longer a British colony. If that was the case, he had misjudged their mood – not for the first time. Most of them simply welcomed the chance to escape from the suffocating holds for an hour. Any humiliation was totally lost on them.

Christopher wasn't to know, but the *Lisbon Maru* followed much the same route round Hong Kong's west and south coasts as that taken by the cargo launch that had ferried Topsy into internment back in January. He was joined at the ship's port rail by Martin just as they were passing Repulse Bay.

'I've happy memories of that beach. We had some great times there; me learning to swim, you showing off what a good swimmer you are.'

Martin laughed. 'You were a quick learner, Chris. Mind you, you had a great teacher. But look at it now. Deserted.'

The Repulse Bay Hotel came into view. They had downed many a gin sling up there on the heights looking down from the north end of the bay.

Christopher pointed to the hotel flagpole. 'It hurts to see the Rising Sun up there. It makes me want to be here when we return and take the bloody rag down.'

The *Lisbon Maru* passed frustratingly close to the mouth of Tai Tam Bay. There, close to the shore of the Stanley Peninsula and, it seemed, almost within touching distance, the new prison loomed over the internment camp that had sprung up around it. For the past nine months Christopher had woken each morning telling himself that Topsy was still alive. If so, she was there, somewhere among the scattered buildings contained within that narrow, pear-shaped peninsula. Just to stand there, leaning on the ship's rail, able to see what he'd only been able to imagine since the surrender on Christmas Day, he felt closer to her and more determined than ever that for her sake he would survive everything thrown at him. For Martin, the scene had a different significance. He pointed towards a small hill close to the remains of a pill box.

'That's where the Japs shot me. Halfway up that bit of high ground. We held it for a while, then were overrun. I lost some good blokes there. Honestly Chris, I really don't know if it was worth it.'

Chapter 18

1 October: Under Attack

Christopher crawled to the edge of the upper sleeping platform in Number 2 hold, on his way clambering over Martin Weedon who was wedged in on the bunk beside him. It was six o'clock and the hatch covers had just been flung open to mark the beginning of another day at sea. He stood awhile beside the ladder leading up to the deck, filling his lungs from the inrush of fresh sea air. He had spent the last two hours waiting for this moment, unable to sleep, cramped for space, struggling to breathe, desperate to escape – if only for a few minutes – the foul, stench-laden air he shared with nearly one thousand others in the hold. They had been shut in since the hatches had been closed at eight o'clock the previous evening. Many were so weak that they lacked the will and the strength even to think about stirring from this hellhole. So they lay there, some of them in their own filth, and they swore and groaned and shouted their despair into the semi-darkness. Some just prayed for an end to it all. Not all of them, though. Any random gathering of British soldiers will contain those who are born entertainers and lifters of spirits. For them, no scene is so dark, no situation so grim, that they go unheard. One of them in Number 2 hold had managed to keep hold of his mouth organ and had led some remarkably tuneful singing into the late evening. Regimental songs had mingled with all the London favourites, while down in the depths of the hold the Royal Scots, not to be outdone, had responded with 'Flowers of Scotland'. Other groups played noisy games of cards, gossiping away and laughing with gusto at jokes they'd all heard before. Christopher hadn't been alone in thinking how absurdly unreal it was. There they were, many of them half dead, no better than slaves in this stinking hold of a Japanese slave ship that was taking them to labour for their lives in the home of their captors, and yet they were having the sort of sing song you might expect to come across in the NAAFI on the evening of pay day.

They'd been at sea for four days, and this had been the pattern ever since they had left Honk Kong fading away into the haze behind them. But as soon as he hauled his head above the hatchway, Christopher could see that something was different about today. There was now scarcely room to pick his way across the deck between the casualties who had been exiled to life under tarpaulin there. Diphtheria had sneaked its way onboard, despite the obvious early cases having been evacuated back to Shamshuipo before the ship had sailed. Two days out of Hong Kong, twelve cases had been identified, but too late to stop its inevitable spread in the fertile air of the ship's holds. It was now poised to take its deadly toll. Scores of sufferers lay silent on the deck, waiting to die. There might have been some hope for them back in the sick bay in Shamshuipo, but here on the *Lisbon Maru*, the medics could do no more than watch over their last hours.

Christopher made his way towards the foredeck for his early morning rendezvous with the latrine. He caught sight of Monkey Stewart who was standing amongst the diphtheria sufferers and talking to one of the medical officers. Not for the first time, Christopher wondered where the Colonel got his strength from. He was in the grips of dysentery and the strain of leadership was beginning to tell on him.

On the foredeck there was already a queue for the latrines, as there would be for use of the one water tap and then, after the morning roll call, Christopher would queue again, mess tin in hand, for what had become their usual shipboard breakfast of rice and onion soup with a slice of bully beef. Come late afternoon, the queues would form again. That was what prisoners of war did, even at sea.

*

That night, the USS *Grouper* patrolled on the surface. A bright moon lit a calm sea. It was a good night to be a hunter armed with twenty-three torpedoes. The boat had moved to an area of sea south-east of Shanghai. From there she could hope to intercept Japanese merchant shipping operating between that city and Hong Kong. It was also an area astride the sea route between Hong Kong and Japan. Ships from Hong Kong would predictably hug the Chinese coastline for as far as possible, but once they reached as far north as Shanghai, they were faced with a five-hundred-mile dash across the open East China Sea to Japan's south-western ports such as Moji and Nagasaki. Lieutenant Commander Rob McGregor and his crew were still feeling the frustration of a failed mission three nights ago. They had sighted a potential target but had been unable to approach it close enough to engage it. They were thirty days through a two-month patrol and they still had only one kill to their name. If they felt fatigue after a month at sea, it was balanced by a desperation to sink enemy ships. Bitter memories of the humiliating losses at Pearl Harbor only ten months ago still sharpened their appetite for patriotic revenge.

At around four in the morning, McGregor was alerted to the approach of a Japanese freighter heading north. There was no sign of any escorting warships. For an hour *Grouper* shadowed the freighter which continued to head NNE at around nine knots. McGregor was tempted to close in on the target but the bright moonlight made it too dangerous. On the surface, *Grouper* had twice the speed of the freighter which meant she had time to get well ahead of the target and simply wait for it to come within range. McGregor ordered full speed ahead. An hour later, with dawn about to break, the submarine stopped some ten miles off the chain of small islands at the east end of the Zhoushan Archipelago. She turned to face the way she had come, then submerged and waited.

*

An hour before dawn, Lin Agen followed his father, Shengtian, down the rough, stone steps of the harbour in Qingbang. His father was limping badly these days, and there was a hint of a bend in that once proud, straight back. They weren't the first of the village fishermen to rise early that day. Already the harbour was alive with the sound of around twenty boats being prepared for the day's fishing. It was much the same activity that their ancestors had practised over the centuries, and the latest generation of island fishermen went about the routine with an easy familiarity. Some of these boats had been repaired after the last Japanese punitive raid back in February, but memories of Japanese troops running amok across the island were still bitter and fresh. The weather forecast for the next two days was favourable, but tomorrow night the wind was expected to rise. They needed to make a big catch today and tomorrow.

Close by to the west, similar scenes were being enacted in the harbours of Qingbang's sister islands, Huangxing and Miaozihu. The three islands ran out into the East China Sea at the extreme eastern end of the Dongji Islands, so when Lin Agen and his father pushed their sampan away from the quay and paddled out from the sheltered harbour, only the vast expanse of the open sea lay between them and Japan to their north east. To the south, two hours steaming time away, the *Lisbon Maru* approached on a heading that would see her pass within twelve miles of Qingbang.

*

As Christopher made it back from the latrines to Number 2 hold in time for the morning roll call, the *Grouper* waited at periscope depth less than two miles away. McGregor had made his assessment. As far as could be seen, the target was a freighter of around seven thousand tons. Large numbers of Japanese soldiers could be seen on its aft deck, so the chances were that the ship was doubling up as a troop carrier with its cargo being restricted to the holds. The guns mounted fore and aft posed a threat to be respected and although the target ship was not escorted, they were so close to the shore that anti-submarine warplanes could be on the scene within minutes of take-off from their coastal bases. He needed a first-time kill followed by a rapid withdrawal fully submerged. Which is why McGregor was worried. The Mark 14 torpedo was unreliable. It was prone to running deeper than intended and the detonator was liable to fail. The risk of a miss or of a hit but no explosion was uncomfortably high.

On the *Lisbon Maru*, Christopher stood by the ladder leading from the upper tier of Number 2 hold to the open hatch above, making the most of being close to the only source of fresh air.

At the same time, Lieutenant Commander McGregor gave the order to prepare the *Grouper*'s first three torpedo tubes for firing. Then he paused, took a deep breath and calmly gave the command. 'Fire one.' Within seconds, six hundred pounds of explosive were headed towards the *Lisbon Maru* at a speed of forty-six knots. At ten second intervals, two further torpedoes were on their way. The eighteen-hundred prisoners in the holds of the *Lisbon Maru* were now within two and a half minutes of their fate being decided.

*

Captain Kyoda had yet to rise from his bunk, and in his absence the bridge was manned by his First Officer, Niioka Gentaru. Also on the bridge were three lookouts. All four of them were on full alert, shutting out the distractions of the early morning activity on the deck below them, concentrating keen eyes on the surface of the sea. They were aware that dawn and dusk were especially dangerous times. Niioka noted with satisfaction that the crews of both guns were at action stations.

None of them saw the first torpedo before it struck the port hull amidships and bounced away without exploding. The Diehards and Royal Scots in Number 2 hold heard it strike the hull outside but had no idea what they had heard.

Christopher turned to Martin and Ewan Graham, another Diehard officer. 'What do you think that was?'

Before either of them could answer, they were distracted by a loud hiss that seemed to pass below the ship. Within seconds it was followed by another.

On the bridge, Niioka sounded the torpedo attack alarm. Alerted by the impact of the first torpedo, those on the bridge watched as it ran out of control on an erratic course away from the ship. They scanned the surface to the west of them, certain that the danger was not past. Sure enough, they spotted the approach of a second torpedo, too close and too late for the ship to turn out of its path. By the time Captain Kyoda made it to the bridge, the second torpedo had passed beneath the ship, followed by a third. He ordered the ship to turn sharply to starboard.

*

In the control room of the *Grouper*, it was obvious to McGregor that too much time had elapsed without an explosion. The target had been missed. He made a snap decision to fire a fourth torpedo and ordered it to be set at a shallower depth.

In the dark holds of the *Lisbon Maru*, the prisoners were unaware that the ship was under attack. Christopher was sure that something was up. He climbed the ladder and poked his head through the hatchway. The scene was much as he had left it on his return to the hold for roll call. At that moment, the fourth torpedo slammed into the ship's port side, just to the stern of midships, and blew an eight-feet wide hole in the hull. The *Lisbon Maru* shuddered and then lurched to a stop.

When the sound of the explosion reached the *Grouper*, McGregor ordered the boat to periscope depth. He needed to confirm a hit and then take evasive action. All he could see through the periscope was that the target ship had turned to starboard and had stopped. At that moment the *Grouper* came under fire from the *Lisbon Maru*'s forward gun and McGregor ordered the boat to dive. He would wait before attempting a second attack.

*

On the *Lisbon Maru*, peering out from the open hatchway of Number 2 hold, Christopher watched as pandemonium broke out on the decks. Their Japanese guards seemed to be in a state of panic, running aimlessly this way and that, screaming orders that were lost in the din created by the forward gun which was firing shell after shell in the direction of land. Christopher grinned with satisfaction as he spotted a terrified Niimori scamper towards the bridge as fast as his short, plump legs could carry him. Some prisoners had been caught on deck by the attack, either using the latrines slung over the ship's rails or queuing for the tap up on the foredeck. Others had been assigned to prepare the prisoners' breakfast. For them, the scene above the holds had suddenly become a dangerous place to be. Some of the Japanese troops began joining the guards at the ship's rail, pointlessly firing their rifles out to sea at an enemy that none of them could see. The stern gun now joined in the shooting spree. The severely sick prisoners who had been removed from the holds over the course of four days were soon bundled back down below deck.

Within minutes of the attack, all prisoners were shut in the dark, airless holds where there was no sanitation, no food or water, and no escape from close confinement, limb against limb, with hundreds of diphtheria cases. They had last had food at four o'clock the previous afternoon and only the lucky few had tasted water from the tap that morning. All that was left for them was speculation. They listened for signs. There was no engine noise. The shooting had stopped and they could no longer hear the noise of panic on the decks above them. At first, only the eerie sound of the sea lapping against the ship's hull disturbed the silence. Then ominously, the ship began to creak and groan and something heavy began to thud against the bulkheads, as if objects were being sloshed around in water.

When they had first boarded the ship, the prisoners had found piles of life jackets dumped in the holds. At the time, the prospect of the ship sinking had not been at the forefront of their thoughts and not much interest had been shown in them. Besides, there were only enough of them for half their number. The jackets had proved useful as pillows but suddenly they were being viewed in a new light, and not only by the non-swimmers.

In Number 2 hold, Sergeant Frank Waldron was sitting on a platform close to the bulkhead separating them from Number 3 hold. He called for quiet. The Gunners were tapping a message in morse. Their hold was taking in water.

*

What they didn't know was that the *Lisbon Maru* had been crippled when its twin propellers were damaged in the explosion. She was now completely immobilised, without power, both her engines already flooded.

On the bridge, Captain Kyoda confronted Lieutenant Wada and the commander of the Japanese troops and demanded that they get a grip of their men. He had radioed for assistance and had been informed that a destroyer and a merchant ship were heading their way. They would be with them within the hour. He intended to transfer the Japanese troops onto whichever ship reached them first and would then have the *Lisbon Maru* towed to shallower waters. Wada insisted that the prisoners should be kept locked in the hold. He feared that if they forced their way on deck, they would create chaos, even threaten to take control of the ship.

*

In the *Grouper*'s control room, McGregor had a decision to make. An hour and a half had passed since the fourth torpedo had hit the target and he wasn't sure of the outcome. The action was certain to attract Japanese warships and warplanes to the area, in which case the sooner Grouper made her getaway the better. But he was reluctant to leave the scene without confirmation of a kill. He made his decision. They would come to periscope depth, ready to fire a fifth torpedo which would be set at a depth of six feet, much shallower than the first four.

His next sight of the *Lisbon Maru* through the periscope told him only that she had stopped. *Grouper* was now within less than a mile of her target and even from a position that close, he could not yet see signs that the freighter was sinking. He gave the order, 'fire five' and then watched and waited.

*

On the bridge of the *Lisbon Maru*, Kyoda was alerted by the port lookout's shouted warning that another torpedo was heading the ship's way. With the ship immobilised, Kyoda could do nothing except brace himself for the impact. It never came. The torpedo fizzed its way beneath the ship's bow section and carried on harmlessly out to sea. He turned to use the ship's radio to urge the destroyer to make best speed and noticed with distaste that Niimori was lying flat out on the floor of the bridge, shaking with fear.

*

Lieutenant Commander McGregor was known to his crew as a leader who kept a cool head when the boat was in action, but when it became obvious that the fifth torpedo had not exploded, they were treated to an outburst from their commander that did full justice to the accumulated anger and frustration of all sixty of them. McGregor was in no mood to give up. He decided to shift the boat's position and have one last attempt to deliver a killer blow. He would get as close to the target as he dared and fire a sixth torpedo set to run on the surface.

It was just after 9.30 before he was satisfied that the *Grouper* was in a good position to fire again. There was no time to waste. He could see a light bomber circling over the freighter and it was only a matter of time before it was joined by others. The torpedo was only seconds on its way from one of *Grouper*'s stern tubes when the submarine crash-dived to a depth of one hundred feet. Her crew heard an explosion, but there was no time to return to periscope depth to confirm a hit. The boat's maximum speed when submerged was nine knots and she needed every one of them now as she headed towards the open sea. McGregor knew that he had little time to put as much distance as possible between the submarine and the target ship. In ordering the final torpedo to be fired at surface level, he had calculated the risk of giving away his position and had concluded that it was a risk worth taking. The consequences were not long in making themselves felt. Three depth charges exploded close enough to rock the *Grouper*. The hunter was now the hunted.

*

From the bridge of his stricken ship Kyoda breathed a sigh of relief. The destroyer *Kuri* could now be seen steaming towards him. This entire voyage had been stressful for him and not only because he was haunted by the memory of having been sunk twice already during this cursed war. A passenger manifest that included eighteen hundred potentially rebellious enemy prisoners shut in his ship's holds was worry enough without the addition of eight hundred volatile infantry soldiers still flush with victory and heading home on leave. The presence of Wada and Niimori hadn't helped. Although it was his ship, he felt intimidated by them. Altogether, this had been a nightmare of a voyage, even before that torpedo had struck and left his ship adrift without power and fighting for her life. It was almost an hour since he had watched that last torpedo pass harmlessly beneath the ship's bow. Could he dare hope that they were no longer under attack?

The answer came with a frantic warning from the port lookout. This time the threat was in clear view. In a direct line towards the bridge, the wake of a fast-approaching torpedo scarred the surface of the sea with a long, white streak. The crew of the forward gun needed no order from the bridge. They opened fire. Shell after shell sought its elusive target but still the missile came on. At four hundred yards from the ship, the sinister dark shape of the torpedo was now distinguishable against the bright spray that marked its passage. Within seconds, it would be too close for the ship's gun to depress and engage it. At two hundred yards from its target the torpedo exploded and vanished within a dense upheaval of foam and spray. The sound of the explosion reached Kyoda at the same time as the bridge was peppered with shrapnel. The crew of the forward gun began to celebrate, beside themselves with excitement. They had saved the ship from what could have been a swift death.

The *Kuri* was now within half a mile of the scene and at her full speed of thirty-six knots. The track of the sixth torpedo had given away the rough position of its launch from the *Grouper*, and the destroyer now headed straight for it. Within minutes, three of its depth charges were launched, too late to damage the American submarine but close enough to convince McGregor that it was time to leave.

*

It was around seven o'clock when Lin Agen and his father reached their chosen area for the day's fishing some eight miles offshore from Qingbang. His father had inherited the family's knowledge of the local fishing grounds gathered by countless generations, and this spot rarely disappointed in its yield of fish. They were not alone. Just a few hundred yards to the east of them, framed against the low, autumn sun, their neighbour Chen Xinghua had already cast his nets, while to the north of them Liang Agou and his son were already hauling one of their nets inboard. No other vessels were in sight. Their horizon to the east was barely three miles distant, and the larger ships rarely passed this close to the islands. When the fourth torpedo fired by the *Grouper* exploded against the hull of the *Lisbon Maru*, the sound that reached Lin Agen and his father could have been that of a muffled rumble of thunder announcing the approach of a storm from beyond the horizon. They glanced towards the eastern sky. Not a cloud to be seen. They knew only too well that storms could arrive with little warning in this area of the East China Sea, but the peak season for storms was well behind them and the forecast had given no hint of one. Lin shrugged his shoulders; perhaps they would never know what they'd heard. When they returned to the village later that day, they would ask their fellow fishermen what they made of it.

There was no confusion about the sound of gunfire that next drifted their way, carried on a steady breeze from the north-east. In common with other Dongji fishermen, Lin Agen's experience and knowledge of the world at war were confined to the Japanese armed occupation of his own country and to all the consequences that even these remote island communities had been unable to escape. So when he and his father heard that distant rumble of an explosion over the horizon followed quickly by the sound of gunfire, the possible explanations open to them did not include an American submarine attacking a Japanese freighter that was transporting hundreds of British prisoners from Hong Kong to Japan. Not that the two of them needed an explanation. Gunfire in these coastal waters meant only one thing – trouble from the Japanese.

Lin Agen was all for hauling their nets in and heading for home. It was just over two years ago that he'd been badly shaken by his encounter with Japanese marines when fishing alone, and the memory of it still made him feel sick. His father, though, was reluctant to abandon the day's fishing so soon after it had just begun. He was more fatalistic about living under Japanese occupation. If there was trouble, at least it was out of sight. So they continued fishing. Lin Agen scanned the sea around them; Chen Xinghua and Liang Agou had not moved either. Perhaps he was worrying without reason.

Two hours later a Japanese warplane approached from the mainland and passed low overhead before beginning to circle just over the horizon. Within minutes, the sound of gunfire reached them, this time followed by what was clearly an explosion, far sharper than the dull rumble that had left them puzzled last time. The gunfire stopped abruptly. Lin Agen noticed that Liang and his son were standing in their boat looking towards the north. Lin followed the direction of their gaze. Less than a mile away, a large warship steamed fast towards the sound of the gunfire. Lin Agen turned to his father. It was time to go.

*

Captain Kyoda's experience of two sinkings had prepared him well for the situation in which he now found himself. His was the clearest head on the bridge of the *Lisbon Maru* as many of those around him were on the verge of panic. To him, the priorities were obvious. His ship needed to be protected against further torpedo attack. The disabled freighter was a sitting duck for any enemy submarines, so the first duty of the *Kuri* was to keep them at bay. He watched with relief as the destroyer made straight for the area from where the last torpedo had been fired and launched three of her depth charges. Kyoda knew that the destroyer carried more than enough depth charges and launchers to keep circling the *Lisbon Maru* for a few hours until more escort ships arrived. He was confident that his ship was not in imminent danger of going down. If they could get pumps down into the rear holds, there was a good chance he could win enough time to off-load the eight hundred soldiers and some of his crew and tow the ship into shallower waters. The guards would have to stay for as long as the prisoners remained on board. As for the prisoners, they would have to take their chances if he had to order abandon ship. He knew there were only enough lifejackets for half of them, and the ship's four lifeboats would be needed for the crew and the guards. He needed to talk about the prisoners again with Wada and Niimori.

Both Wada and Niimori were all for locking the prisoners in the holds and letting them go down with the ship if she sank. Niimori was motivated by his sadistic contempt for the prisoners whereas Wada was driven more by a personal fear of them. He had twenty-five guards to keep control of nearly two thousand prisoners who he knew from experience were constant trouble. It had been bad enough keeping on top of them in the controlled environment of Shamshuipo Camp, but here on a sinking ship it could easily turn into a nightmare in which old scores would be settled if they were given half a chance. Wada demanded that the hatches to the holds should be closed and battened down, but Kyoda would have none of it. The prisoners could be kept in the holds, but the hatches would remain open. They had to let air into the holds and allow water to be lowered to the prisoners. He agreed that none should be allowed out to use the latrines and that the worst cases of sickness would have to remain below. Wada fumed and stormed off the bridge to give his orders to the guards. Kyoda had not heard the last of him.

Throughout the morning, more ships reached the scene. Two transport ships that had been converted to serve in wartime as gunboats came alongside for the transfer of the Japanese troops. The swell caught one of them and drove her against the *Lisbon Maru*, crushing the two port lifeboats. Kyoda cursed his luck. That left him with only two lifeboats for the crew and Wada's guards.

By late afternoon the transfer of the Japanese troops had been completed and a naval tugboat and a salvage vessel had the *Lisbon Maru* under tow, heading at a painfully slow pace towards the shallow waters of Hangzhou Bay. Kyoda was allowing himself to hope that they might be able to beach his ship. She was beginning to list to port and the pumps could not keep up with the amount of sea flowing into the engine room and aft holds, but they might just make it. Now that the Japanese troops had been transferred, there remained the problem of what to do about the prisoners. As the next hour crept by, Wada was becoming more and more agitated. The departure of the eight hundred troops had left him feeling even more vulnerable and tormented by the prospect of his small force being overwhelmed by hordes of desperate prisoners if the ship came close to sinking. He made his decision. Kyoda might be in command of the ship, but he was in command of the prisoners. He would countermand Kyoda's decision to keep the hold hatches open.

The daylight was fading when Kyoda noticed that Wada's guards were closing the hatches and securing them by stretching canvas covers over them and roping them down. He went through the motions of protesting but inwardly knew that it was pointless. The guards were under Wada's control and not his, and he was powerless to intervene. Besides, he had the fate of his ship to worry about. He convinced himself that the prisoners were not his concern.

*

The prisoners had awoken that day expecting nothing worse than one more day of unremitting tedium and miserable discomfort on their journey to captivity in Japan. In every sense they were hardened to life as prisoners of the Japanese and their expectations of each day were accordingly low, but the daylight hours of 1 October had inflicted a new order of horrors and indignities on all of them. Deprived of water and any semblance of medical care, the worst of the diphtheria cases died that morning and remained in the holds amongst the living. Others lay unconscious or too weak to care; they had simply given up the fight and for them the end could not come soon enough. In the early afternoon, the Japanese lowered buckets of foul-tasting water into each of the holds with instructions that the water was for the sick. Crude ventilation chutes had been inserted into the hatch openings, but with each passing hour the air in the holds grew hotter and the stench of sweat, urine and excreta ever stronger until even the fittest of the prisoners struggled for breath. Only rage and his despairing sense of duty to the men under his command could have given the ailing Monkey Stewart the strength to climb to the hatchway from where he demanded to speak to Wada. Wada strutted to the hatch accompanied by Niimori. Stewart protested as strongly as he could. He demanded to know what was going on. Was the ship sinking and, if so, how were the prisoners to be rescued? His men needed food and water and access to the latrines. The worst of the sick should be returned to the deck and the dead should be buried at sea. A gloating Niimori grinned as only he could grin and began tapping Stewart on the shoulder with his stick. His message was uncompromising. Stewart would find out what was happening soon enough. There would be no food because the ship's kitchen had no power. The latrines were no longer in use. More buckets of water would be lowered and once empty the buckets could be used in place of the latrines above deck. As for the dead and the dying, their place was with their fellow prisoners. And with that, he and Wada turned their backs on Stewart.

*

In the early evening, when it seemed that conditions in the holds could not possibly get worse, they did. As the hatches were covered and then battened shut, the prisoners lost their one source of light and fresh air. Their helpless separation from what was happening beyond the confines of the hold was now complete. Some of them lost hope, too, but they were few. Most embraced a sod-'em-all determination to overcome whatever was thrown at them. No matter that they had not eaten since yesterday. No matter that water was so scarce that they sipped the last precious drops just to moisten dried-up lips and sluice it around their mouths before returning it to their water bottles. No matter that some of their best mates now lay moaning somewhere in the dark of the hold, mere dying wrecks of the men with whom they had stood shoulder to shoulder during day after day of battle. No matter that they had to fight for each breath of the foul, stinking air that stung their lungs. No matter that they might be spattered with the filth of some wretched dysentery sufferer above them because there were no latrines and the buckets were all full. No matter that even if they survived, their future was as forced labour in Japan. For them it was all about clinging on to life at all costs.

*

That evening, on the top tier of Number 2 hold, Monkey Stewart gathered his Diehard officers around him. They were soon joined by the RSM, Robert Challis, and Lieutenant John Potter, a young St John Ambulance officer who spoke fluent Japanese. Stewart had also summoned a young officer in the Royal Army Service Corps, Hargreaves Howell. Knowing that Howell had already been shipwrecked twice in his young life, the Colonel had greeted his arrival on board by remarking: 'I shall blame you if it proves to be third time unlucky.'

Number 2 hold might have become a scene from hell itself, but Stewart was still very much the commanding officer as he outlined the situation as he saw it.

'Gentlemen, in the absence of any contact with the Japs on deck, we can only speculate about what's going on. It's almost certain we've been hit by a torpedo, but we've no idea about the extent of any damage. We need to assume the worst and plan for it. And the worst is that the ship will sink and those bastards will let us all go down with it. I'm afraid to say I think they're well capable of doing that.

This is what we need to do. Mr Challis, I want you to set up a system for communicating with the other two holds. We need as much information as we can get, and we need to share it. Apart from the Japs, the biggest threat to getting out of this alive is panic amongst our own ranks, and panic feeds off a lack of information. Every single man in the three holds has to be kept in the picture.'

He turned to Lieutenant Potter. 'John, I need you to help me keep in contact with the Japs. Somehow, we've got to achieve that. Niimori is the only English speaker and there's no point in relying on him. We need to know what's going on and persuade them to let some air into the hold and give us some food and water.'

Stewart paused. A sick man, he was already struggling for breath in the stifling heat of the hold.

'All of you, we must plan how to break out of here. The Japs are sure to get their troops transferred to any rescue ships, but the guards may be forced to stay until the last minute. The priority is to find a way of breaking open the hatch covers. Hargreaves, I want you to be responsible for working that out. If we can do that, we'll have to take our chances with the guards. If they fire at us, we'll have to overwhelm them with sheer numbers.'

Howells tried to clear his mind. Forcing open the hatchways would have to be done in two phases. First, he would have to chip away at the wooden hatch lids until they were so weakened that they could be forced open. That would be difficult enough, but it would have to be done without alerting the Japanese sentries on deck. Once a gap had been made, the next phase would be to slash through the canvas covers and the ropes that were tying them down. The first stage would take hours of patient work but making the final breach through the canvas covers would have to be achieved in seconds.

'I'll need something sharp and tough,' he announced, more in hope than expectation.

*

In 1928, Bill Speight had been a twenty-two-year-old butcher's assistant in Croydon when he met up in The Dog and Bull for a beer or two with a school chum who was on leave after a tour in China with the Diehards. That was enough to change the course of his life. The next day, he had dropped into the local recruiting office and signed on. He had decided not to tell his mother, just yet. Four weeks later he had found himself at the Diehards' depot in Mill Hill, doing everything at the double and being shouted at. He had never regretted it but had stuck with his old trade by becoming an immovable presence in the battalion butcher's shop. He was happy enough. He had discovered that cutting up meat in places like China, Palestine, Egypt and Singapore was less boring than doing it in Croydon. Apart from that, he wasn't much bothered. When it became clear that the Japanese would attack Hong Kong, he had been extracted from the butcher's shop and drafted into Christopher's Z Company of odds and sods. His new role was as a member of a Vickers machine gun team, but he had refused to be separated from his treasured butcher's knife. He had carried it everywhere during the battle for Hong Kong and had smuggled it undetected into Shamshuipo Camp. He treated it with reverence and kept it razor sharp.

Now, half asleep in a dark corner of Number 2 hold, waiting for someone to tell him what to do next, Private William Speight was about to find himself in a position of prominence for the first time in his hitherto unremarkable fourteen years of service under the Diehard colours. Christopher remembered seeing Speight using his knife on board to slice up bully beef for the prisoners' tea meal.

Christopher tapped Howell on the shoulder. 'I suggest you get the RSM to track down Private Speight. He's somewhere in this hold and has something you will find useful.'

Chapter 19

2 October: Sinking

Just before six o'clock the next morning the first light of the day confirmed what Kyoda had already begun to suspect – the *Lisbon Maru* was within an hour or two of sinking and had no chance of reaching Hangzhou Bay. She was listing heavily and her stern was dangerously low in the water. With the ship's bow rising clear of the surface, the hull was bearing a weight for which it was not designed; his ship was close to breaking her back. Half of his crew, accompanied by an anxious Niimori, had been transferred with the last of the troops, but Wada and his twenty-five guards remained on board. Kyoda made his decision. He ordered the tow lines to be released and briefed Wada. One of the supporting ships would come alongside and take off the remainder of his crew. What did Wada want to do about his guards? This posed Wada with a dilemma. His priority was to save his own skin, but even he could not leave without his guards, and if they abandoned ship with him the prisoners would be left with time to escape. He made his decision. All but six of the guards would be transferred to another ship. Six of them would remain on the ship to prevent the prisoners from breaking out. They were to base themselves on the bridge and shoot any prisoners trying to escape on deck. They would be issued with life jackets and life belts and would be rescued from the sea.

*

In Number 2 hold, Lieutenant Howell and Private Speight had worked throughout the night on breaching the hatch covers. They had taken it in turns. Holding onto the ladder with one hand whilst hacking away at the underside of the wooden lid asked too much of muscles already weakened by months of malnutrition. They had not eaten for a day and a half by now, and the last drops of warm, polluted water left in their water bottles brought little relief to parched throats. At first they had changed over every half an hour but as the hours passed, they could scarcely manage ten minutes between rests. The stale air was without pity and had made their task even harder. In all three of the holds, prisoners were losing consciousness through lack of oxygen in the air. But despite everything, by eight o'clock Howell and Speight had prised the last splinter from the hatch lid and exposed the underside of the canvas covers.

Monkey Stewart had kept himself awake, following their progress through the night, offering encouragement when most needed. He promptly reconvened the group that had met the previous evening. It was almost pitch black in the depths of the hold, but just enough light filtered through the canvas covers for Christopher to note that Stewart wore his peaked service cap and held his silver-tipped cane under one arm.

'Good old Monkey,' he whispered to Martin Weedon. 'Setting standards even in this hellhole. How does he do it?'

Stewart addressed them all. 'Gentlemen, we don't usually single out individuals for praise, but I make an exception in this case. Thanks to Lieutenant Howell and Private Speight we have a way out of here. We are in their debt.'

This signalled a bout of back-slapping which left a sheepish Private Sleight not knowing where to look. He wasn't used to being the centre of attention and just wanted to find a space where he could lie down for a rest.

'And I must also mention a third hero in all this,' continued Stewart. 'Bill Speight's knife shall henceforth enjoy the status of Excalibur amongst us Diehards.'

They all cheered and laughed.

Stewart issued his orders. They needed to be clear and simple, and they were. The prisoners in Number 1 and Number 3 holds were to be kept in the picture. When the time came, the breakout would be through the Number 2 hold hatchway. The first to break out would open the other hatchways. Lieutenant Potter would be in the lead group tasked with negotiating with any Japanese still on board. If any guards remained and tried to prevent their escape, they were to be attacked, whatever the cost. Any questions? There were none.

*

An hour later the *Lisbon Maru*'s stern grounded on a sandbank and the ship listed violently to port. That was enough for Stewart. Whatever the situation above deck, it was time to break out of the hold.

He turned to Hargreaves Howell. 'Time to go. Get us out of here.'

Howell needed no encouragement. He had prepared himself for this moment. He had worked out precisely how best to attack the canvas covers and ropes. Speed would be critical. The aim had to be to get as many fit prisoners as possible up through the hatchway before any guards could intervene. He had nominated himself to be the first to exit the hold and make for the covers over the other two hold hatches. John Potter would be close behind him.

Monkey Stewart had insisted that the Diehard officers should remain on the upper level of the hold. They were to be amongst the last to leave. An example needed to be set in order to avoid a panic-stricken scramble for the one ladder leading up to the hatchway. He made one exception. He needed an officer to be amongst the first on deck to assess the situation and take command of it until he made it out of the hold himself.

He had made up his mind. 'Christopher, you're in better shape than any of us. I want you to lead the breakout once Howell and Potter are clear of the hatchway. The priority is to prevent the Japs from interfering with our escape from the holds. Martin and Ewan, I need you here to help control the rush to get out. I'm worried about Jim Whitham. He'll need help to get up the ladder. Between you, make sure he makes it.'

Standing on the top rung of the wooden ladder in Number 2 hold, Howell lunged the knife through a gap in the wooden hatch lid and made a first slit through the canvas cover. Then another, and another. He braced a shoulder against the lid and thrust as hard as he could against it. The lid gave way at its centre and he was through, his head and shoulders above the canvas. He glanced around him. No sign of anyone, but the deck at the stern was already awash with the sea. The ship was listing heavily to port and as he turned his head to look over the port rail, he could see land. As his eyes adjusted, he could see what appeared to be several islands in the distance. Between the *Lisbon Maru* and the islands, several Japanese ships were lurking. He called down through the hatchway to Monkey Stewart at the bottom of the ladder and briefed him on what he could see. Stewart had heard enough. He turned to Potter and Christopher. Right. Break out. And good luck.'

Howell wriggled his way out on deck, tense with the expectation of coming under fire. Still nothing. He sliced the ropes and ripped the canvas cover away from the hatch lid. That hatchway was now fully open. He dashed to the hatch over Number 3 hold. The sea was only feet away from it. He slashed at the ropes and the canvas cover, exposing the hatch lid. It was secured with bolts. By now, Potter had joined him. Between them they kicked the bolts back and hauled the hatch lid open. Within seconds, prisoners from Number 2 and Number 3 holds were out on deck, blinking in the sunlight after hours spent in the dark holds, desperately trying to orientate themselves. Christopher was among them and saw Potter heading towards the bridge. Potter had spotted Kyoda, who appeared to be alone on the captain's bridge immediately below the top level of the bridge superstructure. The first shots thumped into the deck around the hatchways. Potter staggered, then fell and was dragged to the nearest cover. The shots were coming from the bridge. The prisoners from Number 2 and Number 3 holds were nearest to the bridge and they now swarmed towards the source of the firing. Some fell but enough survived the short dash to storm the bridge, inflamed with rage and a burning desire for retribution. It was as if all the humiliations, indignities and pain inflicted by the Japanese over the previous nine months, together with the squalid inhumanity of their treatment on the *Lisbon Maru*, had to be repaid in the moment. Thoughts of personal survival gave way to a lust for revenge – this was their first and perhaps last chance to satisfy it. In the face of such a primordial frenzy, the six Japanese guards had no chance; they were overwhelmed by sheer numbers and their bodies thrown into the sea.

Whilst the guards on the bridge were under attack, Howell tackled the hatch cover of Number 1 hold. It had already been partly opened from within the hold and was soon freed, enabling the Navy prisoners to join the growing number of prisoners milling around on the deck. Christopher directed a group of Diehards towards the ship's life-rafts. They were all that remained of the ship's life-saving equipment. They needed to be released and thrown over the port rail. Then he remembered Lieutenant Potter. He found him, slumped unconscious under the ship's steam pipes. Christopher had comforted enough dying soldiers in their last moments to know that there was nothing to be done – Potter had been hit twice and was beyond saving.

The deck of the *Lisbon Maru* aft of midships was by now completely submerged. It was clear to Christopher that too many prisoners were aimlessly crowding the remaining deck space, uncertain what to do next, reluctant to be among the first to abandon ship. That all changed within seconds. There were by now around ten Japanese vessels of various type and size at the scene, and all but one, the destroyer *Kuri*, were keeping station between the sinking ship and the nearest island several miles to the west. Now that it was clear that the prisoners had broken out of the holds, some of these ships began to pour rifle and machine gun fire onto the *Lisbon Maru*'s decks. With the doomed freighter listing heavily to port, the prisoners massed on the decks had nowhere to hide. Even amid the noisy chaos on deck, Christopher could hear the familiar crack and thump of incoming bullets. Men began to fall. The prisoners needed no further encouragement to take to the sea; the rush to abandon ship began of its own volition. Some simply climbed over the ship's rail amidships and allowed themselves to be washed into the water, others launched themselves from closer to the ship's bow and hit the surface hard from a height of thirty feet or so. A few had the presence of mind to pause long enough to dismantle the wooden latrines before plunging into the sea clutching their own makeshift life raft. Christopher crawled to the hatch over Number 2 hold where Monkey Stewart was dragging himself onto the sloping deck, his role in the hold below now done. Moments before, panic had threated to turn the evacuation of the hold into a disastrous free-for-all until his shout of 'Steady the Diehards, remember who you are' had restored calm. Christopher grabbed his commanding officer by the hand and hauled him clear of the hatchway. Incredibly, but typically, even at this moment of desperate chaos, he still wore his cap and carried his regimental cane. Close behind Stewart, Jim Whitham emerged through the hatchway, pushed from below by Martin Weedon and Ewan Graham. Despite his wounded legs, Jim regarded himself as a strong swimmer and had at first refused the offer of a life jacket. Martin had insisted that he wear one. Stewart ordered Martin and Ewan to help Jim into the sea and then watched as the three of them slid off the listing deck and began to drift away.

'You next Christopher.'

Some of the old fire in Stewart may have been doused and his body weakened to the point of exhaustion, but that calm voice, that hard-as-steel stare had lost none of their compelling authority. Christopher was loathe to turn his back on the Colonel and just leave him there, but he knew there was no point in arguing.

'There's nothing more you can do here, Sir. Why don't we leave together?'

Stewart looked him in the eye. 'That wasn't a request, Christopher. It was an order. I won't be far behind you.'

With that, Christopher half slid, half crawled to the ship's rail. Once there, he climbed unsteadily to his feet and stood knee-deep in the water, pausing to look back and watch Stewart lurching across the sloping deck towards the bridge. Christopher turned to look towards land. By now hundreds of prisoners were in the sea, each one fighting his personal battle for survival. Some were swimming with strong purpose, intent on distancing themselves from the sinking ship before she went under. Others just bobbed between the waves, head and shoulders above the surface, drifting with the current which carried them towards the Japanese ships that lay between them and the distant islands. Some clung precariously in ones and twos to bits of wreckage and he could see one group of four survivors lying flat on one of the life rafts, uselessly trying to paddle with their hands. The sea had already claimed too many of them. They lay face-down, lifeless, tugged and pulled this way and that at the whim of the waves, mere human flotsam from a doomed ship. The survivors were battling more than the sea alone.

Two large Japanese patrol boats were ploughing aggressively to and fro amongst the survivors, seemingly intent on running them down. From the rails of two auxiliary warships, riflemen were shooting at survivors in the sea while a machine gun on another ship continued to seek more victims amongst the diminishing ranks of survivors who remained on the *Lisbon Maru*'s decks.

The scene confirmed Christopher's suspicions; the Japanese were determined that no prisoners would survive to tell the tale. He banished any thought of being rescued from the sea. He made up his mind; he would keep clear of the ships and think of nothing else but reaching those islands.

He drew a deep breath and calmly waded off the *Lisbon Maru* into the East China Sea. It was mid-morning on his second wedding anniversary.

Chapter 20

2 October: In the Sea

Once in the sea, Christopher was surprised how calm he felt. He cast his mind back to those happy hours spent with Topsy at Repulse Bay in the summer months before the war had begun. Now, in a benign sea, far from the nearest land, he said a quiet thank-you for those swimming lessons. He let himself drift away from the *Lisbon Maru*, carried by the flow of a tidal current running towards the islands. If he felt fear, it was of those vessels that had gathered at the scene. He defied the normal instincts of a survivor in the sea and avoided drawing attention to himself. He could see that the current was taking him on a course that would cross the bows of the large patrol boat that was last in the line of vessels. Far too dangerous. If he could steer his drift so that he passed astern of the ship, there would then be nothing between him and the nearest of the islands. He nearly collided with a survivor clinging to a piece of wooden hatch cover. He recognised Private Tom Stickley from Z Company.

'Room for one more on this luxury cruise if you want,' Stickley yelled at Christopher.

'No thanks, I'm fine. Good luck.'

Christopher watched as Stickley drifted away towards the patrol boat. Members of the crew were at the port rail and had lowered a rope into the sea. Stickley was drawn to it like a moth to a lamp. He let go of the wooden hatch batten and grabbed the rope. He lacked the strength to haul himself up the rope but as he clung to it, the crew members began to haul him up the boat's side. Stickley was within feet of the boat's rail when they let him drop. As he floundered in the sea beneath them, no longer supported by his makeshift life raft, they jeered and taunted him with gestures. Christopher watched, sickened but helpless. Within a few strokes he was well clear of the boat's stern and had evaded attention. When he next looked, Stickley had disappeared.

The next minutes passed unbearably slowly for Christopher. As if the challenge of the sea was not enough, he felt like the human quarry in a depraved hunt. He kept the patrol boat's stern rails in view, expecting any moment that someone on board would spot him. He was in luck. On board the Japanese ships, most eyes were trained on the patch of sea between themselves and the *Lisbon Maru*.

The current continued to carry him westwards until he felt it safe to tread water whilst he took stock. He was beginning to tire and had barely started his swim to safety. Before abandoning ship he had removed his canvas shoes but already his shirt and shorts were clinging to him and forcing him to use up energy just to stay afloat. He discarded them, swallowing some sea water as he did so. He paused for one last look back towards the *Lisbon Maru*. Already all that could be seen of her was her foremast. He was looking into the sun and struggled to see clearly, but he could just make out a man up on the crosstree, clinging with one arm to the rigging and waving defiantly with the other. Christopher made himself watch as the man went to his death and the last of the *Lisbon Maru* sank from his view.

*

Quite a crowd had gathered on top of the shallow cliffs on Qingbang's east coast. It was late morning and none of the island's fishermen had taken to the sea that day. They had noted the number of Japanese warships that had gathered far out at sea and had dismissed any idea of fishing that day. Whatever was going on out there, it was not a place to be. Lin Agen was amongst those watching. He and his father, Shengtian, had gone to the cliff top together but his father had quickly decided that he had better things to do than stand around speculating with others about what might be happening out there. As far as he was concerned, it was another day's fishing lost. Lin Agen inhaled the excitement. Others of his father's generation remained there, keeping a vigil that they felt obliged to keep. There could be men in trouble out there at sea, and it was not in their blood as fishermen to ignore them. All the stalwarts of the Qingbang fishermen were there. Between them, Zhao Xiaoru, Tang Ruliang, Chen Yonghua, Weng Azhou and Xu Yusong had more than 150 years' experience of fishing these waters. They knew every turn of the tide and current, every perilous rock, every safe landing place in a sudden storm. With his father gone, Lin Agen mingled with them.

It was towards midday when the first debris came into view of the villagers. A tangle of wood and rope was thrown by the waves onto the rocks below them, followed by items of clothing and a life jacket. Then a lone swimmer was spotted, perhaps two hundred yards from the shore. He was struggling to make headway. Each of those Qingbang fishermen watching the scene below knew only too well the challenge he faced. Although the tide out at sea was flowing to the west, once close to the shore it sped up and swept northwards. They had known almost from birth that no matter how calm it might be out at sea, close to the shore the waves always grew stronger and bigger as the deep water of the open sea met the inshore shallows. The swimmer was battling his way across the strong tidal flow and through waves that threatened to pick him up and dash him onto the rocks immediately below them.

Lin Agen pointed further out to sea. 'Look. There's another one. No, two of them.'

Sure enough, just beyond the first swimmer, two more were being swept inshore. That was enough for Zhao Xiaoru and other island elders. It was the duty of Qingbang fishermen to help anyone in trouble at sea, whoever they might be. Within half an hour, thirty sampans were being launched from the island's fishing harbour, the Lin family's boat amongst them.

*

Christopher was beginning to struggle. He had no idea how long he had been in the water. Six hours? Seven? For the most part he had floated on his back, checking every now and then that the tide was still carrying him towards the islands. At first it had been easier than he had feared. None of the patrol boats had come close to him; they were still milling about closer to the spot where the *Lisbon Maru* had sunk. The sea was still warm in early October and although there was a powerful swell running, it was smooth and taking him where he wanted to go. At one stage he had grabbed hold of a wooden batten and hung onto it for a while until he realised that it was taking more out of him than just allowing himself to float while gently paddling with his hands. It seemed an age since he had last seen other survivors. His fight for survival had become a lonely, seemingly endless journey, just him drifting alone in the daunting vastness of the East China Sea.

The islands that beckoned him grew closer and closer, but never quickly enough, always tantalizingly out of reach. He knew that his strength was fading and with it his confidence was beginning to drain away. As he tired, simply staying afloat had become more of a struggle and he'd swallowed too much sea water for his own good. He was shaken to realise how easy it would be to panic, or even to just let go of life. He'd never felt that before. Ever since he'd become a prisoner, he'd been driven by a fierce determination to survive, come what may. He had witnessed fellow prisoners in Shamshuipo Camp and on board the *Lisbon Maru* simply give up the fight and had always assumed that somehow it would be different for him. For one thing, he would be letting Topsy down; he had her to live for now.

But now, for the first time, he began to doubt himself. He tried to remain calm. He forced himself to recall all those sacrifices made in battle, those bitter months of humiliation and deprivation stoically borne in Shamshuipo and the still vivid horrors he had survived in that dark, stinking ship's hold, and then asked himself, what was the point of letting go now?

It was as the Qingbang fishermen were putting to sea that Christopher began to feel the tug of the current changing. He trod water long enough to get his bearings. He had been aiming at the left-hand edge of the nearest island and had not needed to do much more than let the tide take him towards it. Now he could see that he was heading towards the centre of the island and the current was edging him still further north. The swell was no longer as smooth, and he was beginning to rise and fall with the waves as the surface became more disturbed. He had a fight on his hands.

*

When Britain's war with Germany was declared in September 1939, Arnold Topliff was twenty years old and earning a living joining electricity cables for Derby Corporation. It was his first job since leaving school and he was reasonably content in it. No doubt if war had not come along, he would have stuck at it and would have still been joining cables together somewhere in Derby instead of swimming for his life close to the shore of Qingbang Island. But war had come along, and like many young men of his age he had enlisted to fight in it. The Royal Signals needed linemen like him, and within months Signalman Topliff was helping to lay line in Hong Kong in preparation for the battle that everyone seemed to believe was coming. During the fighting back in December, he had the dangerous job of repairing breaks in the field telephone lines caused by shelling and bombing. In the process he had seen Monkey Stewart and Christopher Man in action on Leighton Hill and they had seen him doing his job when under fire. It had been a case of mutual respect thoroughly earned. So Topliff had been relieved to find himself allocated to Number 2 hold on the *Lisbon Maru*, crammed in with the Dichards. As a Derbyshire man through and through he had grudgingly come to accept that those Cockneys with their funny way of speaking weren't so bad when you got to know them.

He had been a champion swimmer at school, which explained how he came to be the first survivor to be spotted by the Qingbang fisherman gathered above the cliff face. He had jumped from the *Lisbon Maru* as soon as he escaped from the hold. Throughout those grim days on the ship, he had kept close to a fellow signalman, George Carroll. They had done their recruit training together and had watched out for each other ever since they arrived in Hong Kong. Carroll was a good swimmer, too, but they had quickly lost touch once in the sea.

Strong swimmer as he was, Topliff managed to avoid being swept north by the inshore current, but once he reached within a short distance of the shoreline, he discovered that he had little control over where the surf was going to dump him on those uninviting rocks. He was about to throw himself on the mercy of the waves and let the gods decide where and how he landed when he spotted a rocky promontory where the water was much calmer on its lee side. He struck out strongly and reached it without too much trouble. He grabbed onto a smooth slab of rock and hauled himself out of the sea. He was numb with relief. He had made it. It was as if all the suffering of the past nine months was being expelled from his body by this simple act of resting, head between knees, on the pale rocks of Qingbang.

His thoughts soon turned to his fellow survivors. For any of them who made it this far, this spot gave them a good chance of getting ashore in one piece. Either side of him were sharp rocks lashed by a rough swell. As far as he could see, the entire coastline was similar. The cliff face here was not steep and there was bound to be a way to scramble up. He climbed unsteadily to his feet and looked out over the near sea. There, just beyond the surf, were two swimmers faced with the same problem that had confronted him only minutes before. Topliff took off his vest and waved it above his head. One of them was quick to spot him and acknowledged with a raised arm. Topliff watched as they steered clear of the surf and made it to the lee side of the small promontory. He knelt and helped pull them ashore. They were too exhausted to do anything more than flop onto the large slab of rock. It was only as he reached out a hand to the second swimmer that he recognised George Carroll.

*

Out of sight of the three survivors as they recovered their strength close to the northern tip of Qingbang's east coast, the first of the island's fishing boats headed out from the fishing harbour further south. Lin Agen and his father rowed their sampan with a steady, well-practised rhythm which belied the good speed they were making out into the open sea. All around them were the rest of the island's fishing boats, each man scanning the sea. None of them yet understood what had happened further out from the shore. It was enough to know that there were men whose best chance of survival lay in being picked up in the open sea before the inshore current carried them too far north.

It was not long before Lin Agen and his father spotted their first survivor close to a mile out from the shore. Private John Jennings had just seen Bert Robertson, a fellow Diehard in A Company, slip beneath the waves and fail to reappear. Jennings had watched him grow weaker and weaker for some time. He had seen him go under twice before but each time he had struggled clear, gasping for air. Jennings had been powerless to save him, being close to exhaustion himself. He swore out loud in frustration, mad with himself that he could only look on as Robertson drowned, and just as mad with the fates that had let him make it this far and then abandoned him this close to safety. Well, they weren't going to mock him the same way. Using his anger, he struck out towards the shore.

Five minutes later he lay, stark naked, on the floor of the Lins' sampan. He would never have made it if they had not seen him. He was too tired even to haul himself over the sampan's gunwale. Lin Agen and his father each had to take a hand and haul him into the boat. At least one question had been answered. The survivors were not the hated and feared Japanese. But who was this foreigner they had saved? Jennings spoke no Chinese at all other than what had been necessary to navigate the bars and other delights of the Hong Kong night scene. Anyway, that was Cantonese which would have been unintelligible to fishermen of the Zhoushan archipelago. As for Lin Agen and his father, they knew only their own language. In their community, only a handful understood any other. Lin Agen knew of one, a relative who had returned home from overseas boasting that he could speak English.

Jennings numbered off his fingers, closed and opened his fists several times and pointed further out to sea. The message was clear. There were many like him out there. Within minutes, Lin Agen and his father had helped a second and then a third survivor into their boat. All around them, other fishermen were doing the same. It seemed that the patch of sea between one and two miles of the shore was dotted with men at various stages of survival, all of them fighting their own personal battle for survival. Some were drifting on their backs, letting the tide take them where it wished, too drained of strength to do anything else. Others still clung to bits of wreckage and a few continued to swim. None of the groups of prisoners who had initially taken to life rafts and large pieces of wreckage could be seen; they had been easy targets for the Japanese patrol boats.

When Lin Agen and his father had picked up a total of eight survivors, it became clear that their sampan could take no more without serious risk of foundering. Lin

Agen steered the sampan around and headed for home. He had tried to indicate to the survivors that he and his father would make a repeat journey once they were safely ashore, but he was not sure they had understood. A blur of orange caught his eye, ahead of them to the right. His first thought was that it was yet another life jacket; the sea seemed littered with them. But as they drew closer it became clear that it was a survivor. In fact there were two of them, clinging to a piece of wreckage. They spotted the sampan and began waving to attract attention. The Lins needed to make a quick decision. Their boat was already dangerously low in the water. The nearest sampan to theirs was beyond shouting distance. By the time they had dropped their survivors and returned, it might be too late to find these two again. Father and son exchanged glances and, without speaking, knew that whatever the risk, there was no question of leaving them to their fate.

During the breakout from Number 2 hold, 'Ginger' Howell had been wounded by a rifle shot from the guards on the *Lisbon Maru*'s bridge. He was now so weak that he had to be hauled into the sampan. His companion was perhaps the luckiest of many lucky survivors. Andrew Salmon, a young NCO in the Royal Artillery, was one of the few to escape from Number 3 hold. He owed his life to Howell on two counts: it was Howell who had freed the bolts on the hatch cover of Number 3 hold just as it was being swamped by the sea, and just now the Lins' sampan would have passed them by if Lin Agen had not spotted Howell's mop of ginger hair.

The Qingbang fishermen had decided to land any survivors on a gently shelving beach on the north-west of the island. There would be no surf there and a convenient track led down to the edge of the sand. Other islanders would be there to lend help once the survivors were safely ashore. Lin Agen and his father gestured to their passengers to keep the balance of the sampan by lying flat and then began rowing strongly for the northern tip of Qingbang.

*

For the first time in his life, Christopher believed that he was about to die. Even when the battle for Hong Kong had been at its fiercest, he had shared that common soldier's belief that death was for others. Not now, despite being so close to making it to that shoreline barely one hundred yards away. He had reconciled himself to accepting that only a lucky random wave would pitch him onto the rocks and leave him still in one piece, but now it seemed he was to be denied even that desperate last chance. He no longer had any control over where he was heading, having spent every drop of energy that remained to him in battling across the left-to-right pull of the inshore current. And it was now a struggle lost.

He was within minutes of being carried clear of the northern tip of the island. As far as he had been able to see, there was nothing but open sea beyond that point. He was coughing up a mouthful of swallowed sea water when from behind him a forearm grabbed him under his chin followed by a loud shout into his ear. 'It's alright mate. I've got you. Just don't struggle.'

Standing on the slab of rock he shared with his two fellow survivors, Arnold Topliff had watched the lone swimmer's struggles with growing concern. At one moment he had thought that the man in trouble less than one hundred yards offshore would be picked up by a fisherman's sampan that was heading towards the north-east tip of the island, but the two oarsmen in the stern of the boat had failed to see him. Topliff could see that the swimmer would soon be level with him. There was no time to waste. Once past him, there would be no hope of retrieving him. He dived into the calm water in the lee of the rocky outcrop and swam strongly out. At first he couldn't see him. Where the hell was he? Then a flash of white caught his eye; there he was, only ten yards from him, flailing arms, the top of a white vest and a head turned away from him.

By the time Topliff pulled Christopher to safety, he had nothing left to give. He trod water and watched as George Carroll and the other survivor heaved Christopher onto the slab of rock. He then attempted to haul himself out of the water but only a grab of his hand from Carroll prevented him from slipping back. Arnold Topliff had done what he could to help his comrades in arms. Three of them owed him their lives. It was now time to look after himself. He had had enough of the sea to last him a lifetime. He voiced his thoughts to Carroll.

'George, I need to get off these bleedin' rocks. I won't be happy until we're up there.' He pointed towards the top of the cliff.

George Carroll was already one step ahead of him. 'Don't worry, Arnie. While you were giving your Johnny Weissmuller impression, I found us a way up out of here.'

He addressed all three of them. 'Right, time to move. Follow me.'

The four of them stumbled, barefoot, across the rocks that fringed the foot of the cliff. The soles of their feet had been softened by several hours spent in the water but by now they were beyond caring about the pain. All that mattered was getting up there. Christopher was too exhausted to think for himself. He simply kept his eyes on Carroll's heels and followed. Within minutes they gained the gentle slopes of smoother rock and grassy scrub and then it was just a few yards on all fours to the crest. Once they reached level ground, they threw themselves down onto rough grass and just lay there, breathing in the air of freedom, blissfully uncaring about what awaited them next.

Chapter 21

2 October: Stanley Camp

Some seven hundred miles to the southwest, Topsy was quietly celebrating her second wedding anniversary in Phyllis Newnham's room within the grounds of St Stephen's College. The room was tiny, having previously served as a storeroom within a block of classrooms, but Phyllis had it all to herself on the ground floor that she shared with twenty other women. It was her haven. She'd made an effort to make the room her home. She had scrounged several scraps of material and had stitched them together to make a pair of curtains for her one window. They didn't match, but that scarcely mattered. There had been enough left over to make three small cushion covers which she'd stuffed with straw and pine needles from the red pine tree in the college garden. The cushions had more than a decorative purpose. Her block, like all the others, had been stripped of its furniture before their arrival in the camp, which meant that everyone had become used to squatting cross-legged on hard floors.

Topsy envied Phyllis her privacy in a room of her own, but there was a drawback about this block; it was so close to where the massacre had taken place. On her frequent walks around the camp, Topsy always gave the college as wide a berth as possible, keeping close to the camp edge. The Japanese had tried to hush the atrocity up, but word had leaked out. The work party that had arrived in early January to prepare the site as an internment camp had found the burnt remains of the victims and they'd also come across one of the few eyewitnesses who had survived to tell the story. So Topsy knew enough about what had happened in the makeshift hospital to feel uncomfortable this close to it. It was as if the place refused to let go of the barbarity it had witnessed. Phyllis was better at shutting such things out of her mind, but for Topsy this part of the camp would always be a sinister spot.

Topsy expected her second wedding anniversary to pass unnoticed, but Phyllis had done her best to make sure there would be a celebration of some sort. For the past two weeks she had ferreted around the camp, gathering bits and pieces so that at the very least there would be a cake of sorts and a present to wrap. She had begged a favour from her most reliable contact outside the camp and called in a few favours of her own from within it. She had remembered the date of Topsy's anniversary as clearly as if it had been her own. After all, it was down to her that Monkey Stewart had relented and given Christopher permission to marry. She had not told Lance what she was up to. After all, Lance himself had refused Christopher permission to marry. Not that it had mattered in the end; during the wedding ceremony Lance had whispered in her ear. 'By the way, I know all about your role in this. Monkey told me the day after you spoke to him.'

Topsy and Phyllis were easy company for each other and often drew comfort from talking over their fears and hopes with a kindred spirit. And they were kindred spirits, sharing a strong bond as wives of Diehard officers who were known to have survived the battle.

They both agreed that by far the worst thing about their captivity was not knowing anything about the world outside the camp perimeter. They had become accustomed to being hungry all the time, to having only the bare minimum of clothes, to the loss of freedom and to the futility of their day-to-day life, but it was the not knowing that drained their spirits. They had been prisoners at Stanley for nine months and in all that time neither of them had received a letter or card from their husbands. Not even a message had been delivered via their precarious contacts beyond the barbed-wire perimeter. From time to time they received an allowance from their husband's pay, and the presence of a familiar signature on the payment slips had assured them that Lance and Christopher were both alive and still in Hong Kong. But that was as far as it went in terms of knowing what was going on. There were rumours of course, but they only made matters worse. They raised and dashed hopes in equal measure but were impossible to ignore. One rumour had reached them only last week. It was said that a shipload of prisoners at Shamshuipo had sailed three weeks ago from Hong Kong, bound for labour camps in Japan, and was due to be followed soon by a second transportation. If true, this was bad news. It added uncertainty to their already uncertain lives. Were Lance and Christopher amongst those transported? Would they be better or worse off in Japan? Would the internees be transported to Japan, too? Or was there a chance that they would be repatriated like the Americans had been three months ago? Worst of all was the thought of being separated from their husbands by such a distance. Despite the lack of any contact with them only a handful of miles away in Kowloon, the prospect of being separated from them by hundreds of miles somehow seemed to make the separation feel absolute.

Topsy was by nature a private person. She had told no one that in her darkest moments she was still tormented by the memories of her own encounter with terror at the University Hospital. She tried as best she could to shut them out of her life but every now and then they invaded her. She had resolved early on to deal with her demons in her own way. One day, Christopher would know, but no one else. Not even Phyllis. She had been a nurse at a different hospital. She needed no telling of what it had been like for some of them when the Japanese had arrived late on that dreadful Christmas Day.

The early autumn sun was dropping slowly over Stanley Bay as the two of them sat side by side on the floor, backs propped against the wall, each one deep in her own thoughts.

It was Topsy who broke the silence. 'Thank you so much for remembering my anniversary. I have to admit that at one stage I thought I would never make it this far.'

Phyllis gave her a quizzical look. 'You surprise me. I always thought you were amongst the most positive of us here.'

Topsy shook her head. 'There were times in those first few days when I really did think that most of us would die in this place. Perhaps I was good at hiding it. One day I would be up and the next day down. And I mean really down, completely emptied of hope. It wasn't that I was prepared to give up, it was just the sense that I simply wouldn't be strong enough to get through it. The whole world had been turned upside down and had suddenly become unrecognisable. All the familiarities of life had been obliterated and in their place was a brutal anarchy. But the good thing about what we've all been through is that I now know for certain that we will survive all that this camp can throw at us. There's no way that the Japanese can win in the end.'

Phyllis nodded in agreement. 'I've felt the same for some time now. Like you, at first I was terrified by their brutality. And they seemed unbeatable. They were winning everywhere. But bit by bit, the more I saw of the Japanese the more I could see their weaknesses and the ways we could outwit them. And we have. Look at us now; we're better off than we were, and it's no thanks to the Japanese. It's not that they have softened, it's because we've learnt how to exploit their incompetence and stupidity.'

'Absolutely,' said Topsy. 'It's hard to understand how they can have been so successful in war. They've been hopeless at organising even the simplest of things here. Not only that, they're so easily corrupted, too. I know that we've had to select our targets carefully, but when you think of it, it's been easy to bribe some of the guards, even the camp officials. I can hardly believe the risks some of them have taken for the sake of a few extra yen in their pockets.'

'Mind you,' added Phyllis, 'they remain unpredictable and dangerous. What frightens me most is their volatile mixture of hysteria and brutality. I'd always thought of the Japanese as being self-controlled, but they've been quite the opposite. They are so unstable and hysterical. It takes only the slightest miscalculation on our part to set them off, and then they react so brutally. And it hasn't just been us on the receiving end; look at their treatment of the Hong Kong Chinese. Women and children bayoneted and shot on the streets just for being in the way.'

Phyllis paused as her voice faltered and her eyes moistened as they both quietly recalled images of what they had seen in those dreadful days that had immediately followed the colony's surrender.

'I can never, ever forget those scenes or forgive the Japanese for them.'

Topsy allowed a few moments to pass in silence. She, too, felt the tears coming.

They were interrupted by the wail of the air raid siren at the adjacent prison. A few days ago new orders had been posted on the various noticeboards around the camp. For the first time they included instructions about what the internees should do in the event of an air raid. The instructions were short and simple. They could not have been anything else since there were no shelters. On the sounding of the alert, all internees were to go to their rooms and remain there till the all-clear. Failure to follow this instruction would be punished by a withdrawal of privileges.

'What privileges?' had been Topsy's response when Daisy had drawn her attention to the notice. 'I wasn't aware that we had any.'

The new orders had been greeted by the internees as good news. For some time there had been rumours that the Americans had begun to set up air bases in those parts of China that remained under the control of the Nationalists. Topsy was typical of many internees in not daring to believe these rumours for fear that they might raise false hope, but the issuing of new orders seemed to add weight to them.

Topsy gave Phyllis a hug. 'I'd better go. I don't want to lose my privileges.' She dashed out of the block, clutching the multi-coloured woollen hat that Phyllis had knitted for her as an anniversary present. The sound of the siren began to die. Back in December in the Naval Hospital it had been a sound they had dreaded. Then it had been the inevitable prelude to yet another ordeal by bombing. Now, as she ran towards Block 15, fear was mixed with hope. Could this be the first sign that the Japanese were not having things all their own way?

Back in her room, she lay on her camp bed and thought back to her first wedding anniversary. She could picture their celebration dinner at The Peninsula as clearly as if it had been yesterday. She wondered whether Martin and Tony were able to help Christopher celebrate their second anniversary today. Had they even survived the battle? Were they all being held in the same camp? There had been no word of any of them. It was known in Stanley Camp that most of the British prisoners of war were held in Shamshuipo, but the unconfirmed rumour that the officers had been moved to another camp in Kowloon was still doing the rounds. She tried to picture Christopher in Shamshuipo, but the image that came to her was of the barracks she had known. It was there in the Officers' Mess that she had been made to feel so welcome by Christopher's brother officers and the other wives at their Christmas Ladies' Night nearly three years ago. Wherever he was now, she just prayed he was safe and thinking of her on their special day.

Chapter 22

2 October: Qingbang Island

Christopher hauled himself to his feet. He had lost track of time. He had no idea how long he had lain there. All that mattered was that he was alive. He knew just how close to drowning he had been and was still shaken by the experience. He threw his head back and sucked in the air, savouring the pleasure that such a simple act gave him. The sea had washed away the grime and stench of those wretched days in the *Lisbon Maru*'s hold but the memory remained fresh. Whatever time it was in the afternoon, the sun was still warm but not strong enough to dry his sodden underwear. He desperately needed a drink after nearly two days without one. Come to that, he had not eaten for two days either, but being permanently hungry was so much a feature of life as a prisoner that it mattered less than the need to drink fresh water and moisten lips already cracked and blistered by the sun and several hours in the sea. He stood awhile, unsteady, finding his bearings. The island stretched as far as he could see to the south with a ridge running down its spine. From where he stood on that ridge the ground sloped gently to either side, enabling him to see that the island was scarcely a quarter of a mile wide. It was so narrow that he could see down to the island's western shoreline opposite to where he had been brought ashore. A sandy beach, horseshoe-shaped, was the scene of much activity. Sampan after sampan was discharging survivors into the shallows and then heading out around the north-west tip of the island. Already a mixed crowd of islanders and survivors had gathered on the beach.

'Hello Sir. Glad you made it.' Christopher turned around. It was a fellow Diehard, Sergeant 'Dusty' Miller of the battalion's signal platoon. Christopher extended his hand. He felt embarrassed.

'Sergeant bloody Miller. How did I not recognise you? Forgive me. I was too done in to note who'd rescued me. I'm glad you made it, too. Where are the other two?'

Miller pointed down to the beach. 'They've gone to see what's going on down there. The Chinese seem to have set up a sort of reception party. The blokes left me as your minder. You'd passed out. By the way, they're both signallers. What with me, you've fallen in with a bunch of Scaly Backs.'

They made their way down to the beach. The word had spread quickly across the island that hundreds of men were in the sea and that they were enemies of the Japanese. The Qingbang community had responded without a second thought. Those island leaders not manning the fishing boats had deployed to the island's most accessible landing point. They had been joined there by several women who took with them such items of clothing that could be spared. They carried food, too. Not much, because they did not have much. A few baskets of dried fish and raw sweet potatoes. There would be time later to boil some of their small store of rice. A crude standpipe close to the beach offered fresh water which some of the women, all dressed in black trousers and black blouses, were carrying down in buckets, coolie-fashion.

By the time Christopher and Sergeant Miller reached the beach, more than a hundred survivors had gathered there. They made an extraordinary sight. None of them had shoes of any sort. Most of them wore nothing more than shorts and vests. A few were completely naked. Many were well on the way to recovering from their ordeal in the sea and already had a sense of purpose, asking themselves what next and swapping stories of their survival. A few had been left so crushed that they were incapable of any initiative; they just sat there, heads between knees or curled up on the sand, waiting for someone to tell them what to do.

The Qingbang islanders were a practical people. Their life was hard but simple. They were used to being faced with problems and sorting them out for themselves. When it became clear that their small island was about to host many more than a few survivors, the senior men were quick to identify their priorities. The first was to provide food and shelter before nightfall. Some survivors, perhaps up to fifty of them, could shelter in the island's Tian Hou Temple. Tian Hou was Goddess of the Sea and Patron of Chinese fishermen, and like any other fishing community, Qingbang had built a temple in her honour. For those survivors who could not be sheltered in the temple, room would have to be found amongst the island's family homes. Not every family could be counted on. They would be sympathetic towards the survivors, but memories of the last brutal Japanese reprisal raid, back in February, were still raw, particularly amongst those families who had borne the brunt of it.

But if providing food and shelter for the night was the immediate task, the elders who had gathered at the beach also had to decide what to do about the survivors the next day and beyond. Their shared instinct was to get them off the island and into the hands of the Chinese Nationalists as soon as they could organise it. Zhao Xiaoru was Qingbang's equivalent of the village elder. The advance of old age had long since brought an end to his livelihood as a fisherman, but he had the respect of the community and the authority to speak on their behalf. He and others of his generation knew that Miao Kaiyun would be keen to help. Miao was a senior figure in the national resistance corps and lived on a nearby island. He would know best how to organise ferrying the survivors to the interior. They needed to get a message to him tonight. Others were more cautious, Weng Azhou amongst them. His two sons were at that minute out at sea helping with the rescue. When they had dropped off their first load of survivors, they had reported rescuing men in the sea within easy sight of the Japanese ships. The Japanese were sure to come looking for survivors, and if they did there was no way they could be kept hidden. He had a point. Qingbang was barely two miles long and less than half a mile across at its widest. It would be impossible to hide even a handful of survivors if the Japanese put search parties ashore.

The elders decided to meet that night. In the meantime, they needed to organise the survivors who were already ashore. They also needed to search the island's east coast. There could be men who had survived the surf and the rocks. They would need help.

Christopher could feel strength returning to his body and his spirits rising. An elderly woman offered him a sweet potato which he shared with Sergeant Miller. Never had a raw vegetable tasted better. But even more memorable and restorative was their first taste of Qingbang's fresh water. Both he and Miller cupped their hands and greedily swallowed mouthful after mouthful from the buckets carried down to the beach by the island's women. Christopher looked around him for familiar faces. There was no sign of Monkey Stewart, nor of Martin Weedon. He was especially worried about those two and Jim Whitham. Christopher had last seen Martin and Ewan Graham helping Jim into the sea. The Colonel had been severely weakened by illness, and neither Martin nor Jim had fully recovered from their wounds. They were hardly in the best shape to swim all the way as he had just managed to do. Other than Christopher, there had been nine Diehard officers on the Lisbon Maru and he could see none of them here on the beach. Come to that, the only officer he recognised was 'Ginger' Howell. Christopher limped over to where Howell was talking to Zhao Xiaoru and another islander.

'I didn't know that you speak Chinese, Hargreaves.'

Howell grinned. 'I'm having trouble with the local dialect.' He pointed to the tallest of the two islanders who wore a military-type peaked cap.

'This is Mr Xin; he speaks good English. I think he's the only islander who does.'

Mr Xin was Lin Agen's relative who had learned his English while serving in the Chinese navy. He had been sent for by Zhao Xiaoru as soon as the first survivors had been landed ashore and identified as British. He enjoyed good face amongst the Qingbang community because of his military career and he was obviously as pleased as punch to be of service. Christopher pointed to his hat. Xin's face lit up. He proudly explained that he was wearing his navy hat, complete with the twin-anchor cap badge of the Republic of China Navy. He kept it well hidden at home since the Japanese invasion, but it was only right that he should wear it now. Xin introduced Christopher to Zhao Xiaoru and explained that they needed to arrange matters with the survivors on behalf of the island. They wished to help but they feared what would happen if the Japanese came looking for them. One thing was clear to Christopher; there was no chance that the Japanese would not come for them. They had intended all along that the prisoners would go down with the *Lisbon Maru*. Why else would they have shot at those who had made it into the sea? The Japanese would now know that some of them had been rescued from the sea by these fishermen. They were bound to conclude that at all costs the prisoners must not be allowed to escape further to the Chinese mainland and tell their story to the world. In Christopher's mind, there was no question of trying to hide here on this small island; it would be far too dangerous for the islanders themselves. He asked Xin to make this clear. The survivors would be grateful for any food and clothing that could be spared and for shelter for the night, but if the Japanese put soldiers ashore, he would arrange for all the survivors to gather and give themselves up.

Xin interpreted as Zhao Xiaoru explained his plan. He would lead up to fifty survivors to the temple where they would be fed and sheltered for the night. Other elders and some of the women would lead the remaining survivors to find shelter for them within family homes. They needed to move quickly, before last light. In the meantime, the island's fishing boats would continue to look for more survivors at sea.

*

Christopher woke from a deep sleep just as the first of the morning's light found its way through the temple's small windows. Last evening, he had been given a long, quilted coat which had kept the worst of the night's cold away. He ached all over from lying on the bare stone floor, but that was a small price to pay for all those hours of unbroken sleep. He could not remember when he had last had anything like a proper sleep.

He had no idea how many survivors had made it to this island. The elders had talked of hundreds, but he acknowledged to himself that they may have been exaggerating. One thing was certain; whoever these islanders were, he and his fellow survivors were indebted to them. Xin had explained that some of the first sampans to deploy had been fired on when they had approached too close to the Japanese ships at the scene of the sinking. It had been too risky to search for survivors that far out, but the sea within three miles of the island had been full of survivors as well as wreckage and bodies.

In Monkey Stewart's absence, Christopher sensed that it was up to him to assume the Colonel's role. He had seen for himself how important it had been to maintain some sort of normal chain of command during those hard days spent on the *Lisbon Maru*. Monkey Stewart had led like a man possessed, and all those on board had responded heroically, whatever their cap badge. Without the Colonel's leadership and the military hierarchy beneath him, Christopher doubted many would have survived the sinking and all that had preceded it. The need for leadership and discipline was no less urgent now. Possibly hundreds of survivors were strewn haphazardly across this small island, many of them scarcely knowing where they were and what to expect next. Their hosts were torn between their instinct to help the survivors and their terror at the thought of how the Japanese would react. Just before Christopher had finally slept last night, two of the survivors had reported that they had seen the Japanese helping survivors onto the rescue ships. They appeared to have stopped shooting at them or running them down. That seemed to indicate that someone in the Japanese chain of command had ordered survivors to be rescued. If so, that could be a good sign of what Qingbang could expect when the Japanese came looking for them.

Christopher took his first, shaky steps out of the temple and felt the weight of leadership settling on him once more as he braced himself for the day ahead.

The weather had changed overnight. Rain had swept in on a strong, chill wind from the north-east. The sea which yesterday had been in merciful mood was now whipped up and angry. As Christopher took in the scene, he thanked the good luck that had saved so many lives the day before. He for one could never have survived amongst the waves which were now hurtling towards the island's shore.

The islanders had dug deep into their store of rice so that wherever the survivors had slept that night – some of them crammed into the temple and its grounds, others given a space in fishermen's huts, outhouses and haystacks – they all began the day with a breakfast of boiled rice, dried fish and sweet potato. They wore an eccentric assortment of clothing. Many had emerged from the sea naked and now wore primitive loincloths improvised from hessian sacks and other scraps of rough material. Others had been given baggy, black trousers. A fortunate few now wore a padded jacket or thick shirt. The people of Qingbang had responded to the sudden arrival of all these strangers with extraordinary generosity. Faced with so many men being thrown under their care by events they did not fully understand, they had given what they could spare, and in some cases still more.

*

When the Japanese came, it was in the form of three warships which took up station as close to the island's coast as the shallow inshore waters allowed. With cold, deliberate menace the ships trained their guns on Qingbang. It was late morning. Christopher and the island's elders had come to a decision. At the first sign that the Japanese were coming for them, he would lead the group of survivors who had spent the night in the temple to the beach where the sampans had put most of them ashore. They would assemble there and wait to hand themselves in. The elders agreed to put the word out to those islanders who were providing shelter. The message to all survivors was clear; assemble on the beach and don't do or say anything that would give the Japanese cause to abuse the people of Qingbang.

By the time the first contingent of Japanese came ashore, around two hundred survivors were gathered on the beach close to the north-west corner of the island. Christopher couldn't help but feel proud of them. They stood around as if they hadn't a care in the world, telling how they had survived, sharing jokes, asking after comrades they had lost touch with. Despite the cold, they had handed back most of the clothing that could be identified as having been given them by the islanders, so they presented a somewhat comic sight, with their assortment of underclothes and improvised loincloths. Christopher noted that most of them were in much better shape than when they had landed; food and water followed by a night's sleep seemed to have done much to restore yesterday's exhausted bodies. For the first time since leaving Hong Kong they were clean. Spirits seemed to be high despite the certainty that they were about to be recaptured. All but a few had quickly come to accept that there was never any real chance of total freedom; it was enough to have escaped the sinking with their lives. But not all were in a good state. Some had been carried to the beach, unable to make it without support. They sat around in small groups, grim-faced and listless. Some had been injured either when escaping the holds, abandoning ship or being dumped by the sea onto the rocks of Qingbang's east coast. Others had been so weakened by days and weeks of sickness that survival at sea had used up their remaining reserves of strength and willpower; they simply had nothing left to give. Christopher spoke to some of them in the hope that words of encouragement would help, but it was all too obvious that without medical treatment they had little chance of making it much further.

The Japanese came ashore with an ostentatious show of aggressive intent. They were marines, about one hundred of them, their rifles with fixed bayonets pointing at the survivors. Two of them each carried a large flag, as if in the vanguard of a charge against the enemy. They were led by officers brandishing their swords amid a din of shrieked commands and whistle blasts. Christopher detached himself from the large group of survivors and calmly walked out to meet the landing party. The Japanese officer in command was accompanied by the familiar figure of interpreter Niimori who was in his element; here was the opportunity to inflict further humiliation on these British prisoners. The marine commander yelled a question at Christopher and Niimori translated. 'Do you surrender?'

Christopher resisted the temptation to laugh. Only the Japanese could fail to see the absurdity in the question. Here they were, two hundred or so emaciated survivors, nearly all of them dressed in nothing more than underclothes, facing heavily armed Japanese marines on a beach covered by the guns of a Japanese warship two hundred yards offshore. He carefully explained that the survivors would cause no trouble. None of them would attempt to hide and in any case the islanders had refused to help them. Christopher had no idea if Niimori interpreted his words accurately, but the marine commander's response indicated that he did not believe what he had heard. He barked orders to his officers. Around twenty marines shepherded the survivors at bayonet point into a corner of the beach whilst the remainder fanned out across the island.

The prisoners were ferried out to one of the ships in groups of twenty. Christopher stayed until the last boatload were boarding. He wished he could thank the islanders for their kindness on behalf of all the survivors who had found themselves cast ashore amongst this generous community of fishermen and their families. As it was, not a single Chinese face was within sight. Christopher was about to climb aboard when Niimori summoned him. The interpreter demanded a bow from Christopher, prodding him in the chest with the stick that he carried everywhere.

He gave Christopher one of his familiar sneers. 'It is an offence for prisoners of war to try to escape. I want you to know how lucky you have been to be spared by the Japanese Imperial Forces. You would have saved Japan much trouble if you had all gone down with the ship.' Christopher bit his lip and said nothing. There was no point in provoking Niimori. The islanders were in enough danger as it was. He left Niimori on the beach, waded into the shallows and climbed over the gunwale of the waiting boat. The next stage of his troubled journey to Japan was about to begin.

Chapter 23

3–5 October: Where Next?

Christopher climbed unsteadily up the gangway of the large vessel and joined the throng of fellow Qingbang survivors on the deck. Armed Japanese sailors herded them towards the ship's stern and indicated that they were to stay there. Already on board, shivering in the driving rain, were groups of survivors who had been picked up the previous day from the sea close to the *Lisbon Maru*. They had been lucky. The ship that had hauled them to safety was a gunboat of the Imperial Japanese Navy, manned by naval personnel who looked down with distaste on their country's soldiers. The Japanese navy had been trained by the Royal Navy during the early years of its formation, and successive generations of officers and ratings had inherited many of the British naval traditions and attitudes. The ship's officers had disapproved of the conduct of the Japanese soldiers who had prevented survivors from boarding other ships and shot at them in the water.

Christopher looked for a space. The deck was already packed tight with survivors. It was going to be a matter of squeezing in as best he could.

'Chris, over here.' It was the familiar voice of Martin Weedon. Christopher looked around. There, in the corner by the ship's stern rail, a raised hand waved. He stepped carefully over several prone survivors before he reached what turned out to be a small colony of Diehards. As well as Martin Weedon, RSM Bob Challis and Sergeant Frank Waldron had both been pulled from the sea the day before and had found space for themselves here on the aft deck. And there, fast asleep, propped up against a bollard, was Private Bill Speight. Christopher asked the first question to come to mind. 'Has he kept hold of his butcher's knife?'

Frank Waldron grinned. 'No, we've declared Excalibur as having been lost at sea. Speight is inconsolable.'

They were all keen to hear news of who had survived and who had not. Christopher reminded them of how much they all owed to Lieutenant John Potter and confirmed that he had died of his wounds before they had abandoned ship. He briefed them about events on Qingbang, and drew a subdued cheer from them when he related how he and Dusty Miller had made it ashore.

Martin Weedon had good and bad news for Christopher. 'I'm sorry to tell you that Jim Whitham didn't make it. Ewan Graham and I both lost sight of him once we were in the sea.'

Christopher was reluctant to give up hope. 'Are you sure? He could just be missing.'

'I'm afraid there's no doubt, Chris. Private Viner and two others later saw him face down in the water. Viner's over there if you want to ask him.'

This news came as a body blow to Christopher. As a friend, he had encouraged the young banker to join the Diehards on an emergency commission just before war was declared. Unreasonably, he had felt personally responsible for him and had argued that Monkey Stewart should leave him off the list for transportation to Japan. In his view, there was no way that Jim's wounded legs would stand up to forced labour. But Jim had pleaded to be put on the list; he hadn't wanted to be made a special case.

Martin placed a reassuring hand on Christopher's shoulder.

'There's better news about the Colonel, though. Monkey has survived. He's on another ship.'

Christopher sighed with relief. 'How do we know?

Frank Waldron joined in. 'I saw him. In fact quite a few of us saw him. He was drifting along on a half-submerged life raft. Sitting on the dry bit, calm as you like. Would you believe it, still wearing his bleedin' cap. We watched someone throw him a line and pull him on board. I tell you, we were all half dead but we managed to give him a cheer.'

They went on and on, these reports of survival and tragedy. Some had been seen dead in the water, others in their final struggles, desperately clinging to whatever bits of wreckage, however useless, that had come within reach. Some had made it past the Japanese ships but had been carried too far north of the islands. One non-swimmer had been seen drifting out towards the open sea astride an empty water tank; another, poor old Private Alex Tait in A Company, had been caught around the neck by a boat's tow rope and been strangled while being dragged along. Some survivors confirmed seeing fellow Diehards being shot in the water, while others reeled off a string of names of those who had been pushed back into the water by Japanese soldiers on the rescue ships, as Christopher had seen happen to Private Stickley.

For the rest of that day they lay there huddled together, cold and hungry, under a leaking, makeshift tarpaulin cover, whilst the ship continued to search for more survivors on the several small islands that lay to the west and south of Qingbang. The drill was simple. The ship would lie off an island whilst launches landed a search party and brought any survivors out to join those already on board, the latter watching with interest, anxious to learn which of their fellow prisoners had survived. As the daylight hours crept by, each small island searched seemed to produce its survivors, mostly in ones and twos, each with their story to tell.

*

Three days after the *Lisbon Maru* had sunk, the Japanese called off the hunt for further survivors. Christopher and his fellow survivors from Qingbang had spent another wretched night, bitterly cold, tormented by the drip drip of rain through the leaking tarpaulin cover and soaked from time to time as the spray from the rough sea washed across the deck. Sleep had been out of the question. For two of them, it had been their last night. They had survived all the horrors that had been inflicted on them since their defeat in battle just over nine months ago only to succumb quietly to diphtheria, their death unnoticed until first light. They were tipped into the East China Sea with a prayer for their souls and as much dignity as could be mustered in the wind and the rain that swept across the deck of the Japanese warship. Christopher could do nothing but seethe with anger. Their deaths could have been prevented by even the most basic of medical treatments, but at all stages of the sea journey from Hong Kong, the Japanese had callously rejected Monkey Stewart's demands that the sick should be treated.

Overnight the warship had set a course for Shanghai. It was now one of a small convoy of vessels carrying survivors to a port where they could be loaded onto a single ship for their onward passage to Japan. The prisoners had been told nothing of this. They just wanted to get ashore somewhere, anywhere. They were cold, wet and in many cases suffering from sea sickness. They were also weak with hunger. They were fed twice that day, the same as the day before, each time with a ration of two biscuits and a cigarette tin of warm, soya bean milk. That was the daily ration. There were no latrines, only buckets. With dysentery and diarrhoea rife amongst the survivors, as fast as the buckets were emptied over the ship's side they were filled again.

Christopher shared a grimace with Martin Weedon. 'I don't know which is worse, claustrophobia in the *Lisbon Maru* hold or exposure on the deck here.'

'It depends whether you prefer your misery hot or cold' was Martin's wry response. 'I just want to feel dry land under my feet. Anywhere will do; I've had enough of life at sea to last me a lifetime.

*

The Huangpu River is a tributary of the mighty Yangtze. It flows northwards through the centre of Shanghai and on to Woosong, a drab, shabby port town close to where the Yangtze empties into the East China Sea on the southern fringe of what we know as the Yellow Sea. Just outside Woosong, the first boatloads of survivors from the *Lisbon Maru* shivered on a bleak railway wharf, waiting for the last of their comrades to arrive. Some had waited there for two days now. They were penned in like a flock of sheep, completely in the open with no shelter. On board the ships that had brought them here, the Japanese sailors had largely left them alone. There had been none of the ill-treatment or humiliation that had been inflicted on them by Wada's soldiers on the *Lisbon Maru*. There had even been acts of kindness and on at least one of the naval ships those prisoners who had died on board had been buried at sea with appropriate honours being paid. But that had all changed the moment they had docked in Woosong. As the first prisoners walked down the gangway, waiting for them on the quay were Japanese soldiers. The mood had become one of familiar menace. Any clothing received from either the ship's company or the Chinese fishermen was torn from the prisoners. The luckiest among them had managed to retain their issued shirt and shorts, but they were few. Most had only underclothes or makeshift loincloths which they had come to refer to by their Japanese name, *fundoshi*. Many were completely naked. None had footwear of any sort.

The scene was one of utter misery. The wind was still from the north-east, bringing with it the first flurries of autumn snow. Already, several prisoners were lying unconscious from hypothermia on the concrete floor of the wharf. Those suffering from dysentery could be seen from time to time scuttling to the side of the quay to squat and relieve themselves directly into the harbour water below. There happened to be some medics amongst the survivors, but they had nothing by way of medicines or dressings and could offer no relief to the sick and the injured.

Monkey Stewart was amongst the sick but was doing all he could to hide his failing health from those who looked to him for leadership. His peaked cap had survived the sinking and he wore it, correctly set and defiant, as a sign that they all still had a military leader. By his side, Company Sergeant Major Edwin Soden had assumed the role of the Colonel's right-hand man in the absence of RSM Bob Challis. Not that he looked the part. He was wearing nothing more than a *fundoshi*. Chinese fishermen had pulled him from the sea and put him ashore in Qingbang. He and a group of survivors had been sheltered in a shed belonging to one of the island's families and had slept the night on piles of smelly fishing nets. In the morning the wife of the shed owner had decided that a skimpy fundoshi was not sufficient cover, even for a shipwrecked soldier. She had presented him with an old overcoat, much to the amusement and applause of the women who had come to give the survivors some food. As soon as he had set foot on the quayside in Woosong, the coat had been ripped off him.

Stewart had been impressed with Soden during the battle for Hong Kong. His company commander and two of the platoon commanders had been killed early in the battle and Soden, although only recently promoted to CSM, had responded like a seasoned warrior. Stewart thought back to the early days of captivity in Hong Kong when Soden had led the remnants of his company in refusing to sign a promise not to escape. It had been a recklessly brave act of defiance that had led to their mock execution and could easily have ended in tragedy. Although Stewart had reprimanded Soden for staking his men's lives against the satisfaction of standing up to the Japanese, he still harboured a quiet admiration for the spirit that had driven him. One thing he did know. Soden had what it took for survival: he was tough, stubborn and had a fearless, visceral hatred of his Japanese captors. In the dire circumstances that beset them all on that grim wharf, Monkey Stewart knew he could have no better man at his side than CSM Edwin Soden.

*

The ship carrying Christopher was the last to bring survivors to Woosong. Although it was only early October, a thin, unseasonal carpet of snow lay across the quayside of the wharf. Christopher stood with Martin Weedon and RSM Challis at the ship's rail, waiting for the order to leave the ship. He spotted Monkey Stewart, standing straight-backed on the quayside, ready to welcome them as their commanding officer.

Christopher shared his thoughts with his two colleagues beside him. 'I have to admit that when we abandoned ship I wondered if we would see the Colonel again. I should have known not to doubt it.'

'And still wearing his cap, I see,' observed Martin. 'But he seems to have lost his cane.'

Monkey Stewart was not the only one waiting to welcome the last arrivals to Woosong wharf. There, stepping out of a military staff car and swaggering their way to the bottom of the gangway, were their chief tormentors from Shamshuipo Camp and the *Lisbon Maru*, Lieutenant Wada and interpreter Niimori.

When the order came to leave the ship, Christopher led the way down the gangway. As he stepped ashore, Niimori stood in his way, supported by Wada and several soldiers.

Niimori made a point of prodding Christopher in the chest with his stick.

'Remember,' he hissed into Christopher's ear, 'none of you deserve to have survived. You should have drowned like rats in the sea. You should be grateful that Japan's Imperial Forces have heroically saved you.'

Christopher said nothing and edged his way past the interpreter, followed by Martin. RSM Bob Challis was still wearing a shirt which Niimori ordered him to hand over to one of the soldiers. Challis refused and was promptly kicked in the groin by Niimori before being dragged away and stripped of all clothing.

This set the tone for the unloading of the rest of the survivors. As they made their way onto the quay, individuals were selected – seemingly at random – for a punch or kick as punishment for imagined offences. The message was clear: they were no longer survivors of a sinking at sea; they were what they had always been since the beginning of the year, dishonoured prisoners of war who were now back under the control of the victorious Japanese imperial army.

That evening they were all loaded onto open Chinese junks where they spent the night. They took it in turns to sleep because there was not enough room for everyone to lie or sit down at once. They had been given no food and had no blankets to help keep the intense cold at bay. By morning, five of them had died of exposure.

At dawn, they were forced back onto the wind-swept quayside for a breakfast of rice in warm water. They had no mess tins or cups, so the food was spooned from a large metal container straight into their cupped hands. Monkey Stewart was still queuing for his breakfast when Niimori arrived and beckoned him over. Stewart was given his orders. He was to prepare the prisoners for a *tenko*. The procedure would be the same as for the parades they were used to in Shamshuipo. There were to be no exceptions. A full roll call needed to be held.

An hour later they all formed up along the quay, Stewart to their front, awaiting the arrival of Lieutenant Wada. Some were too weak to stand, but if they fell they were set upon by guards and forced to their feet again. Stewart remonstrated with the Japanese NCO and was slapped in the face for his pains. The mood of the prisoners began to turn ugly. Many of them had by now reached the point where they had simply had enough. A rumble of protest ran through the assembled ranks, accompanied by the shaking of fists. The Japanese had set up a machine gun at each end of the quayside and the gunners now released the safety catches, looking nervously at their NCOs.

'Stand fast. Leave it to me.' Stewart's command had an instant effect on his men. He may have been weakened by sickness, but his presence had lost none of its authority. When Wada and Niimori arrived, Stewart made straight for them.

He made it clear that they were close to having a mass rebellion on their hands. There would be carnage on the quayside and they, Wada and Niimori, would be to blame for it. They would be in trouble. They were responsible for bringing an important source of labour to Japan and would be seen to have failed. Both the Japanese were taken aback by Stewart's outburst. They were more vulnerable to being held to account here than in Hong Kong where they had basked in the protection offered by the unchallenged authority of Colonel Tokunaga. Well, Tokunaga's writ did not extend this far, and Stewart knew it. He gave an undertaking to Wada which Niimori did not enjoy translating for him. If all his men were fed that day and issued with clothing, and if the severely ill were taken to Shanghai to receive medical treatment, he would guarantee an orderly, cooperative response by the prisoners to their onward transportation to Japan. Failing that, he warned, there could be a bloodbath right there and then on the quayside.

Stewart's message hit home. By early afternoon, every prisoner was being issued with clothing. First they were lined up to be sprayed with disinfectant. The clothes given them were not new, and most recipients concluded that it was better that they didn't know from whom they had inherited them. There was no sign of shoes or boots, so they were all condemned to remain barefoot. They were issued with a thin cotton shirt, a rough corduroy tunic and loose trousers which tied around the waist and ankle. Every single item was heavily infected with lice. Then, they were made to line up fully clothed to be sprayed again. By late afternoon, they had all been served with cups of rice and onion soup, and the senior medical officer amongst them had negotiated with Niimori the selection of seriously ill prisoners who were to remain in Shanghai, accompanied by one of the medics.

By evening, the Chinese junks had been cleared from the quayside and a rusty transporter pulled alongside in their place. Christopher paused from picking the lice from his shirt and looked up. The name *Shinsei Maru* was just visible amongst the rust and grime of the ship's bow. They were all loaded during the night. The decks were occupied by Japanese troops, and the prisoners once more found themselves down in a ship's holds. The ship was filthy and the air in the holds was already foul with the stench of vermin. Christopher and Martin stuck close to Monkey Stewart. All three of them found themselves deep down in the hold, lying on wooden boards. A bare lightbulb hung above them, suspended from a beam on the end of a wire. By its feeble light they could see that their boards were set above heaped layers of coal. They were in the ship's bunker.

At first light next morning, the *Shinsei Maru* set sail for Japan. The final roll call had been taken just before the prisoners had climbed aboard the previous evening. Ten days had passed since 1,816 of them had sailed from Hong Kong. As darkness had descended on that desolate wharf in Woosong, their names had been called and fewer than a thousand had answered. They left behind around twenty sick comrades to fight for their lives in Shanghai. Those who had not answered to their name numbered more than eight hundred. Of Stewart's Diehards, 152 had been lost. They either lay entombed in the *Lisbon Maru* or drifted lifeless somewhere in the East China Sea.

Chapter 24

Japan

They took two days to cross the East China Sea to Moji, a port which served as the gateway to Japan's Inland Sea. Not all of them made it that far. Lieutenant Kenneth Young had gone down with diphtheria soon after boarding the *Lisbon Maru* in Shamshuipo. Perhaps only he knew how he had survived several hours in the sea after the sinking and then the privations inflicted on them during those two days of misery on the quayside in Woosong. Monkey Stewart had wanted to leave him for treatment in Shanghai but the young officer had insisted that he could make it all the way to Japan with the rest of them. He died the first night at sea. For the final hours of his life he had been unable to eat or drink, so those closest to him had helped to ease his suffering by dipping chopsticks into water and letting the drops fall into his mouth. At dawn, the six surviving Diehard officers carried his body to the stern rail. Monkey Stewart led them in a prayer and Christopher paid a brief tribute before they released him into the East China Sea.

Life for the prisoners on board the *Shinsei Maru* was much as it had been on the *Lisbon Maru* in the days before the sinking. They spent most of the time shut down and crammed into airless, foul-smelling holds, with barely enough to eat, limited fresh water, no medical facilities and allowed on deck only to use the improvised latrines slung over the ship's rails. It was all too much for some, and Kenneth Young was not alone in being buried at sea. For those who remained, there was one significant extra burden to bear – fear of another torpedo attack. They all knew how lucky they had been that only one torpedo had hit the *Lisbon Maru* near the stern. The *Shinsei Maru* was even more of a rust bucket, and it was obvious to them all that a torpedo strike anywhere near midships would send her down in a matter of minutes. Unable to dismiss that thought from their heads, not many prisoners were able to sleep during these final two days at sea.

As soon as the *Shinsei Maru* had tied up in Moji, she was boarded by newspaper reporters accompanied by a civilian interpreter. The Japanese had identified a propaganda opportunity in the safe arrival on Japanese soil of so many survivors of an American act of war. The interpreter was directed to Monkey Stewart as the commander of these men.

Christopher watched as the Colonel stiffened into a pose familiar to them all. It was one he adopted when confronting Japanese officialdom on behalf of his men. The forward thrust of his head accompanied by aggressive finger-jabbing and the hurling of insults had become familiar features of these confrontations in Shamshuipo, but here in Japan the object of Stewart's anger turned on his heels in shock, and slunk away, a thoroughly cowed figure.

Christopher and Martin joined Stewart by the ship's rail. 'What was that all about?' asked Christopher. Stewart briefed them. The Japanese press wanted to hear from the prisoners' own mouths their contempt for the cowardly American submarine commander who had attacked a defenceless ship carrying prisoners of war, and their praise for the master and crew of the *Lisbon Maru* and for the Japanese navy who with great gallantry had risked their own lives to save those of their prisoners.

'I told them what they could do with their request. I've told the RSM to put the word out. We can't stop the reporters from speaking to the men, but the message is clear: nobody is to go along with this farce. It would amount to collaboration.'

Their first faltering steps ashore in Moji were accompanied by a collective sigh of relief. As Monkey Stewart and RSM Challis led them down the gangway to the quayside, Christopher voiced what many of them were thinking.

'Who'd have thought we'd be so relieved to set foot as prisoners in the land of our captors? I can hardly believe we've made it.'

Martin nodded. 'You're right. It's really weird. The last two days have been a nightmare. I'm just happy to feel the ground under me, even if it's some Godforsaken Nip town.'

They were shepherded onto the dockside railway siding and left to wait, guarded by Japanese soldiers. The reporters and the hapless interpreter had gone, their mission a failure. There was no sign of anybody in authority. They were given no orders, no idea of where they were going or when. Christopher and Martin looked for Monkey Stewart. There he was. Ever the commanding officer, hat still in place, he was moving through the groups of prisoners, exchanging comments and gestures as he went.

Christopher nudged Martin. 'We've come to think of him as indestructible, but I worry that he's running on empty by now.'

Stewart signed to the two of them to join him and made his way towards a bollard. He needed somewhere to sit.

'No sign of Wada and Niimori, I see,' observed Christopher. 'Perhaps they've done their job.'

'I shan't miss them,' replied Stewart. 'Which reminds me. I've been meaning to mention something to you two for some time. The more I see of the Japs, the more I'm convinced they will lose the war. It might take a couple of years, but this will all end. When it does, there needs to be just retribution. They need to be held to account. Tokunaga for what we saw of him in Hong Kong, and Wada and Niimori for their treatment of us in Shamshuipo and on the journey to here. We're talking about serious war crimes. We need to record the evidence whilst it's still fresh in our memory. I'm not sure I'm going to make it much further, and if I don't, I look to you two to take things on from me. You will be the senior Diehard officers here. With you and the likes of RSM Challis and CSM Soden, what's left of the battalion will be in good hands.'

Christopher was about to interrupt him, but his Colonel beat him to it.

'And by the way, don't even think of telling me that I'll be fine. I don't want any of that nonsense. I'm just facing facts.'

This was said accompanied by one of those withering looks that clearly signalled 'end of discussion'.

They waited on the railway siding for hours, without food or water or any sign of what was to happen next. Christopher was just beginning to sense that they might be in for a repeat of their experience at Woosung when a train inched its way down the track towards them. Martin Weedon gave Christopher a surprised look. 'I can't believe this. The way we've been treated so far, I expected to be shoved into open cattle trucks. But look at this; proper carriages with seats.'

They were crammed in, fifty of them and four armed guards in each carriage. The most severely ill amongst them, around thirty in number, were separated from the main body and helped into the lead carriage. Daylight was fading fast when they pulled out of Moji only to stop within a few miles. Christopher looked out of the window. They had stopped alongside a station platform where a group of Japanese soldiers stood chatting amongst themselves beside three military trucks. The reason for the stop soon became clear; the sick prisoners in the lead carriage were being transferred. Christopher watched with a mixture of anger and sadness. They made a pathetic sight. Young men who should have been in the prime of life but were now old before their time, many of them close to death.

The train jerked itself into motion and edged its way out of the station. They had barely left the suburbs behind when an elderly Japanese civilian pushed a wheeled trolley into the carriage and began issuing each prisoner with two small cartons.

Christopher opened the first of his. 'Guess what. It's rice. But at least it's warm.'

Martin opened one of his cartons with an exaggerated flourish. 'But look at this. There's some fish, and a bit of cabbage, and this must be our favourite seaweed. Japan might not be so bad, after all.'

They passed a cold and uncomfortable night without a chance to stretch their legs, but spirits were high amongst the lucky few who were not laid low by sickness. There was a sense of excitement in the air, generated by the novelty of a train journey and a curiosity about their still unknown destination. With daylight came their first sight of the landscape at the western end of Honshu, the largest of Japan's principal islands. Cristopher looked to his left. The dark green, forested hills offered the most subtle of hints that in a month's time they would be ablaze with a brilliant display of reds, oranges and yellows. The rice harvest was underway, the flat fields and terraces dotted with women bent double over their rows, their huge, bell-shaped hats bobbing up and down as they went. Christopher's thoughts drifted to boyhood memories of early autumns spent among fields and woodland on the edge of the North Downs. The hop harvest would have just ended there. As a boy he had helped out in the fields with the picking and then in the oast houses where the hops were stored in sacks before being dried. He smiled to himself as he remembered the gangs of women who each September exchanged their lives in London's East End for four weeks' work in the hop fields of Kent. They would have been driven back home by now. He could picture them climbing into open-top lorries for the return journey, exchanging saucy banter and singing at the top of their voices. He wasn't to know it at the time, but he was destined to share life as a soldier with men who could be the brothers, husbands and boyfriends of these tough, spirited women.

To Christopher's right, from time to time the shoreline of the Inland Sea came and went from view but whenever the train approached one of the sea's coastal towns, the guards pulled down the blinds.

Christopher was curious. 'I wonder what they don't want us to see. Perhaps they don't want us to know where we're going, but I don't see why.'

Martin glanced around their carriage. 'Perhaps they want to spare the Nip civilians the sight of us lot.'

*

It was in the early afternoon of 11 October that they began their march from Kobe railway station to wherever they were going to begin their lives as prisoners of war in Japan. They now numbered around five hundred, including the Diehards who had boarded the *Shinsei Maru* in Woosong nearly four days ago and then survived the sea passage. Their column snaked its laboured way through the streets of Kobe, a busy port just twenty miles west of the city of Osaka. Christopher looked to his right and had to smile. Martin was marching at his side, covered from head to foot in coal dust. Christopher looked much the same; there had been no chance of a wash for any of them since their rescue from the sea nine days ago. They weren't really marching. Monkey Stewart had drummed into them that they would be on public display and needed to show that they weren't an ill-disciplined rabble, but unshaven and filthy as they were, without shoes and with their lice-ridden, ill-fitting clothes hanging shapelessly on their emaciated bodies, they were never going to impress the civilian population with how smartly they marched through their town. For the people in the streets this was their first sight of British prisoners of war, and they weren't sure what to make of them. Christopher recalled the dispirited, humiliating march from Hong Kong Island to Shamshuipo Camp after the surrender at the end of last December. Then they had been pelted with stones and taunted by insults hurled from the many Chinese who had been quick to shift their allegiance to the victors. This was different. He shared his thoughts with Martin.

'I feared we might get a rough reception from the people here, but they seem more bemused than hostile.'

Martin had come to the same conclusion. 'I even saw a smile here and there. Mind you, we must make a comic sight; just look at us.

They came to a playground in the centre of the town and were ordered to halt and form up. They were to be addressed by their new commandant. A military staff car drew up and the prisoners were given their first sight of Captain Morimoto Yasuji. Short and fat, he swaggered his self-important way to the front of the parade. It was meant to be an entrance that would impress his future prisoners, but it succeeded only in prompting an outbreak of barely suppressed sniggers and amused mutterings amongst their ranks. Monkey Stewart was quick to spot the danger. The Japanese could be counted upon to react badly to any sense of loss of face, and for the prisoners, especially the Diehards amongst them, irreverence and causing loss of face was in their nature. A volatile clash of cultures would not be the best way to begin what could be years of captivity here in Japan. Stewart turned and fixed the entire parade with a stare familiar to them all. He had no need to shout a command. He held his stare until the parade fell silent, then turned, saluted Morimoto and reported the parade present to him. Morimoto launched into a long harangue, his words interpreted by a thin, middle-aged civilian whose reedy voice struggled to make itself heard. Morimoto introduced himself as the commander of Kobe prisoner of war camp. All his prisoners would be treated according to the military code of Bushido. In return they were to show respect by bowing to Japanese officers and NCOs and saluting their guards. Failure to do so would be severely punished. They were to learn to count in Japanese and understand Japanese words of command. Even work parties would be given their orders in Japanese. Morimoto paused to allow his gaze to wander across the parade. He strutted along the front rank of prisoners, randomly jabbing individual prisoners with the point of his cane. As he resumed his speech, his sweaty, round face twisted into a sneer of distaste. He found them dirty. They had a responsibility to keep themselves clean. No wonder so many of them were sick if they neglected themselves.

'Unbelievable,' Christopher whispered. 'We've not seen a bar of soap since leaving Shamshuipo.'

Martin's response drew a smile of recognition. 'All this reminds me of my first day at boarding school; the housemaster instructing us to wash behind our ears and change our socks each day.'

Morimoto launched himself into a tiresome litany of dos and don'ts, with each pronouncement working himself further and further up towards a crescendo of indignation and threat. His voice grew steadily shriller, the jerking of his head and the throwing of his arms less and less synchronised, like a marionette whose strings were being pulled by a drunk. The interpreter made no attempt to emulate Morimoto's theatricals and simply carried on delivering his translations in the same bored monotone, his face empty of expression.

Finally, Morimoto had a reminder for them. Some of them may have fought with honour in battle but all honour had been lost when they had surrendered. They had killed and wounded sons of Japan and were lucky that their lives had been spared by the merciful Imperial Nippon Army. With that, he turned on his heels and left them to it.

Daylight was fading by the time they covered the short distance to their new home. They came to a halt in the evening shadow of two red-brick warehouses close to the waterfront. Christopher looked up. His spirits sank. All the windows were boarded up behind iron bars. This was grim, far worse than anything he had pictured to himself during the long journey here. Shamshuipo Camp had been a shambles when they were first imprisoned there, but they had made the most of it. At least there had been open space and light there, but here there was none of either. They were crammed anyhow into dark, cold rooms and were issued with thin blankets before their Japanese guards left, bolting the warehouse doors shut behind them. Christopher found himself on the second floor in the same room as Martin, Monkey Stewart, Ewan Graham and young Ralph King who had been commissioned only months before the battle. The sixth surviving Diehard officer was Cyril Cheesewright, known at his request as Charles, but he was too sick with beriberi to join them. The Colonel was in a bad way and no longer able to hide it. He gathered the four young officers around him.

'You know the form. We need to get a routine going right now; just like we did in Shamshuipo. Get hold of the RSM and senior ranks. They're probably onto it already but get involved yourselves.'

Sleep would not come easily that night. Christopher lay uncomfortably on the bare, wooden platform that was his bed, unable to stretch out to his full length in the limited space available to him. They had all had an evening meal of a small loaf of bread, a rare treat. It had been washed down with a cupful of hot water, itself something of a luxury. The sick had been found space on the ground floor in a makeshift set of wards that were devoid of medicines and drugs. Christopher was exhausted and depressed. He felt unwell and feared that he might be about to go down with dysentery. He clung to the belief that Topsy was alive and still in Hong Kong. He wondered what she knew about his fate. He tried to picture her going about her life as an internee, but he struggled to form a clear image of a possible internment camp on the Stanley Peninsula. He had once taken Topsy to see the fort at the peninsula's southern tip but had given the grim prison and its adjacent infrastructure barely a glance. That had been two years ago, a whole world away from now.

A prisoner died that night. He was a naval warrant officer who had escaped from the bow hold of the *Lisbon Maru* and had managed to swim to Qingbang. Christopher remembered chatting to him on the beach there, both of them still scarcely able to believe they had survived. His death was the first of ten in that grim first week. Each day the worst of the sick cases were packed off to hospital in Osaka, crammed together in the back of open-topped trucks. A further two died before they could be sent from the camp in Kobe. They were both Diehards. Christopher and Martin watched as their bodies were folded up, forced into wooden barrels and then loaded into a hearse. The two officers had been given permission to accompany the hearse to the crematorium on a hillside that overlooked the town. They stood there in a small clearing amongst the casuarina trees, heads bowed in respectful silence, as the bodies were carried inside. Monkey Stewart saw it as his duty to go with them, but even he had to accept that he was not up to it. The next day Christopher and Martin were driven back to collect the two small wooden boxes that held the ashes. They vowed that, one day, they would be buried and commemorated somewhere fitting. In the meantime they would rest amongst their own.

*

On the tenth day of their captivity in Kobe, Monkey Stewart summoned his Diehard officers and RSM Challis. He told them he was being ordered into hospital in Osaka. He would be back, but in his absence Christopher and Martin would share leadership of the Diehards in the camp. When the time came for him to leave, Christopher and Martin accompanied their Colonel to the warehouse gates. They helped him up into the back of the waiting truck. They knew then that this was to be his last journey and that Monkey himself knew it, too. He sat there, wedged in amongst a group of sick prisoners. He still wore his cap and did his best to sit upright. Two Japanese soldiers lifted the tailgate into position and the truck pulled away. Christopher and Martin saluted him and Monkey raised his hand to his cap in response. That was the last they saw of him.

It was shortly after reveille the next morning that Yusui, the Japanese interpreter, informed Christopher that Stewart had died overnight. The cause of death had been certified as heart failure.

'More like a broken heart,' was Martin's response when Christopher gathered the Diehard officers to break the news. 'He loved his Diehards as a father loves his kids, and it broke his heart to see what was happening to them.'

'That and the fact that he was simply worn out,' added Christopher.

The news spread rapidly throughout the camp. There was not a man amongst them all, whatever his cap badge, who did not respect the man who was known to them all as Monkey. And it went beyond respect. As fighting men they were not given to sentimentality, but even so, he had a very special place amongst their affections. For all the Diehards he would always be the commanding officer who could terrify you with one of his looks but who had made sure you were well prepared for the battle to come and, when it did come, had been there at your shoulder, whenever and wherever the fight was at its fiercest. No matter what your regiment or service, if you had not seen Monkey Stewart on the battlefield, you would have seen him on the parade ground of Shamshuipo Camp, out there in front of you all, standing up for you, holding the Japs to account. You would have seen him dragging himself across the sloping deck of the *Lisbon Maru*, urging those who hesitated to abandon ship before it was too late, making sure that he was one of the last to leave. The chances were that you would have exchanged a few words and shared a joke with him during those miserable days on the Woosong quay where he had summoned up what remained of his strength to move amongst the ranks and help keep spirits up. All the hardships you had endured, he had shared with you, and more. He had led you by example and you could not ask for much more than that.

They were of course used to death. Since the start of the battle in Hong Kong ten months ago, the loss of life had been an ever-present feature of their lives. They had all lost someone close, whether on the battlefield, in the sick bay or in the East China Sea. But the loss of Monkey Stewart was a body blow which left the entire camp in deep depression.

*

'Boys, you need to listen to this.' Christopher waved a newspaper to draw the attention of his roommates. It was evening, and they were back in their room after a day's labour in Kobe docks. With Monkey Stewart's death they were now down to five in number, with Charles Cheesewright still in the hospital wing. The newspaper in Christopher's hands was the English edition of *Japan Times Weekly*. The Japanese were ruthless in denying the prisoners any independent news of the outside world, but the *Japan Times Weekly* was a tightly controlled arm of the government's propaganda machine. Letting the prisoners read it was designed to undermine their morale.

'It's the Nip version of the sinking. It's priceless. Listen.' Christopher began reading from the front page.

The report ran to two pages. It painted a story of Japanese heroism in the face of a cowardly American attack on a transport ship carrying British prisoners of war. With brutal callousness, the barbaric Americans had abandoned their comrades to die in the open sea, but many prisoners had survived thanks to the courage and humanity of the Imperial Nipponese forces. Those who had survived were full of praise for the gallant Lieutenant Wada and Captain Kyoda but still seethed with anger at being betrayed by the Americans.

Christopher paused from reading out loud from the newspaper.

Ewan Graham shook his head in disbelief. 'All this is straight out of the Joseph Goebbels handbook. It's hard to know whether to laugh or get angry about it.'

'It's probably what we expected,' Christopher responded. 'And it's up to us to somehow make sure that the true version is recorded and reaches the world outside. We owe it to those who didn't make it.'

Chapter 25

October: Stanley Camp

Like many of the rumours that swept through the camp from time to time, nobody was sure where this one started. Since the originator could not be traced and questioned, no one could judge whether it was true or yet another of those that petered out and were never verified.

But this one was different. It seemed to tie into other rumours that had preceded it and had one consistent thread; a Japanese ship had sunk on the way to Japan whilst transporting British prisoners of war from Hong Kong. Apart from that, the rumour had taken on different embellishments. All prisoners had survived. None of them had survived. The ship had gone down in a hurricane. It had been bombed by Chinese Nationalist aircraft. An American submarine had torpedoed it.

Topsy and Phyllis went together to the camp headquarters and demanded to know what was known by the Japanese authorities. They were told to disregard rumours that had been started by troublemakers.

Just a few miles to the north in the Japanese army headquarters, Colonel Tokunaga was in an even worse temper than usual. As the officer responsible for all prison camps in Hong Kong, he had been handed a big problem just when he least needed it. He had lost two key enforcers with the departure of Wada and Niimori at a time when he already had trouble enough. Unrest was spreading within camps that were hopelessly overcrowded and ridden with disease. Now this. When the first reports of the attack on the *Lisbon Maru* had reached Japanese headquarters in Hong Kong, the decision had already been taken in Tokyo that the incident should be hushed up, but it soon became obvious to Tokunaga that the news was certain to leak out. Rumours were already spreading through the camps at Shamshuipo and Argyle Street, making the prisoners even more troublesome. Now he had confirmation that the rumours had reached the internees at Stanley. The policy needed to change; they had to manage the news, not hide it.

Tokunaga didn't have to wrestle with the problem for long. The day after Topsy and Phyllis had been sent on their way by the officials in Stanley Camp, the decision was taken out of Tokunaga's hands when Tokyo authorised publication of the official version of the sinking. Before the end of the day, copies of the English edition of *Japan Times Weekly* dated 20 October 1942 were pinned up on the notice boards of all camps under Tokunaga's command.

It was early evening when Topsy came off shift in the camp hospital and headed for her room. She noticed a small group of women gathered round the notice board just inside the entrance to the British canteen. Joyce Bassett was one of them. She gestured for Topsy to join her.

'Topsy, I'm afraid it's not good news. You'd better read it for yourself.'

The first few lines gripped Topsy with an ice-cold fear and left her numb with shock. She had to force herself to read on. It was the same newspaper report that Christopher and his brother officers had read amongst themselves with a mixture of amusement and indignation. But they had known it for the grotesque nonsense it was. For Topsy it was devastating, the more so because it offered more questions than answers. The propaganda was so clumsy, so amateurish, that it left her not knowing what to believe. What was certain was that it didn't tell the whole story. The Japanese were holding something back and that meant it was something bad. She didn't even know if Christopher had been on board. There was no mention of where the prisoners were from. If they were from Hong Kong, the odds were that Christopher was among them. The report talked about many prisoners being rescued, but that could mean just about anything. Fighting back tears, she hurried towards Block 10. She needed to check if the news had reached Phyllis.

*

Four days later, Topsy was changing the dressings of a patient in the camp hospital when the air raid sirens began to send their chorus of alarms into the early afternoon air above Hong Kong. Yesterday, the alert had been a farce. The first bombs had already fallen on the docks in Kowloon and a confused dogfight between American and Japanese fighters was well under way before the sirens had wound themselves up to their full, mournful voice. From the balcony of Block 15 Topsy had had a good view when two American and four Japanese planes had fought their aerial duel directly above her. She had no idea what type the aircraft were, but the five-pointed star on the wings and fuselage of the American Warhawks and the blazing red sun on the Japanese Mitsubishis made the battle easy to follow. It had all been over in a matter of minutes. She had cheered loudly when one of the Japanese aircraft had fallen, twisting and cartwheeling like a sycamore seed caught in the breeze, until it careered tail-first into the sea close to Lamma Island.

Topsy could remember the fear that had accompanied the Japanese air raids last December, but this was different. There was little point in the Americans attacking their camp. Why on earth would they? They knew that the camp held civilian internees. After all, they had repatriated their own civilians from the camp only four months ago. And it wasn't as if the camp was close to any likely military targets. Her only worries were for the prisoners of war who remained in Shamshuipo or any other camp. For all she knew, Christopher could be one of them. In that case he would be dangerously close to bombing targets such as the power station at North Point, the airport at Kai Tak and the Japanese ships in the harbour. Wherever Christopher might be, Topsy was sick with worry about him. The absence of news was a daily torment. All that anyone in Stanley Camp knew about the sinking of the *Lisbon Maru* was what they had read in that Japanese newspaper report pinned to the camp notice board.

The sound of the island's warning sirens gave way first to a brief silence and then to the distant high-pitched howl of dive bombers attacking targets far to the north. The muffled crump of exploding bombs sounded deceptively harmless from a distance, but Topsy knew better; she only had to think back to those dark times last December when she had felt for herself the terrifying violence of bombs and shells falling close around her, day after day.

By the time the all-clear was sounded, it was time for her to be relieved. Phyllis was one of the nurses coming on shift and had news for her.

'You and I are on the list to receive our cash allotments tomorrow morning. They want us at the camp offices at ten o'clock.'

*

It was not a long queue, but like most procedures organised by the Japanese it seemed to take ages. They were called forward according to their block number, so Phyllis was ahead of Topsy in the line of women queuing to receive their money. Like many of them, Topsy had spent an anxious night. They were accustomed to seeing their husbands' signatures and date on the form that accompanied the payment. These signatures had come to be taken as confirmation that their husbands were alive and held somewhere in Hong Kong. So far, Topsy had received three of these payments and each one had had Christopher's signature on the form. The most recent was dated early in September. She had learned that the *Lisbon Maru* had sailed from Hong Kong for Japan on 27 September; so she knew that if the signature on her next payment form was dated later than that day, it would tell her that Christopher was still in Hong Kong. She watched anxiously as Phyllis emerged from the office holding her small envelope high above her and smiling broadly. Seeing Topsy, Phyllis rushed over to her. She was keen to share her good news, but very much aware that Topsy was still waiting for hers.

'Bless him, Lance signed the bloody thing four days ago. He must still be here. I'm so relieved. I do so hope you get the same good news about Christopher.'

Topsy gave her a hug. 'Please wait for me. Good news or bad, I need you to be here when I get it.'

When her turn came, she climbed the stairs of the camp offices and was directed towards a long wooden table. Three officials from the Japanese Foreign Department sat behind it, talking amongst themselves. One of them paused and reluctantly acknowledged Topsy's presence.

'Onamae?'

Topsy responded with her name. He handed her a brown envelope and gestured her on her way with a flick of his hand. Topsy waited until she was clear of the building before opening her envelope. It contained more money than she was expecting, but that was of no interest. She unfolded the form and looked for the precious signature. It was not there. At that moment she knew that Christopher had boarded the *Lisbon Maru*.

Chapter 26

Christmas: Kobe House

Christmas Day – a year to the day since they had begun life as prisoners of war after Monkey Stewart had carried a white flag to the Japanese headquarters. That day, Christopher and Topsy had shared their last desperate moments together at the university hospital and Martin Weedon had led a counter-attack on the Stanley Peninsula until a bullet had whacked into his right shoulder and felled him in his tracks.

Snow had fallen on Christmas Eve and now lay in a thin blanket over Kobe. Not that Christopher could see it; the warehouse windows remained shuttered. He could feel it though. His bout of dysentery had left him weakened and the damp cold was pitiless, seeping through the thin blankets wrapped around him. There were rumours that the Japanese would issue them with greatcoats, but they had been given no winter clothing at all.

There was not much for any of the prisoners to celebrate. Christopher and Ewan Graham had returned to the camp in Kobe only two days earlier. Back in early November they had both been sent to the military hospital in Osaka, suffering from severe malnutrition and dysentery. They had been loaded into open trucks for a nightmare journey of more than two hours, huddled close together for some protection from the hail and rain that lashed them every mile of the way. By the time they reached Osaka, two of their number were dead. The hospital had been set up beneath the stands and terraces of the city's sports stadium. The facilities were crude but better than those in the warehouse in Kobe. Crucially, the patients were in the care of a Royal Navy surgeon lieutenant and a team of trained medical orderlies. Christopher remembered nothing of his first two days in Osaka. He had arrived there in a state of utter collapse. By then both he and Ewan Graham were suffering from exposure and had been carried from the truck to their beds by some of the prisoners from the nearby camp who had volunteered to work as orderlies in the hospital. It was mid-morning when Christopher first woke to his new surroundings. He became aware of a familiar voice.

'Morning Sir, welcome to Osaka.' It was Colour Sergeant Bill Poulter, one of the few Diehard senior NCOs who had survived the sinking and had made it to Kobe.

'The surgeon commander told me to wake you up. Apparently, they need to clean you up.' He paused and then added with a grin 'And I can smell why.'

Christopher smiled. 'Yes, I feel a real mess. How long have I been here? And remind me, what are you doing here?'

'You arrived here on Wednesday and it's now Friday morning. I was on the same truckload that brought the Colonel here three weeks ago. I had diphtheria, but I was one of the lucky ones and pulled through. I reckon I'm fit to go back to Kobe.'

Christopher's memory stirred. 'Talking of luck, that's your second dose. I don't think you'll ever know how you survived that Jap ambush down near Bennet's Hill.'

Poulter laughed and pointed to the scars on his neck. 'And I've still got bits of the grenade in me to prove it. Some of it's still in my arse; I don't know what my Doff will make of it.'

Christopher wanted to know how Monkey Stewart had died. There were rumours in Kobe that he had been mistreated. 'And the Colonel?'

Poulter shook his head as he recalled the scene three weeks earlier. 'It was obvious when we arrived here that he was on his way out. And he knew it. So I stayed close to him. He just died in his sleep early in the morning. There were four of us Diehards here and we made sure he had a proper coffin, not one of those bloody apple barrels. We put his cap in the coffin with him. Then a Sapper helped us carry him to the hearse. It was the best we could do. The Nips wouldn't let me go with him.'

Christopher nodded in approval. 'Thanks for that. At least he had a Diehard send-off.' Poulter paused on his way out and called back over his shoulder. 'By the way Sir, we took his cap badge out of his cap. The Colonel wanted you to have it. I've got it in my bed space.'

*

Despite the cold, Christopher was relieved to be back in Kobe, just in time for Christmas. He had missed the companionship of his fellow Diehards.

Not much had changed for the better. Prisoners continued to die like flies. On his first evening back in Kobe House, Christopher had sat down with Martin Weedon, Ewan Graham, Ralph King and RSM Challis and had tried to make sense of the various roll calls that had been taken since they had been put ashore in Woosong. When they compared notes, they made grim reading. Of the 358 Diehards who had boarded the Lisbon Maru in Hong Kong, only 206 had answered to their names during the first roll call in Woosong, and seven of those had been left behind to be treated in Shanghai. Kenneth Young had died at sea which meant that 198 had boarded the train in Moji. By Christmas Day, twenty-one of those Diehards had perished. The worst of it was that their deaths were preventable. The right medicines and the right food would have saved them. Beriberi, diphtheria and dysentery were the main killers, each disease inflicting its own distinct agonies on its victims. Beriberi dragged even the strongest of prisoners down into despair and drained them of their will to survive. Only last week one of them had ended it all by throwing himself down the warehouse lift shaft. Some might have been saved by a diet that provided them with the required vitamins and other essential nutrients, but the meagre ration was a bowl of rice with cabbage and turnip soup twice daily, a small loaf of bread no bigger than a bun and the occasional issue of seaweed as a bonus. On non-working days, the ration was halved, as it was each day for prisoners too sick to work. That meant no bread, only a bowl of thin vegetable soup at midday, and a half bowl of rice in the evening. Meat or fish was issued once a week alternately at just over half an ounce per man.

If starvation was kept at bay, it was achieved haphazardly and no thanks to the Japanese. Welcome as they were, Red Cross parcels were too infrequent to keep prisoners from starving. In any case, Morimoto denied the Red Cross access to the distribution of their parcels which meant that his own camp staff kept some parcels for themselves and broke into others to steal the more attractive items. In their desperation, the prisoners deployed the self-preservation skills they had learned in their months of captivity in Shamshuipo. The Japanese could be bribed despite the certainty of severe punishment if caught. Once a guard or storeman had been identified as a potential target for corruption, a relationship with them was carefully cultivated until the first favour was received or the first act of trade was made. From then on, the prisoners' contact was hooked by his fear of disclosure. The prisoners were paid each month in military yen according to their rank. The sums were miniscule, but when pooled they were enough to provide the basis for trade. While Christopher and Ewan Graham were in Osaka, Martin had recruited Tae, one of the regular Japanese sentries in their block of the warehouse. Soon he was exchanging their military yen for the standard Japanese currency and bringing them small quantities of food, typically a packet of margarine, some fruit, a jar of fish paste, even cheap whisky or wine. Tai was running a high risk and he overcharged them accordingly.

Kobe House offered ways to smuggle in food and other priceless extras which had not been available in Hong Kong. In Kobe, the provision of working parties presented a new opportunity to be exploited. When permanently hungry prisoners were sent to unload ships in the harbour and carry the contents into stores and warehouses, the outcome was inevitable. Prisoners soon became expert at pilfering the ships' cargoes and hiding even large items on their persons. They developed and perfected techniques for defeating the searches carried out when they returned to camp after a day's work. The Japanese camp officials were not entirely unaware of what was happening beneath their noses but by the year's end an improbable *modus vivendi* seemed to have evolved. The captors were prepared to tolerate a certain amount of smuggling, having concluded that they could not stamp it out. That being the case, they mounted the occasional raid on the prisoners' illicit stores and helped themselves to what they could find. That in turn prompted the prisoners to apply all their ingenuity to ways of hiding their possessions.

*

To mark Christmas Day, Morimoto ordered that each prisoner be issued with two tangerines. He also declared it a non-working day which meant that the rice ration was cut by half and no bread was issued. The Diehards gathered that afternoon, determined that the day should not pass without celebration of some sort. They had no musical instruments and no props, but it was not long before that grim Japanese warehouse echoed to the sounds of old-time, London music hall. Cockney soldiers are not known for their shyness, so it didn't matter that nothing was organised. One by one they stepped forward to offer their impromptu entertainment. Familiar songs were sung and they all joined in the choruses, for all the world as if they were having a Friday night sing song in an East End pub. Some of the born comedians among them jumped up and told their jokes and recited their ribald limericks and it didn't matter that they had heard many of them before, they laughed all the same. Then it was the turn of the mimics. Their own officers and senior ranks were caricatured without mercy but with good nature, and the victims laughed along with everyone else. The same could not be said of the Japanese who were lampooned by impersonations that dripped with venomous mockery. Old favourites such as the 'White Pig' – Colonel Tokunaga, 'Panama Pete' – Niimori the interpreter, and 'Rat Face' – Lieutenant Wada, were instantly recognised, but it had not taken long for Morimoto to join their ranks. He didn't yet have a nickname in common use, but his distinctive fat waddle of a walk and his preposterous air of self-importance had quickly become irresistible targets for mimicry. There were no Christmas presents, but the gathering was a productive marketplace for trading the few possessions they had. Red Cross parcels had been distributed on Christmas Eve, with three parcels for every four men. Some prisoners valued a bar of soap over a bar of chocolate, non-smokers like Christopher happily traded their cigarettes for packets of cheese or dried fruit and Martin eagerly exchanged a tin of beans for a packet of pipe tobacco. He had persuaded Tai to buy him a pipe and was now one of only three prisoners in the camp who owned one. They would all have willingly exchanged anything for news from home. None of them had received so much as a card or letter from their next of kin since the battle for Hong Kong had begun. It was bad enough to be deprived of any news of what was happening in the world beyond their prison surroundings, but worst of all was being shut off from news of their families.

*

Christopher was worried about Martin's condition. On his return to Kobe House after a month's absence in Osaka he had been taken aback at how far his close friend's health seemed to have declined. Martin had dismissed his concerns when he raised them.

'It's just this bloody pellagra that many of us have had. Not surprising really when you consider there's no vitamin B in the stuff the Nips feed us on. And my shoulder plays me up from time to time. Anyway, thanks for asking; I might be feeling rough but I'm coping.'

But Christopher had been right to be concerned. Over the next two days Martin took a turn for the worse. Christopher returned from a working party in the docks to find him still in bed, delirious and shivering violently. Christopher summoned a medical orderly who took one look at Martin and pronounced him to be in an advanced stage of diphtheria. Christopher followed as Martin was stretchered to the camp hospital two floors below. The RAMC staff sergeant was in a foul mood and took it out on Christopher.

'He should've reported sick ages ago. His throat is closing up fast and I don't know what we can do for him without the antitoxin. The Nips just won't let us have the serum that could save the diphtheria cases. I've been promised enough for one patient only and that's for Commander O'Brien, and I won't get that until tomorrow.'

He pointed to an American naval officer lying unconscious in the next bed space.

'And it might be too late for him anyway, poor sod.'

It was too late for O'Brien. He died in the night and the antitoxin that might have saved him arrived eight hours later.

*

As the final hour of New Year's Eve approached, Christopher sat quietly in the dark on the raised wooden board of his bedspace, drew his blankets tight around his hunched shoulders and tried to think of something positive. There was an empty bedspace beside him. The serum intended for Commander O'Brien had been sufficient for Martin to receive three injections. They had saved his life. Although out of danger, he was still seriously ill and would spend new year in the hospital wing of Kobe House.

The near loss of such a close friend had given Christopher a real scare. Like all the prisoners, he had come to accept the death of his brothers in arms as a familiar, almost routine, feature of their existence as prisoners of war, but the recent loss of Monkey Stewart had hit him hard and left him ill-prepared to face another blow. Ever since their time together at Sandhurst, there had been a special bond between himself, Martin and Tony Hewitt. They had shared much fun in Hong Kong before the war, and then the heat of battle had forged an even stronger sense of steely comradeship. Christopher's thoughts drifted to Tony. Good God, it was already eleven months since he had escaped from Shamshuipo with Duggie Scriven and that New Zealander. Had they made it? The odds were that they had made it beyond the New Territories into China, because if they hadn't, Tokunaga would have made sure that the whole of Shamshuipo Camp knew about it.

Night-time was never quiet in the rooms of Kobe House. As for every night, Christopher tried to shut out the moans and curses of the beriberi sufferers two floors below. Thinking of Martin's close call, it occurred to him that it served as an allegory for their lives as prisoners of the Japanese. Their captors were totally indifferent to the welfare of their prisoners. If the prisoners were dying of disease, the Japanese were concerned only to avoid being infected themselves and kept well clear of them. In the absence of any concept of shared humanity on the part of the Japanese, the prisoners' survival and existence depended largely on luck. Christopher was under no illusions; no matter how determined to survive you might be and no matter how resourceful you were in adapting to a life of captivity, your luck could easily run out, with fatal consequences. You were in a contest with the Japanese and the random fall of a thrown dice. If the Japanese shut you in Number 3 hold on the *Lisbon Maru* and not in Number 2 hold, the chances were that you would die like most of those poor Gunners had died. If an American submarine fired several torpedoes at your ship and just one of them hit its target, then around half of you had a good chance of surviving. If a second torpedo hit the ship amidships, then none of you would survive. Once in the sea, it was pure luck whether you drifted towards a Japanese ship that would pick you up or to one that had soldiers on board who would use you as target practice. If the *Lisbon Maru* had sunk a day later there was no way so many of them would have made it to the islands in a sea that had been roughed up by the strong wind. If, like Kenneth Young, you had diphtheria and found yourself beyond the reach of medicine, exposed on the open deck of a ship lashed by rain and cold wind, you died, simple as that. If, like Martin Weedon, you inherited the antitoxin that arrived too late to save its intended recipient, you would survive diphtheria. What terrified Christopher was the sure knowledge that far away on a bleak peninsula in the south of Hong Kong, Topsy was faced by the same forces of Japanese inhumanity and the random intervention of fate, and he could do nothing about it.

PART IV: 1943

Chapter 27

Spring

Kobe House

In Hong Kong, Private Joe Bindon had been known as one of the battalion's best athletes. A talented all-round sportsman and soldier, at twenty-six years old he had been in his prime. As Christopher watched his shrunken, emaciated body crammed into a wooden barrel, he could scarcely recognise him as the young man who two years ago had left all the other runners in his wake in the quarter mile race around the barracks in Shamshuipo. Bindon's death certificate would show that it was beriberi and malnutrition that killed him. The two went together. The prisoners didn't have enough to eat and what they were given had scarcely a trace of vitamin B in it. So in large numbers they were snared by beriberi, no matter how fit they were, no matter how determined they were to survive their imprisonment. The Japanese refused to provide the vitamins and medicines that could have saved the likes of Joe Bindon.

Christopher and the surviving Diehard officers and senior non-commissioned officers lined the street alongside their warehouse prison as the hearse pulled away. That was all they were permitted to do by way of paying their last respects to one of their own.

Christopher shared his thoughts with Martin Weedon.

'You'd think we would have become hardened to this by now. I mean watching men you knew finish up in a wooden barrel and carted off like a bit of rubbish to be burnt. Not me. I still find it hard to take, even after six months of it.'

Martin nodded. 'If we wanted a metaphor for our life under the Nips, Bindon was it. Poor bloke, he just ran out of luck. He was with me at Stanley. You should've seen him taking on the Nips. Brave as a lion.'

'I saw him on Qingbang island,' Christopher added. 'He was one of the few who swam all the way and managed to scramble ashore by himself. He was jubilant at having made it.'

Christopher found his thoughts drifting back to the day in late September when they had all climbed aboard the *Lisbon Maru* in Hong Kong's harbour. The mood had been one of hope mixed with apprehension. Of his brother officers, only four survived in Kobe now. Percy Newton, Jim Whitham and Lawrence Wood, all of them young, had been lost on the day of the sinking. Then Ken Young had died of diphtheria at sea on the way to Moji. Christopher would never forget that bleak, wind-swept morning when they had committed 'Chippie' Young to the depths of the East China Sea. Their last sight of Monkey Stewart had been when he and Martin had seen him off on his final journey to the hospital in Osaka six months ago, but Christopher willed himself to recall other images of him. He could so clearly picture him addressing all seven hundred of them on the square in Shamshuipo, each man's attention fixed on their charismatic commanding officer as if he was talking to each of them personally. Then there was the time at the height of the battle on Leighton Hill when Christopher had looked up to see the Colonel crawling on hands and knees under fire to join him and a Vickers machine gun crew, determined as their commanding officer to be with them at the point where the battle was being decided. Perhaps most poignantly of all, Christopher clung on to that image of the Colonel striding defiantly across the sloping deck of the *Lisbon Maru*, cap set dead straight, regimental cane under his arm, calmly urging his men to abandon ship as the sea washed around his legs.

Back in February, they had watched helplessly as Charles Cheesewright, delirious and wracked by pain, had lost his long fight for life in the camp hospital. Beriberi again. Christopher had asked to accompany the hearse to the cremation site in the hills above Kobe, but Morimoto had refused.

Of course, it wasn't all about his brother officers. Close to two hundred other ranks had perished, Bindon being the latest to have survived the sinking only to die in the months that followed, all of them victims of their captors' callous disregard for them.

RSM Bob Challis stood beside Christopher and Martin, deep in his own thoughts. It had been a bad day. Any day that saw the loss of a Diehard soldier was a bad day, and there had been too many of them, here in Kobe and before. As the battalion's Regimental Sergeant Major, he regarded the death of any Diehard soldier as a personal loss. They were all 'his men'.

It wouldn't have mattered if Joe Bindon had been a pain in the arse instead of the brilliant soldier that he was; as far as he was concerned as RSM, he would have been affected by his death just the same. He felt a soldier's grief as he watched Bindon's final journey begin. Soldiers didn't overdo the grieving. They just tucked it away deep inside themselves; they got over it and got on with it. But that didn't mean that it hurt any the less.

And it was hurting now. There was a numbing banality about the scene, with not even a pretence of dignity; the body folded up and forced into that apple barrel, then rolled to the roadside before being loaded into the open back of a rickety, old hearse by a scruffy Japanese driver and his mate who never stopped chatting away. He watched as they slammed the tail gate shut and then drove off, leaving a trail of smoke and fumes. The matter-of-fact triteness of it all simply added anger to sorrow.

The hearse turned at the end of the street and was gone from view, the cough and splutter of its engine heard drifting away into the hills. Christopher dragged his thoughts back to the present. He reminded himself that all of this had to be recorded. There would come a time when the Japanese would need to be brought to account. Not only that, future Diehards would want to know. He wasn't thinking so much about the battle for Hong Kong; the military historians would take care of that. Rather, it was the sinking of the *Lisbon Maru* and all that had followed. There had been no witnesses to that but themselves and the Japanese. There would be mothers and fathers, wives and girlfriends, sons and daughters who would want to know how the end had come for those who wouldn't be there to tell it for themselves. That mockery of an account they had seen in the Japanese newspaper had to be debunked. If anyone was to record this bit of history, it was down to him to make sure it happened. Martin had managed to keep a detailed diary of their lives as prisoners of war in Hong Kong, but his precious pages had been lost, carried away as the sea had surged across the decks of the doomed *Lisbon Maru*. They were irreplaceable, but their loss made Christopher all the more determined that the story of the *Lisbon Maru* and their lives as prisoners of war in Japan would be recorded before it became blurred by fading memories.

Five of them gathered that evening. RSM Bob Challis sat on the floor in a corner of the room, his back propped against the bare, brick wall on the second floor of the warehouse. Challis knew that the Diehards in Kobe House would need lifting after this latest loss. Experience had taught him that collective morale could be a fragile thing, easily lost and hard to regain. Captain Man had sensed it, too, which was why he had convened this meeting of the command team.

Challis looked around the cramped room. Company Sergeant Major Ed Soden was next to him. It had been Challis's suggestion that Soden should be a member of any Diehard leadership team at Kobe. They had served together in Palestine, Egypt and Singapore and he knew him to be a first-rate soldier. But he also knew him as headstrong. Challis smiled ruefully to himself as he recalled how Soden had taken the few survivors of his company close to being executed soon after the surrender in Hong Kong when they had staged that defiant refusal to sign a promise not to escape. He could afford to smile now, but he had supported Monkey Stewart when he had taken Soden aside and given him a dressing down. He could picture the Colonel now, fixing Ed with that icy glare of his and delivering one of those withering reprimands for which he was renowned.

Challis recalled that Stewart had immediately confided in him.

'I didn't enjoy doing that, Mr Challis. Part of me admired his spirit. Of course I did. But playing Russian roulette with his own life was one thing, playing it with the lives of his men was quite another. And he needed to be told so.'

Challis looked beyond Soden to where Sergeant Frank Waldron was taking his place on the concrete floor of the room. He remembered when Frank had first joined the battalion in Egypt ten years ago as a typical young recruit from London; keen, chirpy, streetwise and sensibly keeping his head down. Frank had acquired an encyclopaedic knowledge of every soldier in the battalion, just what was needed here in Kobe House. He had also secured a useful position for himself in the ration store, working alongside the Japanese ration sergeant, with the result that all British prisoners were getting extra food and cigarettes. They had come close to losing him early that year. He had gone down with diphtheria, badly so. He had lain unconscious in the sick bay, his condition worsening by the day in the absence of any of the medicine that Martin Weedon had been lucky enough to be given. Then, without obvious reason, he had come out of it.

'You had us all worried for a while, Frank,' Challis had joked. 'We thought we were going to lose our best access to extra rations.'

Waldron had chuckled. 'I'll tell you what saved me. I came round one morning just in time to see a Nip soldier place a bleedin' barrel at the foot of my bed. Just so it was handy, like. I thought, sod this for a game of soldiers, they're not going to get me in one of them.'

Challis smiled at the memory. He switched his gaze across the room to the two young captains. In his twenty years as a soldier he had seen countless officers arrive in the battalion, fresh out of Sandhurst at the start of their careers. He reckoned that by now he had developed a good nose for identifying those who deserved to be looked up to and those who didn't. He had no fears on that score about Man and Weedon. As far as he was concerned, no officer could fill the Colonel's shoes, and he didn't expect these two to do so, but he had complete confidence in them. They may have had only a few years of service in the battalion between them, but they had been well led in that time. When it came to showing them the way, they could not have had better commanding officers than Newnham and Stewart. And they had now proved themselves in battle. He thought back to the battle for Leighton Hill. He had been wounded when the Japanese hit the feature with a massive artillery barrage. He had been lucky, and he still had small shrapnel splinters in his back to show for it. He had seen for himself Man's leadership under fire up on that hill and had had his first impressions of the young officer confirmed; here was a born leader in the best of the Diehard tradition. He had the same high opinion of Weedon. A different character to Man, and harder to read, but the Colonel always spoke highly of him. He had finished the battle for Hong Kong badly wounded and in command of what was left of two companies that had been decimated during the heaving fighting in Stanley. The men of B Company who had survived thought the world of him, and that was good enough for him.

Challis kept his ears close to the ground in Kobe House. It was what good RSMs did. He knew what the Diehards in Kobe were thinking almost before they thought it. He knew that they didn't demand another Monkey Stewart. There was no point. He had been unique. But they were happy with the successors the Colonel had prepared for them.

On the opposite side of the room, Christopher was having his own thoughts about leadership. Looking at Challis, Soden and Waldron, he felt a surge of confidence. They made a strong team. Between them they knew every one of the Diehards in Kobe as well as if they were members of each other's family. They knew their strengths and weaknesses. They knew the steady ones and the chancers. In their company, Christopher felt inexperienced. He had celebrated his twenty-ninth birthday only four days ago and it was barely five years since he had first joined the battalion in Hong Kong. But they had been five years like no others. With leaders like Lan Newnham and Monkey Stewart, there had been no need to think back to those lectures on leadership at Sandhurst. He had quietly watched to discover what it was about the two of them that had earned them the respect and trust of their men. When faced with difficult decisions he had often asked himself 'what would Lan or Monkey do?' He no longer needed to do that. He had been hardened by his own experience of battle and all that had followed the surrender. It was as if life had by now prepared him to lead the Diehards in Kobe. It was the way things worked in a battalion. He had learned under inspirational leaders and with the Colonel gone, it was now down to him. He thought back to his and Martin's last view of the Colonel, propped up in the back of that lorry. Monkey had known full well that he would not return. When he had tipped the peak of his cap in response to his young captains' salute, his unspoken words had been 'over to you.'

As Christopher gathered his command team around him that spring evening, he was conscious that he did so as Monkey's successor. He would take possession of Joe Bindon's ashes in the morning. Meanwhile, life for the surviving Diehards needed to carry on. There were matters to be discussed, orders to be issued.

Stanley Camp

It was already hot and dusty beneath the mid-morning sun as the internees at Stanley assembled on the only flat area in the camp where there was room for them all. Women with children formed one group, single women another and the men a third. They had been standing there for half an hour and the children were getting restless. Two miles to the east, a modest wind nudged the warm South China Sea onto the rocks and beaches of Shek O before slipping over the verdant hills of that peninsula and then dropping to a breeze that scarcely rippled the surface of Tai Tam Bay. By the time it reached the camp, it brought scant relief from the heat and humidity of mid-May.

The sudden order issued from the Japanese camp headquarters was that the entire camp was to parade for a roll call. This was unusual. Topsy was intrigued. The internees had become used to roll calls being conducted block by block, without the need to parade as a camp. After sixteen months of captivity they were attuned to being left alone to organise for themselves just about all aspects of their daily lives. If you could shut your eyes to the barbed wire, the lack of food, the exotic improvised clothing worn by most of them and the almost complete absence of privacy and of reliable news of the world outside, you could picture the camp as a small village community. The equivalent of a village assembly hall had been established in St Stephen's and Topsy had already attended two productions staged there by the camp's dramatic society. Church services were held and there had been two weddings so far. The first babies had been born in the camp's Tweed Bay Hospital which was well served by nurses such as Phyllis and Topsy. Topsy was one of several qualified teachers who held classes for the camp's children for up to four hours each day. Sharing so much time with the youngest of them made her realise how quickly so many of them had adapted to their new life and accepted it as normal.

Close to the accommodation blocks, the former prison officers' club had been adapted to serve as a recreation centre. Internees met there to play card games, to exchange personal possessions and food items, to attend hobby classes or simply to gossip. Those seeking more intimate meetings had learned that the cemetery offered the nearest thing to privacy. The cemetery overlooked Stanley Bay. It now held simple wooden crosses marking several new graves that patiently awaited the day when headstones could add their tributes to those whose last days were spent in captivity. For the most part, life in this community went on undisturbed by the Japanese. Which is why the order to parade as a camp was unusual.

Topsy and Phyllis stood side by side.

'Something's up,' said Topsy. 'The last time we had to do this was when those two engineers were caught trying to escape. Back in October. Perhaps there's some good news for us.'

Phyllis was not in her best mood. All she wanted to do after completing a shift in the hospital was to put her feet up for a while. 'Whatever the reason, I wish they'd get on with it. I think the Japs enjoy keeping us waiting.'

Topsy nodded. 'You're probably right. Mind you, it's just as likely to be because everything they try to organise becomes a shambles.'

Phyllis gave her a nudge and pointed to a group of four Japanese who had emerged round the corner of the road that led down from the headquarters.

'Talking of shambles, here come Yam and Nak. And Kadowaki. But I don't recognise the fat one waddling along beside him.'

'Nor do I. And I don't like the look of him.'

Yamashita and Nakazawa were officials of the Japanese Foreign Affairs Department which had taken the camp over from the military within a few months of the surrender. These two men shared responsibility for the administration of the camp. In truth, it was a task for which their experience and training had ill-prepared them. They lacked the brutal arrogance of the Japanese military but, finding themselves out of their depth, they did what came naturally to them; they hid behind a bureaucratic barrier. Most internees knew them only by sight and by their nicknames.

The squat figure in army uniform was Lieutenant Kadowaki, Colonel Tokunaga's right-hand man in the camp. Beside him was none other than Niimori Genichiro, back in Hong Kong where he enjoyed the patronage of Tokunaga and with it the freedom to indulge his sadistic streak and hatred of Westerners. Once he and Lieutenant Wada had handed the survivors of the *Lisbon Maru* over to the authorities in Moji, Niimori had wasted no time in finding a passage back to Hong Kong for himself. Judging from the way he swaggered to the front of the parade, he had lost none of his arrogance and sense of self-importance.

One of the guards carried out a low table and placed it in front of Kadowaki who climbed clumsily onto it and stood there, looking awkward and ill at ease, his face expressionless, narrow eyes coldly scanning the parade from side to side. Topsy giggled quietly to herself. It seemed to her that the more he strived to convey a commanding presence, the more comic a figure he cut. Those stocky, bandy legs encased from ankle to knee in tight puttees didn't help.

Kadowaki signalled for the roll call to begin. The parade quickly fell into chaos. The internees were out of practice. Some had forgotten how to answer when their turn came. Some failed to shout out their camp number loud enough. The guards scurried through the ranks, screaming at offenders, slapping faces of both men and women. Niimori needed no invitation to join in and was soon laying about him with his cane. It took half an hour for the roll call to run its course. By now, Kadowaki had worked himself up into a state of cold fury. The chaotic roll call had caused him to lose face. Topsy felt the menace in his look. This could get dangerous, she thought.

Kadowaki launched into his tirade, lashing the internees with volleys of harsh, staccato shouts that echoed eerily back from the high accommodation blocks behind them. The louder Kadowaki shouted, the higher the pitch of his voice climbed and the more comical it sounded to the European ear. Topsy nervously sensed several suppressed sniggers around her.

She noted that the usual interpreter, Watanabe, was missing from the parade. In his place was that Japanese civilian who gave her the creeps. He seemed to be in his element, gesticulating aggressively with his cane as he interpreted Kadowaki's message in a tortured North American accent.

The purpose of the parade soon became apparent as Kadowaki's face and tone became those of a stern headmaster. He had a reprimand to deliver. 'You have fallen into bad habits. It has come to my notice that immorality is taking place on the roofs of the camp blocks in the evening. This will cease, except between married couples and good friends.' He paused to allow his warning to sink in.

Topsy whispered to Phyllis. 'You'd have to be very good friends to be doing that.'

All round her, giggles were being stifled. Kadowaki continued with his reprimand, Niimori interpreting for him with relish.

'In Nippon and Nippon occupied territories it is customary for civilians to bow to officers and sentries when passing them.'

Kadowaki shook his head gravely before continuing. 'Many of you are failing to bow to Japanese officials and soldiers. It is a disgrace.'

Niimori was enjoying this and had quickly adopted his trademark sneer.

The harangue went on and on. 'Men and women in Nippon are proud to bow to those who serve the Emperor, so unworthy people like you must do the same. But some of you do not bow at all and many do not bow in the proper manner.'

He turned to face the group of women whilst Niimori gestured at them with his cane.

'You women are the worst offenders. You think it is beneath you to bow to a Nipponese soldier. Well, let me tell you, you should feel honoured to bow to them. You must not walk past them. You must stop and bow. I will show you how to bow properly.'

Kadowaki stood with his arms close to his sides and bowed in turn to each group of internees. He did it with exaggerated slowness, bending low from the waist until his head was just above the horizontal. It was his version of what the prisoners of war in Shamshuipo had ridiculed as the 'Giant Panda Salute'.

Phyllis had so far managed to suppress an urge to laugh out loud, but this was more than she could take. She came close to infecting Topsy who was trembling with the effort to keep quiet. She didn't dare risk catching her friend's eye.

'You see how it is done,' yelled Niimori. 'Now you practise. You must bow to each other.'

'Look at Yam and Nak,' Topsy muttered out of the corner of her mouth. 'I don't know how they keep a straight face.'

Phyllis shot her a quick look. 'I daren't look at them. I'm nearly wetting myself as it is.'

Soon the scruffy area set aside for the parade was the stage for an extraordinary sight as more than two and a half thousand internees took it in turn to bow to one another. Some began to treat it as an amusement and were quickly set upon by guards armed with canes. Niimori was to the fore.

When it was all over, Topsy and Phyllis made their way to the canteen for the 11 o'clock meal.

Topsy mused out loud. 'I thought I'd seen everything, but that just about takes the biscuit. If you ever wanted to demonstrate the clash of cultures here, that was it.'

Kobe House

As luck would have it, 16 May was a Sunday and therefore a non-working day. The four surviving Diehard officers followed Albuhera Day custom and at midday hosted fifteen warrant officers and sergeants for the ceremony of the silent toast. In the absence of the silver loving cup, they drank the toast from a tin mug. Instead of champagne, they drank tea, complete with milk and sugar smuggled into the camp for the occasion.

The celebration of their regimental day was due to conclude in the early evening with a gathering of all Diehards in one of the large dormitory rooms. It would be Christopher's role to speak of the battle that had given their regiment its nickname and an identity which they all shared a century and a quarter later. In previous years, he had listened to Lan Newnham and Monkey Stewart speak, now it was his turn. That afternoon, as he sat with Martin preparing what he intended to say, Christopher could scarcely believe that it had been ten years since he, Martin and Tony Hewitt had taken themselves to Spain's Extremadura during a period of leave at Sandhurst. It had been an act of pilgrimage for the three of them. In the village of La Albuera, they had been welcomed as friends and the local wine had flowed. The villagers still talked with passion and gratitude of Spain having been saved from Napoleon, the story having been passed down to them through the generations. The three young officer cadets had walked up a long dusty track and then picked their way through rows of grape vines until they reached the ridge that overlooks the village and beyond. They had shared a long silence there, standing in the heat of early summer on the ground that once held the remains of those who were buried where they had fallen all those years ago. Christopher recalled it as a sobering moment for the three of them. Each of them in his own way had then made a silent vow of loyalty to their future regiment.

'I was thinking back to when we went to Albuhera with Tony,' said Christopher. 'They were happy times.'

'I'm glad we went when we did,' Martin replied. 'God knows, we were so idealistic then and knew bugger-all. We meant it when we made those vows, but we had no idea what it would take to live up to them.'

Christopher nodded. 'Well, we know now. Talking of Tony, I wonder where he is now. Celebrating Albuhera Day somewhere, I hope.'

Chapter 28

Summer

When the Kempeitai came for him in Argyle Street Camp, Lance Newnham was not taken by surprise. He had always known that it would happen one day, and he had prepared for it. Nothing that could compromise him or his fellow conspirators would be found. It was all in his head. They had known the risk they were running and had reckoned that no matter how strict their security measures might be, their luck would probably run out.

When he had handed over command of the Diehards to Monkey Stewart back in May 1940, Lance had been grabbed by the general commanding all the forces in Hong Kong to serve as the senior member of his operational staff. General Maltby had known that Lance was due a break after long service overseas, but war was around the corner and Maltby needed the best man for the job. Lance Newnham was that man.

From the earliest days of his imprisonment in Argyle Street Camp, Lance had refused to settle for spending the rest of the war as a prisoner with no other aim than that of survival. For him, it had always been a matter of how prisoners could play a part in bringing about the defeat of the Japanese.

Soon after Monkey Stewart and the other British prisoners of war had sailed from Hong Kong on the *Lisbon Maru*, Lance had set about establishing a tight intelligence organisation in Argyle Street. Its mission was to establish links with the British Army Aid Group in free China with a view to helping prisoners of war and internees to escape from Hong Kong, and to encouraging attacks on the Japanese in Hong Kong mounted from the territories adjoining the Kowloon Peninsula. Lance had made sure that security within Argyle Street was tight. His agents were organised in sections, each of which was kept in ignorance of the parallel membership and activities of the others. All the threads led back to just one person, Lance Newnham. The weakness of the organisation lay in its dependence on the Chinese and Indian drivers of ration lorries who were used to pass messages to trusted agents operating outside the camps within Hong Kong.

For some months plans had been under way for a mass break-out of prisoners under cover of an attack by Chinese troops commanded by British officers. It was an ambitious plan and Lance had been quick to recognise that it was even more of a risk because it involved sharing details with several agencies. It had been within days of being carried out when the fatal breach of security occurred. Without notice, the regular driver of the ration truck for Argyle Street Camp was allocated a different task and had no time to pass on a warning to his contacts. For some reason, his substitute sensed that something was afoot and reported his suspicions to the Japanese. The outcome had been inevitable. The Kempeitai had arrested the regular driver and begun to interrogate him. After three days of constant torture, the driver had given up the names of Lance Newnham and two of his agents within Argyle Street Camp, Captain Douglas Ford of the Royal Scots and Flight Lieutenant Bertram Gray.

Lance heard them coming before the door to his hut burst open. Six Japanese soldiers, rifles at the ready, were first through the door. Lance stood up, slowly, and calmly nodded a greeting. Two of them grabbed and held him, arms behind his back. They were followed into the room by three members of the Kempeitai, instantly recognisable by the distinctive white arm band with red lettering worn on the left arm. Colonel Noma Kennosuke was head of all Kempeitai in Hong Kong. Short and wiry of build, his close-shaved head, smooth skin and fixed smile made him look far too young to be in command of a force that was feared throughout Hong Kong for its ruthlessness and brutality. Unlike most of his army colleagues, he was immaculate in a uniform which looked as if it had been tailored specially for him. He stopped aggressively close in front of Lance and made a point of inspecting him from head to foot, as if appraising him before deigning to speak to him. Unusually for a Japanese officer addressing a prisoner of war, he spoke slowly and softly. Just a short sentence, then a pause to allow the uniformed lieutenant to translate.

'I believe you know why we are here.' It was part question, part assertion.

Lance looked him straight in the eye and gave him a smile. 'As a matter of fact, Colonel, I haven't the foggiest idea, but I am sure I'm about to find out.'

Lieutenant Imamure Ichiro hesitated. He commanded the Kempeitai intelligence section and knew enough English to translate at a basic level, but 'foggiest ideas' were beyond his competence. Lance Newnham's irony was certainly lost on Imamure, but he had grasped the fact that the English colonel denied knowing why he was of interest. That was the gist of the translated message he passed on.

Colonel Noma paused briefly to reflect on Lance's response. He was no longer smiling. He wasn't there to play games. He gestured with his head to Sergeant Major Yamada Kilchiro for Lance to be taken away. Yamada needed no second invitation. This was what he existed for. He specialised in interrogation, and his techniques included forms of torture which indulged his innate sadism. His usual victims were local Chinese who had somehow fallen foul of the occupying regime, so the prospect of being let loose on an English colonel was something that he relished.

They let Lance walk out of the hut, but once outside he was grabbed and thrown into the back of a van. Douglas Ford and Bertram Gray were inside, crumpled on the floor of the van, both of them bleeding heavily from blows to the head. For them the ordeal by pain had already begun.

An hour later, the van drove through the gate of Stanley Prison and drew to a halt in the prison courtyard. The three prisoners were dragged out and prodded at bayonet point into one of the cell blocks. They had been under guard in the back of the van during the journey across the harbour on the ferry, up across the centre of Hong Kong Island and down through the Wong Nai Chung Gap to the Stanley Peninsula, so they had had no chance to confer on how to react to their arrest. Not that there would have been much to say, beyond offering each other encouragement. Since the formation of their intelligence cells, they had anticipated that the day would come when some of them would be questioned, and they had rehearsed their stories. When the regular ration truck driver had failed to appear for three days running, they had suspected that something had gone wrong, and had met briefly to make sure that their tracks were covered as best they could. Now in the prison, each of them was on his own, confined to a bare, stone-floored cell well apart from each other and with only a wooden bed platform and a bucket for company.

Lance was under no illusions about what lay ahead for him. After a year and a half of captivity in Argyle Street, malnutrition and two bouts of dysentery had left him in ill health, and he was not sure how much physical punishment his body could take. But his moral strength was unimpaired. Even in that first bleak hour when doubts and dark thoughts crept into his cell, he felt the strong determination within him that whatever came his way, the Japanese must not be allowed to win.

Less than two hundred yards distant from Lance Newnham's cell, Phyllis Newnham was playing bridge with Topsy as her partner. They were in the former prison officers' club close to the prison's north wall which lay just outside the camp boundary. For some time she had known that Lance was a prisoner in Argyle Street Camp and took some comfort from the knowledge. Glancing at Topsy, who as a relative novice at bridge was concentrating hard on the cards in her hand, Phyllis counted herself fortunate. She was acutely aware that Topsy had heard nothing at all from Christopher since the surrender eighteen months ago and still didn't know whether he had survived the sinking of the *Lisbon Maru*. As for Lance, she contented herself with the thought that at least she knew he was alive and in Argyle Street.

Some eight miles to the north, Lieutenant Imamure sat at his desk on the first floor of Kempeitai headquarters in the neo-classical supreme court building in Jackson Road. The window to his right overlooked the harbour but he was not interested in the view just now. It was his job to devise a programme for the systematic interrogation of the latest prisoners suspected of spying and conspiring against the Japanese occupation and administration of Hong Kong. This was his big chance to impress his superiors. He was well aware that there was something approaching paranoia amongst the high command about the threat of military intervention from the Chinese resistance, supported by the Americans and the British. It was common knowledge that some form of organisation existed with agents in Hong Kong and the adjacent territories. American bombing of the island and Kowloon had become commonplace, and it seemed to be well targeted. The enemy seemed to know the most valuable cargo ships for attack by bombers and submarines and were obviously getting their intelligence from somewhere in Hong Kong. He simply had to break those who had been arrested as suspected agents. He could rely on Sergeant Major Yamada to do the dirty work, but Yamada needed to be closely directed and firmly controlled. He was a thug and the subtlety of interrogation was lost on him. It would be his, Imamure's, plan that would succeed in breaking the network of agents in Hong Kong, and he could hardly wait to put it into action.

Kobe House

The Japanese guard commander and the duty officer for the day took it in turns to jab their fists into Martin Weedon's face and ribs and stab the tips of their boots into his shins. Not for the first time, Martin fell to the ground and was hauled back onto his feet by two soldiers. The beating had begun ten minutes ago and not once had it paused. Christopher, Ewan Graham and Ralph King could only look on, unable to intervene. They had been forced to watch their brother officer being punished as an example. Martin had been caught by the guard commander sitting on his bedspace in the early evening smoking his pipe. He had paid interpreter Yusui a prisoner's fortune for procuring a precious pipe and it had become a prize possession. Camp regulations prohibited smoking after the evening *tenko* parade. Previous guard contingents had ignored the offence and several other petty rules.

For several months, guards had changed every two weeks without making much difference to the prisoners' daily lives. Increasingly they were left to their own devices when not out on a working party. Snap searches of rooms were sprung on them, usually conducted so inefficiently that little was ever found. On the few occasions that a prisoner was caught hiding a forbidden item, the punishment was usually no more than a bit of face slapping and a period of reduced rations or denial of privileges for all prisoners in the offending room. But that was before the change in the regime. When it came, it had been sudden and brutal. A new guard had arrived towards the end of May and its commander had wasted no time in revealing his taste for violence. His first *tenko* parade for morning roll call had set the tone. Any prisoner taking too long to call out his name and prison number or not shouting them loud enough was set upon. One morning, a young mother with a child had passed on the street close by and failed to bow to the guard commander. Beside himself with rage, he had launched himself at her, slapping her face hard, screaming incoherently as he did so. Searches of rooms had become more frequent and thorough, sometimes being conducted overnight in order to deprive the prisoners of sleep. During these searches, the guard commander's favourite trick was to trip a prisoner and then kick him on the ground.

Worse was to come. An equally violent and volatile camp doctor had arrived, intent on imposing his own petty tyranny. Clearly deranged, he would prowl around the floors of the camp at night, half drunk, wearing dark glasses, a kimono and slippers and carrying his ceremonial sword. Prisoners had soon learned that it was not sufficient simply to bow to him; any bow that was too high was punished by a slap to the face and a blow to the back from the flat of the mad doctor's sword. Matters had been brought to a head by two acts of particular savagery. The doctor had caught a prisoner on duty as a cook eating his own supper in the cookhouse after the evening *tenko*, having been too busy to eat it before. The doctor had launched into the prisoner, lashing him repeatedly across the face with the buckle end of a leather strap until he had fallen unconscious to the floor, his face a lacerated mess. A week later, the doctor had inflicted the same punishment on an Australian prisoner caught smoking after evening roll call. This attack had been even more vicious. The Australian had fallen unconscious three times, and each time the doctor had poured a bucket of cold water over him to revive him and then continued the assault. When it was over, the Australian's roommates had carried him to the hospital wing, his face unrecognisable, his ears cut to ribbons by the buckle's sharp edges.

That incident had left Christopher feeling deeply worried. Both the new guard commander and the doctor were completely out of control. The doctor was an especially dangerous and inflammatory presence. There was a limit to the level of barbarism that the prisoners as a body could be expected to tolerate without retaliation.

Christopher, like many of his fellow prisoners, had stoically come to accept that being on the receiving end of slaps and kicks was a routine feature of life as a prisoner in Kobe, as it had been in Hong Kong, but the sheer weirdness of the Japanese doctor posed an altogether new and more alarming threat. There was a strong risk that prisoners would take the opportunity to deal with him during one of his frequent night-time tours of the block. And if that happened, the consequences for all of them were too terrible to think about.

At the next morning's *tenko*, the doctor's vile temper had not cooled. He had strutted manically up and down the ranks, hitting men across the head with the flat of his sword whenever he saw a prisoner out of line or not standing up straight enough for his liking. Looking around him, Christopher could see and hear the growing unrest of the prisoners on parade. Grim looks were being exchanged and angry words muttered. The Japanese guards sensed the rising tension, too. Rifles were shifted from shoulders to the alert position and the click of safety catches being released echoed across the parade ground. A potential disaster had been averted when the doctor, for no apparent reason, had suddenly turned on his heels and, without even a sign or a word to the guard commander, had hurried from the field, jabbering away to himself and dragging the tip of his sword along the ground behind him. Christopher had breathed a sigh of relief, but he had seen enough. Morimoto must be persuaded to get a grip of the doctor, and of the new guard commander for that matter. As the recognised commanding officer of the Diehard prisoners, he had demanded to see the camp commandant.

The interview had proved to be a farce. Morimoto listened impatiently to Christopher's complaints which were translated by a new interpreter. Yusui had been taken away under arrest to meet an undisclosed fate. His racketeering had been discovered after several months during which he had supplied prisoners with forbidden items, including newspapers, their only source of news. His departure had been a big blow to the prisoners even though they knew him as 'the little rat' who charged them extortionate rates for his services. His replacement's knowledge of English was so poor that he was unreliable as a translator, so Christopher had little confidence that his complaints were being conveyed to Morimoto with any accuracy. Not that the camp commandant was well disposed to listen to them, anyway. He was indifferent to the prisoners' welfare. He wanted a quiet life as commandant and was only prepared to intervene if it was the sole way to avoid trouble. While he didn't go out of his way to encourage violence from his officers and the guard commanders who came and went, his instinct was to turn a blind eye to it.

But he had one weakness and Christopher knew it. Kobe House was one of several prisoner of war camps in the Osaka area, all of them under the command of Colonel Morata. Morimoto was wary of Morata and was especially sensitive about any suggestion that his camp was less efficient or causing more trouble than any of the other camps. It was a question of face. His face. He had come to dread one of those unannounced visits that Morata was prone to make at the slightest whiff of trouble.

Christopher had put it to Morimoto that the conduct of the guard commander and the doctor would not be tolerated by Morata in the Osaka camp. To add weight to his message, he had warned Morimoto that if he failed to control the doctor, it was only a matter of time before the prisoners took matters into their own hands and dealt with him themselves. He could have a riot on his hands. How would it look, Christopher asked Morimoto, if it finished up with prisoners facing a firing squad? It would reflect very badly on him personally.

Morimoto had seemed to take the point and had indicated that he would take care of Christopher's complaint. The result had become apparent that same night. The doctor and the guard commander had stormed through the accommodation floors demanding to know who had complained about them. The prisoners had been turned out for a late-night roll call which had dragged on for hours.

That had been two weeks ago. The days that followed had raised hopes that Morimoto had managed to assert his authority. There had been no more snap searches, no more night-time rambling by the mad doctor and no more beatings. Until Martin had been caught smoking his pipe after evening *tenko*.

The three Diehard officers watched as for the third time Martin slumped to the ground in front of the guard room. This time he was out cold. The soldiers who had been pinning his arms behind him let go of him and no longer bothered to lift him to his feet again. The guard commander emptied a bucket of water over Martin's head and took one last kick at him before signalling to the three of them to take him away. They carried him – naked, covered in cuts and bruises and shivering with cold – back to their room. There, they did their best to clean up his bloodied face. By now word had spread throughout the Diehard soldiers' accommodation and the duty medical orderly had been sent for. Martin came round just as Private William Beningfield poked his head round the doorway and caught Christopher's eye. Beningfield had served alongside Martin in B Company and was one of those who had dragged him to cover when he had been shot in the counterattack at Stanley.

Beningfield handed Christopher a small cardboard box. 'I've got something for the Captain. It's from all of us. We reckoned he'd be needing it.'

Christopher took the package to Martin's bed space and turned to beckon Beningfield to join him. He had already gone. Martin fumbled as he tried to take the lid off the box. He mumbled through swollen lips. 'You do it, Chris. I can't see what I'm bloody doing.'

Christopher removed the lid. Inside the box was a brand-new pipe, filled to the brim with tobacco, ready to be smoked.

Chapter 29

Autumn

Stanley Camp

Autumn. The season of lengthening shadows. The headstones and wooden crosses cast their dark, distorted shapes towards Topsy who sat, chin on knees, on a patch of grass at the edge of the cemetery close to the west boundary of the camp, watching the late afternoon sun dip low behind Lamma Island. Her back rested against a lone casuarina tree. There had been several of them when she had first arrived, but some had been felled to provide firewood for the kitchen stoves during the past winter when the Japanese had switched off the electricity supply. It was the casuarinas and their scent that had first drawn her to the cemetery as a place to sit in peace and quiet. With privacy in the accommodation blocks hard to find, some couples used the cemetery as a place for romantic assignments, but that was in the late evenings. In the afternoons, she could usually count on being alone here for a while.

In the mornings, she still used the rocky outcrop on the east side of the camp overlooking Tai Tam Bay as a personal haven. In the first year of her imprisonment, she had tried to set aside the image of that soldier's body on the beach below, but after a while she had come to regard it as a mark of respect to think of him there. She caught sight of his sister from time to time, but she was not approachable and seemed to be living in a world of her own.

From the outcrop, Topsy could watch the sun inch its way clear of the hills on the D'Aguilar Peninsula opposite. Christopher was somewhere out there far beyond those hills, alive or dead. She still knew only that he had been on the *Lisbon Maru*. Rumour had it that around half of those being transported had survived and been taken to Japan, so she had come to terms with the strong possibility that Christopher was dead. His last words to her had been clear; if he didn't survive captivity, she was to look upon his family as hers. But she had yet to meet any of them. She no longer had ties with Edinburgh, so home without Christopher was an elusive concept for her now.

The breeze began to touch the cemetery with a cool hand, a further reminder of early autumn. It was time to make her way back to her room. Below her, Stanley Bay had begun to shimmer under the low sun. She could never look at the jetty on the beach without recalling that grim January evening when she had first stumbled ashore there. At the time, she had thought that life had all but ended for her. She was far stronger now.

She noticed a large van driving down to the jetty from the direction of the prison. It stopped close to the beach where a Japanese soldier jumped out and opened the back of the van. Two more soldiers were the first to emerge, followed by seven Europeans, their hands tied behind their backs. Topsy couldn't be sure, but she thought she recognised one of them as a former police officer who last year had used his contacts to help Phyllis Newnham pass a message to Lance in Argyle Street Camp. Topsy looked out across Stanley Bay, expecting to see a vessel coming to collect the prisoners. There was no sign of one. The soldiers shepherded their prisoners away from the jetty towards the upper slopes of the beach, barely two hundred yards from where Topsy stood. There, where the beach gave way to low scrub just beyond the camp boundary wire, Topsy saw a freshly dug trench for the first time. The certainty of what was about to happen hit her like an icy blast. She wanted to cry out but was paralysed by the shock of what was unfolding before her. The men walked calmly and deliberately towards the trench and sank to their knees, where they waited, heads bowed. One of the Japanese soldiers thrust the point of his rifle barrel into the back of the left-hand prisoner's head and fired. The prisoner fell forward into the trench as the sound of the shot reached Topsy. She tried to tear her eyes away from the distressing scene below, but she was mesmerised by the sheer horror of it. A second soldier stepped forward and shot the next man in line. The dead prisoner fell to his side rather than forwards, leaving his executioner to nudge his body into the trench with his boot. It wasn't just the barbarism that numbed Topsy; it was the matter of fact, cold-blooded, almost casual demeanour of the soldiers that shocked her just as much. For all the world they could have been dumping the camp garbage into holes in the ground. There was something else that somehow made it even more difficult to watch, and that was the stoical dignity with which each man went to his death. No desperate, futile attempt to get up and run; no last-minute pleading with their executioners; just a defiant and heroic stillness as the last seconds of their lives ran their course.

And so the gruesome ritual went on until the last of the seven had tumbled lifeless into the pit. One of the soldiers went the length of the trench, rifle at the ready, to check for signs of life. Apparently finding none, he rejoined his colleagues as they ambled back to the van, chatting amongst themselves. As soon as they had gone, some of the occupants of Bungalow C, alerted by the sound of shooting close by, emerged from their rooms and began to walk cautiously down towards the boundary wire. Topsy hurried down to join them. As she did so, it dawned on her that this was what the Japanese expected them to do. The victims had been abandoned in their trench, uncovered, precisely because they were meant to be seen. It had been a macabre piece of Japanese theatre which now awaited its audience.

Kobe House

Autumn had drawn the last of the late summer's heat from the streets of Kobe and leant a crisp freshness to the early morning air as Christopher and his working party made their way to the docks. He glanced across at the railway station. A squad of soldiers loitered on the forecourt, milling around the station entrance as if waiting to be told what to do. Ridiculously young. Yet more recruits destined for Moji where a ship would take them to battles far beyond Japan's shores, goodness knew where. Despite everything, Christopher felt pity for them.

It was a year since the survivors from the *Lisbon Maru* had dragged themselves off the train to form up in that same forecourt before trudging their way to their new camp. Only one year. It felt like a lifetime. Christopher pictured them arriving at Kobe House, filthy, hungry and weary beyond words. That first view of the camp had sunk their spirits. Those towering, dark-red brick walls with their barred and shuttered windows had promised a grim future. For far too many prisoners there had been no future to speak of. Even death had not offered them any dignity, just a ride in a shabby hearse, crammed into an apple barrel like a discarded commodity and burned on a remote hillside, out of sight of anyone who had known them in life. Christopher wondered how, when the time came, he might offer solace of some sort – no matter how small – to relatives of those whose lives had ended this way.

For those who had survived beyond those early weeks of captivity in Japan, the year that had followed their first sight of Kobe House had been every bit as wretched as that initial impression had suggested it would be. Christopher considered his own adaptation to life in Kobe House as typical of that of most of the Diehard prisoners. Only a handful had subsided into self-pity, and still fewer had opted out of the collective ethos that all Diehards looked after each other. Up to a point, Christopher had found the prison regime easier to bear as the months passed. He was used to being permanently hungry and awoke each day with the expectation that hunger would accompany him until sleep offered a respite. Having low expectations had made it easier to live with. It was the same with the casual brutality which the Japanese meted out to them as a matter of routine. Christopher had lost count of the number of times he had been slapped hard in the face. The *binta* was a stock response of the prison guards to anyone who annoyed them. It was administered with no more thought than a guard would give to kicking a dog that happened to get in his way. There didn't need to be a reason for it. Christopher had had his share of routine punishment for breaking camp regulations. There were so many of these that some would bound to be broken if a prisoner was to have any sort of bearable existence.

One threat had been removed. The mad doctor had been posted away from the camp. Last month, Morimoto had finally summoned up the courage to deal with him. There had been no sign that he was on his way; one day he was there, going about his routine tormenting of the prisoners, the next he was gone without a trace. When he had gone, it was as if the whole camp had let out its collective breath. Christopher was determined that he would be brought to justice when the war was ended but he had been unable to discover his name.

The sadistic guard commander was also in his sights. They now knew his name.

When the day of reckoning came, Sergeant Morita Hiroyuki would be amongst the Japanese reported as war criminals. Christopher had felt a sense of grim satisfaction when he had added the name of their latest tormentor to his list.

The workdays had come to be welcomed by most prisoners. They helped relieve the utter boredom of camp life and were marked by the issue of a larger food ration for each of the day's two meals. The ration scales had been reduced at the end of the previous winter. Workers were rewarded with a heaped bowl of rice and vegetable soup at each meal, supplemented by one small bread-bun for the day. Prisoners who were too sick to work received only three-quarters of a bowl of rice, and any officer who didn't work saw his ration reduced still further to half a bowl. Unloading of ships provided opportunities to pilfer cargoes of tinned food. At first, Christopher could scarcely believe the sheer quantity of rations that some prisoners managed to smuggle back into Kobe House. Their success seemed to be partly explained by the incompetence of the Japanese when it came to searching the work parties returning to camp and partly by the ingenuity of the prisoners. Christopher smiled to himself as he reflected on how skilled some of his Cockney soldiers were when it came to smuggling. For some of them, a childhood spent living off their wits in London had provided them with valuable training. Later, Christopher had come to understand more clearly how the system worked. It became obvious that the Japanese knew very well that loot was being brought into the camp but they allowed prisoners to get away with it. It was all very simple. Many of the Japanese camp staff were in on the racket and colluded with the Japanese gangers, or *hanchos*, who oversaw the work parties. These *hanchos* were rewarded if their men worked well and they had learned that men worked best if they were allowed to pilfer something for themselves. So the gangers bribed the camp staff not to search the prisoners too carefully. The result was that all parties were satisfied. There had been times when food looted from the docks in this way was all that had kept prisoners from starvation.

Christopher drew his thoughts back to the present. The work party was within minutes of reaching the docks and the next phase of a routine workday would soon begin. He felt a sudden panic. He couldn't remember completing his routine check before leaving his room. It had become a morning ritual. Part of it was to fold his blankets and then check to see that they covered the thin crack in the wooden frame of his bed. He had made a hidden space in the bed frame which now contained a hollowed-out length of bamboo. Rolled up tight within the bamboo cane were items that had to remain hidden from the Japanese.

Christopher cursed his memory. Had he checked? He knew he would now spend the whole working day worrying. Discovery would not only have serious consequences for him but would also mean the loss of three items that were priceless in the context of the *Lisbon Maru*'s sinking. Two of them were reports written in his own hand. One was a list of all the Diehards who had died at sea between their original departure from Shamshuipo and the arrival of survivors in Woosong. His leadership team in Kobe House had been thorough as they probed and questioned their men. They weren't interested in rumour or embellishments, and even second-hand accounts were treated with caution. They established that 150 Diehards had not survived the sinking on 2 October. Christopher had been equally meticulous in his research. It had not just been a matter of making a list of names. Some relatives of the dead would want to be spared the details of how their husband, father or son had died, but many would wish to be able to picture how the end had come. Christopher had personally questioned those Diehards who had witnessed the death of a comrade. By the time that he had followed all leads, he was able to record how one in three of them had died. It made difficult reading. Private George Carrell had been seen swimming strongly close to the *Lisbon Maru* when shot from one of the patrol boats. Lieutenant Lawrence Wood had not given up easily. Sergeant Gilham had seen him some four hours after the sinking, desperately trying to keep hold of a hatch batten but being swept past the islands by the inshore current. The last that anyone remembered seeing of Private

Harry Sansum was in the ship's hold which he had refused to leave because he couldn't swim. And so it went on, this record of what the survivors had seen of their fellow Diehards' last moments. There were fifty-five of them on that list. Of the remainder, there would never be news; they had been there before the breakout from Hold Number 2 and were simply never seen again.

Christopher record did not end there. He had added separate lists for those who had died as prisoners of war in Shamshuipo, those who had been left in Woosong or taken from the train between Moji and Kobe and those who had died whilst imprisoned in Kobe House. Fifteen Diehards had died in those first nine months of captivity in Shamshuipo Camp. The killers were to become familiar to the survivors: diphtheria; dysentery; malnutrition. Exposure had claimed the lives of Privates Willie Bryant and Bill Steele. They had made it to the islands but the sea passage to Woosong had been a journey too far for them. There had been no word of the Diehards left behind in Woosong as too sick to travel further. When Christopher had added Lieutenant Kenneth Young's name to the list of the dead, he couldn't help thinking that 'Chippie' would have stood a better chance if he had been left behind, too. Christopher had been told by the Japanese that of those who had been taken from the train, three had died in Moji and four more in Hiroshima, all of them falling victim to dysentery within weeks of arriving in Japan. Christopher had added the last name only three days ago when Private Charles Pegg had become the fortieth Diehard to die since arriving in Kobe just over a year ago. One day, his father, as his next of kin, would learn that his son had died of malnutrition.

The second hidden report was an account of the sinking of the *Lisbon Maru*. Christopher had felt a duty to history resting on him. The official Japanese report, as recorded in their newspapers, was a grotesque distortion and it was up to him to challenge it. In doing so, he needed to set aside his bitter anger and not allow it to distort his account of what amounted to a mass war crime. His research had to be done whilst memories were still fresh and clear, unclouded by the subsequent clutter of their lives as prisoners and before speculation and storytelling had become accepted as fact. He questioned the survivors from all three of the *Lisbon Maru*'s holds; those who had abandoned ship at the first opportunity and those who had been washed from her decks at the last moment; those who had been picked up by the ships; those who had swum to the islands and those lifted from the sea by the Chinese fishermen. It had taken him three months. At the end, history had gained a dispassionate record of the sinking of the *Lisbon Maru*. It lacked only one thing. A picture.

Amongst the fifty American prisoners held in Kobe House was a young US Navy Lieutenant, Willard Carroll Johnson, who had been taken prisoner in the

Philippines. Johnson was a talented artist who specialised in drawing ships. The Japanese kept the American and British prisoners in separate wings of Kobe House and for the most part the two nationalities tended to keep to themselves. Johnson's special talent would have gone unnoticed if it hadn't been for a chance encounter with Christopher on a quay in Kobe docks. Back in June, the two young officers had found themselves in charge of work parties unloading a Japanese cargo ship and had fallen into conversation. Christopher had noticed that the American seemed to have a fine eye for the detail of the various ships in the harbour and had commented on it.

Johnson had given him an amused look. 'I draw ships. I'm rather good at it. I guess that's why they assigned me to submarines. It helps if you can recognise a ship before you torpedo it.'

Christopher had laughed. He could scarcely believe his luck.

'You're just the chap I've been looking for. I have a job for you.'

A week later, Johnson had begun to draw the sinking of the *Lisbon Maru*. Artist and eyewitnesses had pored over rough sketch after rough sketch until, after two months, Johnson had reported to Christopher that he was satisfied. He could picture the scene with as much clarity as if he had been an eyewitness himself. Another month had passed before Johnson sent word that his sketch was complete. Christopher had called a meeting of the Diehard leadership to take possession of the sketch, not knowing quite what to expect. Johnson brought his work to hand it over in person and when he unrolled it and opened it out, shouts of approval rang round the room.

'I'm sorry it took me so long,' said Johnson. 'The Nips kept springing snap searches on us and I had to be very careful. I had to build it up, bit by bit, whenever I had the chance. If they had found it, that would have been the end of it.'

Christopher had spoken for all of them when he thanked the young American. 'This is far better than any of us could have hoped for, Willard. You've captured it all brilliantly. It's uncanny, that's exactly how I remember the ship when I looked back at it from the sea just before she went down.'

The bamboo cane had since survived several room searches but Christopher lived in daily fear that it would be discovered. He had made a copy of his two records and placed them with Frank Waldron for safe keeping, but there would only ever be one Johnson sketch. If the Japanese ever found it, it would be irreplaceable.

For Christopher, the day passed even more slowly than usual in the docks of Kobe. Once back within the camp, he made straight for his bedspace. It was as he had left it, undisturbed.

Chapter 30

December

Stanley Prison

Lance Newnham winced with pain as he picked himself up from the floor of his cell. The guards had half dragged, half carried him from the van in the courtyard and thrown him through the door before slamming it shut, leaving him alone with his thoughts in the semi-darkness. By now he was almost beyond caring what happened to him. That morning, the Japanese had gone through the cynical ritual of a medical examination to certify him fit for trial. The thermometer had shown his temperature as 104F, but it had been recorded as 98F. Yamada had made sure that the months of torture had left little evidence on Lance's face. All the damage had been done to his body and internal organs, and the doctor had not demanded that he be stripped for his examination. The court martial had been a farce, too. He had prepared his defence but had been prevented from putting it before the court. It had been the same for Ford and Gray. The verdict that all three of them were guilty of espionage had been preordained, as had the sentence of death by firing squad. They had no right of appeal.

The torture had begun the day after his arrest back in July. They wanted the names of agents and couriers. Nothing less would be enough. Imamure and Yamada had applied the full variety of techniques contained within the Kempeitai interrogation manual. The infliction of physical pain was at the core of their regime. When they weren't beating him, they gave him the water treatment that repeatedly took him close to the point of drowning. Or they applied electric shocks to where it hurt him most. In the summer months, they left him for hours, tied to a post in full sun, without water. When winter had come, he was hosed with cold water and left naked and shivering in his cell. Each day he had woken up wandering what new form of torture was planned for him, but still they could not break him down.

It wasn't all about pain and terror. They had also tried to get into his mind. They set about lowering his powers of resistance by simply wearing him out.

They allowed him just enough food to keep him alive. They deprived him of sleep until he was on the point of exhaustion and then tempted him with promises. If he gave them names, he could return to his previous place in Argyle Street. He would have good food and receive medical attention. They knew that his wife was in the adjacent camp and offered to take him to see her if he would only be reasonable and cooperate. For five months there had been no end to it. Throughout this time, he was kept in isolation, deprived of any moral support that others might have given him, unable to share his inner thoughts with anyone. Lance had remained defiant, as had Ford and Gray.

Now that the three of them had been sentenced to death, Colonel Noma had one last option. He would let them stew and reflect on the offer of a reprieve if they talked. Day after day, Imamure visited their cells and repeated the offer. Seventeen days after the court martial, Noma lost his patience. Saturday the eighteenth of December dawned clear and still with just a hint of a breeze from the east. Lance sensed that something was up when a prison warder brought him some bread and a cup of hot water. It was the first breakfast of any sort that he had been given since his arrest. They came for him an hour later, a prison warder and two soldiers. As he limped into the prison yard, Lance could see that Ford and Gray were already there under guard. A group of six British prisoners stood close by. Noma had ordered that they should be there to watch the three condemned men being taken out for execution. It was meant to serve as a warning. They included Rex Young, a naval officer whom Lance had got to know well in Argyle Street Camp. Young had been arrested and awaited trial on charges of operating a radio set. The six prisoners edged their way towards Lance and the other two and shook hands with each of them. The guards made no effort to stop them. As he shook hands with Rex Young, Lance felt the need to say something.

'If you come out of this alive, Rex, and anyone asks you how I was at the end, please tell them this. I suppose one should not be afraid to die and I am not. But there is so much that I would still like to do. My son has just qualified as a doctor and I would like to know about him.' He paused, as if there was something else he wished to share, but then thought better of it. 'That's all.'

They were driven down to the jetty on Stanley Bay beach where a naval launch waited. The launch headed south and then east, round the southern tip of Stanley Peninsula before making its way across the mouth of Tai Tam Bay. Big Wave Bay lay on the far side of the Shek O peninsula. Lance knew it well. He and Phyllis had spent many a Sunday afternoon on its wide, sandy beach where the South China Sea first comes ashore on Hong Kong's east coast. When the wind and the tide were right, it had been fun to dive into the surf there. Today there was scarcely a ripple as the launch carefully beached itself. Their graves were freshly dug along the top of the beach, close up against the dense shrub that bordered the sand. The coolies who had dug them stood some distance away, chatting amongst themselves, long-handled shovels in hand, waiting to fill the graves in.

The shots rang out just as Phyllis Newnham was beginning her shift in the camp hospital, barely two miles away.

Kobe House

Christopher shivered in the damp cold of early morning as he lay on the wooden board in his bed space and watched the first snowflakes of the winter drift past the solitary window of the room he shared with the other three Diehard officers. It had been one of the few highlights of the year when back in April Morimoto had finally agreed to have the battens removed from all upstairs windows. The first rays of natural light to invade their room had lifted spirits beyond words. The windows remained barred and judging from the experience of their first winter in Kobe House, it would not be long before the bars and the windowpanes would be covered in ice. Christopher pulled his three blankets closer around him. He had had another rough night. He couldn't remember when he had last had a good night's sleep. In winter it was the cold that kept many of them awake, the cold and the rats. The Japanese had finally agreed to issue the prisoners with greatcoats and Christopher wore his in bed. He also kept his boots on but still the cold denied him sleep. Back in the summer, it had been the oppressive heat, the swarming bugs and the maddening mosquitos that had made sleep elusive. Now, with the coming of winter, the rats that infested the camp had headed indoors. One of them had run across his feet that night. Earlier in the year Martin had acquired a kitten and secured its loyalty by feeding it with scraps of food. The cat had matured into an accomplished rat killer and had provided the room with relief until the mad doctor had discovered it and had it removed.

The first noises of a routine working day began to filter up the stairs from the courtyard. The night guards were coming off duty and being replaced by the day shift. It would soon be six o'clock. Ahead lay yet another dreary day. He was down to go with a working party to continue unloading the cargo ships that had arrived two days ago as part of a convoy escorted by a German warship. The Japanese had banned the prisoners from making any contact with members of the German crew but had been unable to prevent it. Yesterday Christopher had been warming his hands over a brazier on the quay when he was approached by a young German naval officer who had gone out of his way to express his sympathy. He had been shocked to see how emaciated the British prisoners of war had become after two years of captivity. He had pressed a bar of chocolate and a packet of cigarettes into Christopher's coat pocket. As he went on his way, he had called out in near perfect English 'I wish you could be our prisoners in Germany.'

Christopher had been quick to respond. 'Even better if you were our prisoners in England.' They had both laughed.

Last winter each prisoner had been issued with four blankets. These had helped to make the cold nights tolerable but they were of little practical use by day. It had soon become common practice for prisoners to cut one of their blankets and make a waistcoat out of it. Martin had gained a high reputation for his tailoring skills and had earned a useful supply of pipe tobacco in exchange for fashioning waistcoats for other prisoners. When the practice was brought to Morimoto's attention, he immediately added it to the list of things that the prisoners were forbidden to do. From that moment, cut blankets were yet another item that had to be kept hidden in the daily game of cat and mouse played by the prisoners and the camp guards. Christopher's luck had run out only two weeks ago. Returning to the camp from a day spent unloading a freighter in the docks, he had expected the usual casual search which involved turning out the pockets of his greatcoat and being patted down. That day, Morita was on duty as guard commander and had decided to make a point of personally supervising the search of returning work parties. One by one, the prisoners had been ordered to remove their greatcoats. It was fortunate that Christopher's work party had been unloading a cargo of scrap iron and had been nowhere near any of the items that they were usually tempted to risk looting. On any other day, Christopher would have got away with wearing his waistcoat under his greatcoat, but with Morita looking to make trouble, he had stood no chance. Morita's joy knew no bounds. He had found an offender and, best of all, he was an officer. Christopher had been marched to the yard in front of the guard room where most physical punishments were administered. There, he was stripped down to his underwear and his boots removed. He had known what was coming. He had seen it done to others. First came the punches to the face and ribs and the kicks to the shin. Morita took pleasure in delivering these himself, his face set in a smile. Then Christopher was forced to stand holding a bucket full of water above his head. It proceeded as he knew it would. Each time his burning arms ran out of strength, the bucket came to rest on his head. He knew that it might take a further five minutes or it might take ten, but inevitably the pain would become unbearable and he would allow the bucket to spill and fall to the floor. Morita would then hit him again and the bucket would be refilled. An hour had passed before Morita called a halt to the punishment and Martin and Ewan were allowed to carry Christopher back to their room.

Christopher winced as he recalled his ordeal. His ribs were still sore from Morita's punches. But sore ribs and a constant state of hunger were not foremost in his mind as he contemplated the day ahead. Much worse was the anticipation of yet another day of total isolation from Topsy and from the world that lay beyond Kobe House and the docks half a mile away. It was now nearly two years since he and Topsy had shared that last desperate embrace in Hong Kong and in all that time he had had no word of her. No letters, no reports, no rumours, nothing. His hopes had risen a few months back when a small draft of prisoners from Hong Kong had arrived in Osaka. Prisoners returning to Kobe House from the hospital in Osaka had passed on some fragments of news they had picked up from the new arrivals. They told of frequent bombings by the Americans, with Japanese ships being sunk in and around the harbour and close to Stanley. Christopher had mixed feelings about that bit of news. It was good to hear that the Japanese weren't having things all their own way, but the thought of Hong Kong being bombed made him fear for Topsy's safety. Apparently, tens of thousands of Hong Kong Chinese were being deported from Hong Kong to the Chinese mainland, while life continued to be grim for those who remained, with the Japanese routinely carrying out public executions by beheading and shooting. The most disturbing bit of news was that the prisoners of war in Hong Kong had been told there had been few survivors from the sinking of the *Lisbon Maru*. Christopher's heart had sunk when he heard that. If the same news had reached the civilian internees, Topsy was almost certain to presume him dead. She must have known he was on the *Lisbon Maru*. He had written her a letter. Back in May they had been allowed to write a letter of no more than eighty-five words to their next of kin, but Christopher had no confidence that it had ever left Japan.

The absence of any news of Topsy tormented him each day. It was of little consolation to know that all this misery would be over one day. Or would it? Shut off from the rest of the world, the prisoners in Kobe House knew little of how the war was going. Wild rumours ran through the camp, only to be contradicted by the next. Churchill was ill, Churchill was dead, Churchill had travelled to America. The war in the desert had been lost, the war in the desert had been won. Many rumours were simply the result of wishful thinking: the Americans had retaken Singapore; Italy had sued for peace; the Russians were advancing on Germany, and the Japanese were close to agreeing that prisoners of war would be repatriated. Bets were already being taken on when it would be over. Perhaps this coming Christmas would be the last.

Christopher refused to allow these rumours to raise his hopes. Not that he was defeatist. Ever since those early days as a prisoner of war, he had seen enough of the Japanese to be certain that Japan would lose the war. There was no doubting the power of the Nipponese war machine which everyone had underestimated until it was too late. Christopher blamed himself as much as others. But two years as a prisoner of the Japanese had convinced him that as a nation they were a shambles and would be brought to their knees by the same military adventurism that had brought them temporary triumph.

Aside from the rumours, there had been hopeful signs. Most of the ships being unloaded now had half-empty holds and carried much smaller cargoes. On their way to and from the docks, the prisoners had begun to pass queues outside food shops. They had also noticed that the national war effort 's insatiable demand for oil was making itself felt at home in Japan. The streets of Kobe were quieter than a year ago and many of the vehicles were now fuelled by gas from charcoal burners instead of petrol and diesel.

The prisoners were now unloading ships that showed the scars of war. Only last week, a freighter had sunk in the harbour before it could be unloaded. A large German raider, bristling with guns, had been tugged into the dockyard in a battered state and was still there after two months of repairs. Work parties from the camp had noticed that the morale of German sailors who were allowed ashore appeared to be low. Then, last month, the second hospital ship that year had docked in Kobe, bearing thousands of small boxes, each one holding the ashes of a Japanese soldier, their homecoming watched by a sombre crowd on the quayside.

And then there had been the arrival of air raid practices. A rumour had run through the camp at the beginning of the year that Tokyo had been bombed but there had been no reports of it in the Japanese newspapers. So it had come as a surprise when, back in the summer, Morimoto had addressed them all during an evening *tenko* and briefed them on what action was to be taken in the event of an air raid. The next day, anti-aircraft guns had been set up close to the camp and a searchlight installed on the roof of a building opposite. A week later, the sirens had sounded throughout Kobe as the civilian population was subjected to its first air raid practice of the war. Men and women dressed in black cloaks and hoods were put through their paces as air raid wardens, their overseers screaming commands and gesticulating wildly. Equipped with a small hand pump, one team of wardens pumped away until at last their pump produced a thin trickle of water while another tried in vain to put out a piece of burning wood fixed to the top of a step ladder by throwing buckets of water up at it.

Christopher and Martin had watched the chaos with a mixture of amusement and concern. Martin's observation had echoed what was going through Christopher's mind.

'It's pathetic Chris. God help us if the Americans bomb anywhere near the camp and we have to rely on that lot to keep us safe.'

Christopher shared his concern. 'I feel sorry for the local civilians. There's no control, no organisation and the equipment is either primitive or doesn't exist. All those wooden houses, they'll go up in flames if the Americans use incendiaries.'

Christopher's optimism about the outcome of the war, such as it was, rested not on rumour but on all these signs that they had spotted and absorbed as they went about their lives as prisoners. Individually, none of them was conclusive, but taken together, those damaged ships limping into the port, those huddled, sullen civilians queuing patiently for food, those spluttering gas-powered vehicles and those chaotic air raid practices amounted to a clear message: the war had arrived in Japan.

There was another feature of their life in Kobe House that kept Christopher in a positive frame of mind. The spirit of the Diehard prisoners was unbroken. If anything, it was stronger than ever. They were a much-diminished band as 1943 drew to an end. They had seen too many comrades lose the daily battle for survival. Beriberi, diphtheria, dysentery, pellagra, malaria, malnutrition – they were all there on death's grim list of battle honours. Those Diehards who had made it this far were the toughest and the luckiest and they drew strength from each other.

Christopher huddled against the early morning cold, waiting for the minutes to tick away before reveille. Soon, the first sounds of the new guard making their predictably aggressive show of getting prisoners up from their beds would drift up from the floors below. The prisoners would respond as they always did, with their noisy reluctance to abandon the cocoon of blankets that had kept the worst of the night's cold air at bay.

Christopher steeled himself to make a move, then swung his legs out and eased himself gingerly to his feet. He picked his way between the four bed spaces in the small room and wiped the condensation off the windowpane. The bars on the outside were an irritating reminder at the start of each day that they were prisoners. A dusting of snow on the street awaited its first footprints of the day. He pictured the day ahead of him. In two hours' time, after the morning *tenko*, he would lead one of the work parties to the docks. He had come to enjoy that half-mile walk at the beginning and end of the working day. As a prisoner, if you ignored the presence of your armed escort, these walks were the closest you came to normal life. Mind you, it would be damned cold in the docks. That bitter north-westerly wind never seemed to go away in the winter months. He was hungry, and he would stay hungry until the first meal of the day which was six hours away. Unless they could scrounge some food from somewhere. That depended on which company they were assigned to for the day. It was the luck of the draw. If they were sent to work for the Kobe Ship Transport Company, they had a reasonable chance of being offered a hot drink and a biscuit along with the company's Japanese workers, but they couldn't expect any favours from the Nippon Express Company. They were real bastards to work for, whether you were a Japanese coolie or a prisoner of war.

The other three officers in the room were beginning to stir. Martin Weedon's wounded shoulder usually played him up first thing in the morning, so he was never at his most sociable then. Sharing a room with Ewan Graham often reminded Christopher of dormitory life at boarding school where each room had had one boy who insisted on being the last to get up and yelled at the rest to stop making so much noise. Ralph King was the room's quiet man. Back in Hong Kong, when the battle had begun, he was the junior of five officers in Martin's B Company. By the time of the surrender, he had been left in command of it, the rest having been killed or wounded. When the *Lisbon Maru* had gone down, Ralph had made it to Qingbang, but only after being pulled from the sea at the last moment by one of the island's fishermen. Christopher reckoned that if Ralph King was quiet, it was because survival had left him that way.

The first hint of daylight was bringing urban Kobe into view. It looked cold and uninviting out there. Christopher's thoughts turned to Stanley Camp. That southern peninsula of Hong Kong could be a bleak place in winter, too. He wondered if the internees there were any better off than the prisoners in Kobe. If only he knew. Not knowing was the worst thing. A letter, a postcard, a message of any sort from Topsy would make everything else about his wretched life in Kobe House so much more bearable.

PART V: 1944

Chapter 31

Spring

Kobe House

'Tell me, what's it like to share a birthday with Adolf Hitler, Chris?'

Christopher gave Martin Weedon a grin. 'You should know. It's much the same as your sharing a birthday with the Nip Emperor.'

It was Christopher's thirtieth birthday. It would be Martin's twenty-ninth within a few days. Martin had handed Christopher a formal invitation, written neatly on a scrap of paper.

'Captain MP Weedon
Presents his compliments to
Captain CMM Man
And requests the pleasure of his company to
Afternoon tea at 4.30 p.m. on
Thursday 20th April 1944'

Martin had given him a present of a tin of strawberry jam and an egg. The jam had been smuggled into the camp weeks ago by a working party tasked with unloading a Japanese freighter in Kobe docks. Martin had stored it away for the occasion. The egg was a present from the Diehard contingent of prisoners who had bribed one of the guards to produce ten eggs, nine of which were to be shared amongst more than a hundred of them. None of them had eaten an egg since their captivity had begun just over two years ago.

Birthday or not, it was a working day. Christopher and Martin had spent the day shovelling coke for the furnace and kiln of a factory in the outskirts of Kobe. They were each shifting an average of eleven tons per day on a lunch of only half a bowl of rice. At the end of a working day they were exhausted and smothered in coke dust that they washed off with cold water from a hose. There was no soap. They had all been weighed the previous week. At six feet two inches tall,

Christopher's weight was down below ten stones, much the same as it had been when he left his prep school at thirteen.

Martin had recently become worried about his close friend. It wasn't his physical health that concerned him; Christopher had had his fair share of sickness but seemed to have recovered well. No, it was more a case of seeing some of the spirit draining out of him. It was nothing he could put a finger on, just a strong sense that things were getting him down. He could read Christopher like a book by now. He could see that the constant burden of not knowing what had happened to Topsy at the hands of the Japanese was wearing him out. He recognised just how demoralised Christopher had been when he was one of the few to receive no mail last week. Christopher didn't allow it to show, but Martin knew that the blow had hurt him badly. It didn't help that Martin had received a letter from his wife Elizabeth. It had been written more than a year ago. She had made it out of Singapore with their young son just in time to beat the Japanese invasion and was now living with his parents in England. At last he knew they were safe.

No such relief for Christopher. To make matters worse, it was clear from Elizabeth's letter to Martin that his letters written from Hong Kong had not been received, and only one written from Kobe House had made its way home to Martin's parents, a year after being handed in. This only added to Christopher's agony. If letters were not getting through to relatives in England, there was little chance that any of his letters had reached Topsy if she was still in Hong Kong. Other prisoners who had received their first mail told the same story of undelivered letters home. This confirmed their long-standing fear that the Japanese were either deliberately sabotaging the prisoners' mail or, just as likely, were too incompetent to handle it. Suspicions had been fed a few weeks ago when one of the working parties had stumbled upon sacks of prisoner-of-war mail that had been dumped on a mound of waste in Kobe docks.

For his part, Christopher was in the mood to open up to Martin. Normally he kept any negative thoughts to himself. The Diehards looked to him as their leader and being a leader in Kobe House was best served if he didn't share everything that was on his mind. But Martin was a special case. The term 'brothers in arms' was especially true of them. Besides, Martin could be relied upon to be discreet.

'You know, I can hardly believe I'm thirty. I was twenty-seven when all this began. My birthday is such a bloody painful reminder of what a complete waste of our lives these past two years or so have been.'

Martin reflected for a moment before responding. He wasn't so sure about it being a complete waste. 'I know what you mean. We started out as prisoners of war with a clear purpose. It was enough to simply survive. Each day was a matter of staying alive. We learnt to cope with next to no food, to fight sickness with no medicines, to ignore the insults and to ride with the punches and the kicks. On the *Lisbon Maru*, it was enough to grab a lungful of air down in that stinking hold or to make it to the latrine on deck before shitting yourself. And once in the sea, we'd have given anything to make it ashore. But after a time, we've become used to surviving, and staying alive isn't enough anymore. But there is a purpose, Chris, for both of us; we have a wife waiting for us.'

Martin had an afterthought. 'And there's a special purpose for you as Monkey's successor.'

Christopher let his friend's words sink in.

'You're right of course. I suppose what's really getting to me is that there's a war on, and our part in it is done. Finished. We're stuck here, shovelling coke for the enemy. But it's more than that. I'm almost ashamed to admit that I miss the battle. Don't get me wrong. I'm not for one moment glorifying war. We've both seen enough to never wish it on the next generation. It's more a case of recognising that if there's a war to be fought, I was never more alive than when we were fighting in one. Even though in the end we lost.'

Christopher paused, as if expecting a comment. None came.

'There's something I ought to share with you. Yesterday, when I was kept back from going out on a working party, it was because Morimoto had sent for me. It was rather weird. He gestured me to sit down and offered me a cigarette. It was as if he was inviting me to set aside the usual relationship of captor and captive and discuss things like two sensible men. Almost as if the Japanese and their prisoners were third parties. At first he asked me for my view on the origins of the war. Then, did I agree that wars are futile? Had I noticed if Japan had changed since our arrival in Kobe? And, very significantly I thought, did I think the war would end if Japan were given certain concessions, such as keeping some of its new territory? It struck me that he was sounding me out on the possibility of peace by negotiation. Up to that moment, it felt like we were just having a philosophical discussion, but I was intrigued that he wanted to have it. And with me.'

Martin interrupted.

'I can see why it was you. He sees you as Monkey's successor.'

Christopher shrugged his shoulders.

'But then he got to the point. He asked me what I thought the reaction of the prisoners would be if the war ended with Japan suing for peace. Would they be out for revenge? And could he rely on me and the other officers to help keep order?

I thought this an extraordinary question, and still do. It was tantamount to admitting that he thought Japan faced defeat. And bear in mind, he had to ask the question through Ikandaki who kept his deadpan, interpreter's face throughout. I wonder what he was thinking.'

Martin was curious. 'And what did you say in reply; about the men wanting revenge?'

'Oh, I gave him the usual stuff about the British army being a disciplined force and that if the tables were reversed here in Kobe, as officers we would insist on the Geneva Convention being observed. I also told him that I would expect the same of him; that he would keep control of his men. What I didn't mention was that if the likes of the mad doctor and Morita had still been around, I'm not totally confident that I could guarantee their safety.'

'And how did he react?'

'Well, it then got even weirder. He tried to buy me. If I became helpful to him, informed him of guards and prison staff who were being bribed or were helping the prisoners in some way, he could make my life easier. I might even get some letters.'

Martin snorted. 'Nothing short of blackmail. The fact that he thought you might accept probably tells us what he would do if the roles were reversed. We've said it before, most of our problems result from a clash of opposite cultures.'

Christopher nodded in agreement.

'Anyway, in so many words I told him I wasn't interested. And that was that. His mood changed and he dismissed me with a wave of his hand.'

The two friends found themselves reflecting on Christopher's meeting with Morimoto. It seemed to fit with the change they had all noticed in the attitude of the Japanese to their prisoners. It wasn't merely that the mad doctor had gone and been followed by Morita at the end of last year. With their departure, daily life in Kobe House had been emptied of much of its tension, but the change went further than that. It was as if the Japanese sensed that the war was being lost and were preparing to face the consequences.

But if Morimoto's words offered hope, Christopher and Martin were wary of it. They lived on hope, of course. All of them in Kobe House did. But they had learned that hope was a friend that could betray you. It enticed you to think the world was as you wished it to be, and when you discovered that it wasn't, it could hurt you as deeply as an unfaithful lover. More than that, hope fed on rumour in a devilish conspiracy to lure the prisoners into seeing signs that simply weren't there. Mistrustful as most prisoners had become about hopeful signs, they had little else to go on. Reliable news about the war was scarce. Possession of a radio was punishable by death. If any prisoner had taken the risk and constructed one, then Christopher didn't know about it. But all the gossip picked up by the working parties, some of it from sailors off German warships, seemed to point to the defeat of Germany and Japan. Back in September last year, a strong rumour had run through the camp that Italy had surrendered. Christopher had been sceptical, but one morning a column of sullen, dishevelled Italian soldiers had marched past the camp. They were unarmed and guarded by Japanese soldiers who were prodding them on their way at bayonet point.

There were other signs, too. Far fewer ships needed to be unloaded in Kobe, and many of those that did were arriving with smaller cargoes and showing signs of war damage. Only yesterday, a heavy cruiser had limped into the harbour in a battered state, her stern almost under water, her bridge destroyed and her funnel and mast missing. A week ago, the Japanese storeman had mistakenly handed some vegetables wrapped in an English language newspaper to one of the prisoners on duty in the cookhouse. When the paper had been dried out, it was seen to contain reports of allied advances on several fronts. Everywhere the prisoners were deployed to work they could see evidence that the city's infrastructure was under stress. Power failures were commonplace. There were shortages of everything: fuel, spare parts for vehicles, rice, bread, even shoes. The civilian population in Kobe were becoming used to frequent air raid practices, many of them staged during the night. Gangs of elderly coolies were deployed digging crude shelters and one day last week the prisoners had returned from their working parties to find that an anti-aircraft battery had begun to dig in its guns in the field opposite Kobe House. Prisoners deployed to work in the railway sidings reported more and more troop trains passing through on the way to Moji for deployment overseas, each train packed with soldiers who looked too young to fight. Other prisoners working in factories in Kobe and Osaka found themselves with little to do, production having ground to a halt through lack of raw materials and spare parts for machines. The evidence, such as it was, added fuel to the rumours that Japan was losing the war at sea and on land. For most prisoners it had become a question of when, not if, they would be freed. Christopher and Martin were not alone in thinking that when the end came, it might come quickly.

Whatever the cause of it, the change in the behaviour of the Japanese towards their prisoners was real enough. Offences which had previously been punished by brutality were now routinely dealt with by the withdrawal of privileges or a reduction in rations for a limited time. One evening, Martin had again been caught smoking his pipe in his bedspace and had braced himself to receive another beating. Instead, the guard commander had turned a blind eye to it and merely told him not to do it again.

For the first time, books were provided. Christopher had just finished Conrad's *Lord Jim*. When he had first read it at school, he little knew that the next time he would turn its pages would be with the desperate gratitude of a desert traveller slaking his thirst at an oasis.

There had been an issue of clothing, too. For the first time it was all new and clean: for each man an issue of a summer shirt, a pair of shorts and a *fundoshi*.

The death toll amongst the prisoners had started to decline but that was no thanks to the Japanese. Dysentery, pellagra and beriberi remained endemic within the camp and the medicines to treat them continued to be withheld. The national shortage of food was reflected in the camp by reduced ration scales, even for those fit enough for hard work. Without the food smuggled into the camp from the docks by working parties and the black-market which thrived with the connivance of corrupt guards and camp staff, many prisoners would have struggled to survive. If fewer prisoners were dying, it was because the weakest amongst them had succumbed in the first eighteen months, leaving the toughest and the luckiest to struggle on. More than fifty Diehards had died since their arrival in Kobe, each one of them men worn out by life as a prisoner of the Japanese whose neglect and lack of humanity had killed them as surely as any bullet or bayonet. And even in death, there was still no dignity for them. Only two days ago, beriberi had claimed the medical staff sergeant as its latest victim. He had saved countless lives in the camp hospital, including Martin's when he was dying of diphtheria. Yesterday evening the prisoners had paraded on the road outside the camp, all of them determined to be present as he began his journey to the crematorium. As usual, he had been brought out folded into a wooden barrel, but this time there was no hearse. Instead, the barrel had been lifted onto a tricycle and pedalled away by a coolie.

Christopher made his way to the window. It looked out over a field opposite and then beyond up into the hills to where he and Martin had accompanied some of their dead. The two casuarinas that flanked the crematorium were in clear view from here, caught in the last light of the setting sun. For some time, Christopher had made a habit of keeping a tryst with them from this window at the beginning and end of each day. It was his way of reaching out across some two thousand miles of sea to Topsy and keeping fresh his memories of the brief time they had shared together in their home on the slopes of The Peak. The casuarinas never changed but beneath them the familiar dark green of the hills had temporarily given way to the soft pink of sakura blossom. Within a week or two, a late April storm would carry the blossom away and with it the last vestiges of the prisoners' second spring in Kobe House.

Stanley Camp

Topsy leant back against the casuarina tree at the cemetery and looked out beyond St Stephen's Beach, across the stretch of agitated sea towards Lamma Island. The wind was no longer from the east but had shifted to the south as it often did at this time of the year. It had risen, too, and was driving large waves ashore. Even from four miles away, Lamma's coastline was lit up by an unbroken splash of white surf.

This was the first time that she had paused at this spot since being a witness to the execution six months ago. The images had remained too vivid for the place to ever be the same restful spot for quiet reflection that it had once been. Or so she had thought until yesterday. It was the approach of Christopher's thirtieth birthday that had prompted her to think again. That, and a nagging frustration that life was passing her by on terms set by the Japanese. There and then, she had resolved that it was time to set her own terms.

So here she was once again, inhaling that familiar scent of the casuarina as she and Christopher had often done at home on The Peak during those evenings of fading memory. She tried to imagine how Christopher might be marking his birthday.

Six months ago, she had still not heard from him, but she had received news of him. She had never met Christopher's younger brother David, but out of the blue she had received a letter from him. David Man was an official in the Colonial Office in London. Ever since the fall of Hong Kong, he had assisted a new voluntary organisation, the Hong Kong Fellowship, in gathering as much information as possible about Japanese prisoners in the colony and passing it on to their families. It helped that the Fellowship had a dedicated and formidable founder in the person of Beryl Tidbury whose husband had commanded the Diehards before Lance Newnham.

By coincidence, Topsy had received David's letter on her third wedding anniversary. It was short and had been heavily censored by the Japanese, but it had told her what she had been yearning to hear ever since the news of the *Lisbon Maru* sinking had broken – Christopher had survived and had been imprisoned in Japan. But that was all that David knew. He had had no further news of his brother or of any of the survivors.

A month after receiving David's letter, Topsy had at last heard from Christopher. They had allowed him just one hundred words but that had scarcely mattered; just to see that familiar handwriting of his was enough to lift her spirits. It had taken five months to reach her, but at least she knew that he was alive as recently as last summer.

She had carried the letter with her ever since and had reread it each day. From that point on, her life had taken on a fresh lease, but one always tempered by the absence of any other news of him. Five months had since passed without further news. She couldn't help worrying. How were they being treated in Japan? If the Japanese lost the war, what would they do to their prisoners?

Which reminded her. What had they done to Lance Newnham? She and Phyllis Newnham shared the same torment of not knowing the fate of their husbands. It bound them even closer as friends. It was six months since Phyllis had last heard anything of Lance. By then, she had already been put through the mill. Eighteen months ago she had been told that Lance was on his way to Japan. Topsy could remember how relieved she had been, but days later, news of the *Lisbon Maru* had reached the camp, leaving both of them to wonder if their husbands had been on board. Then the news had come that Lance had never left Argyle Street and Phyllis had adjusted to thinking of him being there once again. Then, six months ago, in early October, she had learned that Lance had been arrested during the summer. She had rushed up to the camp headquarters where Yamashita had denied any knowledge of events in Kowloon. It wasn't his business. Since then, there had been no news. She didn't know why he had been arrested or where he was being held. All she knew was that his signature no longer appeared on the chits when she received her allowance.

Topsy's thoughts were interrupted by the distant wail of a single air raid siren drifting across the camp from over the hills to the north. Within minutes, the solo alarm had become a chorus as Hong Kong braced itself for yet another bombing raid. The raids were by now commonplace and the internees had become rather blasé about them. The usual targets were the docks and the airfield way to the north of the camp, or ships coming and going within the island's coastal waters. These attacks seemed to present little or no danger to the internment camp, and most internees would have been happy to carry on as normal during them, but the Japanese and Formosan guards were easily panicked and treated roughly any internees who were slow to take cover.

Topsy headed for her accommodation block as the drone of approaching heavy bombers began to make itself heard above the distant crack of anti-aircraft guns.

Chapter 32

Autumn

Kobe House

All prisoners were made to parade on the field opposite the camp building. Only the sick were excused. Morimoto intended to leave in style and had chosen the second anniversary of the opening of Kobe House as a prisoner of war camp as a fitting date for his departure and the introduction of his successor, Takahaka.

Christopher had mixed feelings about a change of command. He had no respect for Morimoto who had turned a blind eye to the savagery of the likes of the mad doctor and Morita. He also held him to blame, along with Colonel Morata, for the callous neglect that had left desperately sick men dying for lack of even basic medical care. And yet, it was a case of the devil you knew being better than the devil you didn't know. He understood Morimoto and knew how to deal with him, and he sensed that Morimoto in his turn understood his prisoners much better by now. At least Morimoto had not himself set out to brutalise them and for the past year he had gradually allowed the harsher elements of the camp regime to drift. It was as if he had come to realise that he would have a much quieter life if the prisoners were left alone as much as possible under the command of their own officers and senior ranks. As long as they continued to work and didn't cause trouble, Colonel Morata seemed happy and kept off Morimoto's back.

Morimoto gave a brief speech. He had lost much of the swagger with which he had greeted the prisoners on their arrival in Kobe two years ago. That Japan was losing the war seemed to have become taken for granted. The new reality could be seen in his manner and in what he chose to say. He now addressed them as men at arms who had acquitted their duty to their country with credit. He wanted to remind them that they had been treated well and that he and his staff had done all they could to save the sick from dying. This prompted an outbreak of angry mutterings throughout the ranks on parade. Christopher felt nervous. There were some hotheads amongst the Diehards. After all they had been through, it wouldn't take much to push them too far.

Standing next to Christopher, Martin Weedon was thinking the same. 'Why the hell doesn't he just get on with it and hand over to the new bloke?'

'It's all part of the ritual,' replied Christopher. 'They've all got half an eye on what happens to them when it's all over.'

Morimoto finished by bowing extravagantly to Lieutenant Takahaka and took his leave of the parade, eyes fixed on the ground ahead.

Christopher turned his attention to Takahaka. He looked like an older version of Morimoto. It was the same with their guards; their average age had increased during the year as the overseas battlefronts continued to suck the nation of its young blood.

Takahaka's speech took up where Morimoto's had ended. He made a point of referring to the prisoners as honourable prisoners of war. He beamed a broad smile at the parade when the interpreter translated those words, mistaking the ironic cheers with which they were greeted.

Christopher quietly shared his thoughts with Martin. 'Makes a change from being the scum of the earth who deserve to be executed. I can't imagine Wada or Niimori ever bringing themselves to refer to us as honourable.'

Martin grimaced at the reminder of their former tormentors. 'Thank God we saw the last of those two bastards at Moji. I'd give a lot to have them in front of me when this is all over.'

Takahaka drew his speech to an end. He explained that before they were dismissed, they were going to mark the anniversary of the camp's opening with a simple act of respect. Christopher and Martin exchanged intrigued looks. Takahaka first gave the order to face to the east and remove any caps. He then explained that on his command they would all bow to the emperor. He would count to three and then give the command to bow. He warned them that as they would be bowing to the emperor, the brief bow they gave to Japanese officers, the *keirei*, was not appropriate. Instead, they would perform the *saikeirei*, which meant they would bow lower and stay in the bowed position until he ordered them to stand straight again. The prisoners were all accustomed to the usual Japanese words of command, but this was a new one. Without a trace of self-consciousness, he demonstrated the *saikeirei*, his face a deadly serious mask.

'This will be interesting,' Christopher muttered to Martin.

Takahaka drew himself up and shrieked out his command. 'Ichi – ni – san – saikeirei.'

Christopher saw how it would unfold before it even began. There were over four hundred of them on parade. Mostly British, a third of them Diehards, another third Royal Scots. Then there were the Australians, around seventy of them and a few Americans and Dutch. Whatever their nationality, to a man they knew that it was only a matter of time before they were released. That was the problem. Till that day came, the prisoners' collective fuse was shortening by the month, and it was only their shared memory of the uncompromising savagery that the Japanese were capable of that kept their frustration under control. Christopher knew instinctively how his Diehard soldiers would react to being ordered to face east and bow to the Nipponese emperor. Given half a chance, they would turn it into farce. And so they did. It started with scarcely audible mutterings but soon the field opposite their grim prison offered a mass display of ludicrously exaggerated bows accompanied by ribald suggestions of what the emperor could do with his bows.

Christopher was far from certain how Takahaka and his guards would react. He glanced nervously towards the new camp commandant. Takahaka looked shaken. He didn't know what to make of this. It was his first experience of dealing with a large number of war prisoners. The question was written all over his face and in his posture: was he faced with a wholesale act of defiance or was this just the way these prisoners behaved? His guards seemed equally confused and were looking at him anxiously, waiting for an order from him.

He gave it, at the top of his high-pitched voice. 'Kio tsuke'. The call to attention brought the parade to some sort of good order, as it had done for the morning and evening *tenko* parades each day during the past two years. The bowing over, the prisoners allowed the tension that had descended over the parade to loosen and stood quietly in line, waiting to be dismissed.

Later that evening, Christopher held a meeting of his command team. It wasn't just the parade that had prompted him. As they came off parade, each prisoner had been issued with a pamphlet that reminded them of the discipline demanded of them and the punishments they could expect to receive if they offended regulations. Christopher regarded this as a timely reminder.

'I've been thinking for some time that we're entering a new and dangerous phase of our captivity. It's new because it has become pretty obvious to us and to the Japanese that Japan and Germany will lose the war. It may take months, even a year, but they will be defeated. We always hoped that was how it would end, but to be honest, we couldn't be sure. In time we began to believe in our victory and now we know that it's damn near inevitable. And that's why it's also dangerous. Because the Nips know it, too. We've seen the change in them. At first their sense of superiority, even of invincibility, made them think that they could behave as they liked towards us, that there would be no consequences for them. It was the same for the Nip civilians here in Kobe. The war was taking place elsewhere and it was happening to other people. Now that the war has reached Japan, they're beginning to act differently. I should know.'

Christopher smiled wryly and pointed to the bandage around his head. The previous week he had been in the back of an open-topped lorry bringing his working party back from a day's work in one of Kobe's goods yards when it was attacked by an angry group of civilians. Christopher had been hit on the head by a large stone. It was a disturbing sign that public curiosity about war prisoners was turning to public hostility towards them as American bombers were hitting mainland Japan more frequently. Kobe had not yet been bombed, but air raid warnings had become a regular feature of life in the city, adding turmoil to lives already suffering from shortages of food and other essentials. And there was no end to the number of those little wooden boxes being unloaded in the docks as the ashes of their dead were brought home from yet more defeats somewhere beyond the sea.

'What I'm getting at,' continued Christopher, 'is that the camp is set to be a volatile place from now on. It goes without saying, the Japanese remain the masters here but month by month they are more nervous and insecure masters. In my view that makes them more dangerous and more unpredictable. At the same time, our blokes are aware that the tide is turning in our favour. They might be tempted to push their luck too far, too soon. There's a strong risk of a miscalculation that could easily end badly. I think we came close to that on today's parade; it could have turned nasty.

RSM Challis nodded his agreement. 'I had the same feeling out there on the field this morning. Some of our hotheads had me worried for a moment. Giving out the pamphlets as we came off parade could well be a sign that the Nips are worried. When you look at the list of offences and the punishments, it's just a rehash of the camp regulations that were in place when we first arrived here. I think it's Takahaka's way of reminding us of what we can expect if anyone steps out of line.'

Martin was of the same mind. 'As far as I can see, it's the usual story; the punishment seems to be death for everything – even for giving a mutinous look.'

They all agreed that a clear message needed to get out and about. From now on, cool heads were required. There was to be no rash provoking of the Japanese, just a patient wait until ascendency within the camp had shifted. When that time arrived, they would know it.

When the command team had gone, Christopher was left feeling more buoyant than at any time since the surrender of Hong Kong nearly three years ago. At last the process of preparing for freedom had begun. It was no longer a matter of survival alone; from now on it was about getting ready for the day when they and the Japanese would have to manage a new reality in Kobe. There was no way of telling when that would be, but it was coming with a certainty that had eluded him until today.

He had another reason to be in a positive mood. His life had taken a new lease four months ago. At the end of May he had been handed four letters from Topsy. They had arrived out of the blue at a time when he had all but given up hope of ever hearing from her. One letter had taken twelve months to reach him and even the most recent had been written at the end of the previous year. But that scarcely mattered. For close on three years, he had had no word of her. At least he now knew that at the end of 1943 she was alive and in Stanley Camp. The letters didn't tell him much else. They were Red Cross letters, limited to twenty-five words. It was obvious that she had been restricted in what she could write beyond the fact that she was well, sharing a room with two other women and helping in the camp school and hospital. Apart from that, there was scarcely a hint of what her life in the camp was like: nothing about the conditions, the food, how the Japanese were treating them.

Then, two months ago, two postcards from her had arrived. They were Hong Kong government postcards that required the text to be written in capital letters on one side only. The good news was that they had taken only three months to reach him. He didn't know what to read into that. He wanted to believe that the Japanese were taking more care about the welfare of the internees now that they knew they were losing the war and would soon be held to account. But since then there had been no further cards and he had begun to worry again. It didn't help his peace of mind that one of the working parties had returned with a disturbing rumour picked up while unloading a ship that had arrived from Hong Kong. The rumour was that American bombing of Hong Kong was frequently inaccurate and that, during a recent raid, a prison camp had been hit and several prisoners had been killed.

Christopher became aware of the distant sound of air raid warning sirens winding themselves up to full volume. Not that the prisoners could do anything. There were no shelters for them. Christopher watched from his window as the people of Kobe scurried this way and that to their nearest cover and the crews of the anti-aircraft battery doubled across the field to man their guns. It happened so often now that he knew how it would be. Anxious ears would strain to hear the sound of approaching bombers that never came. No bombs would be dropped but it would be several hours before the all-clear was sounded, if at all. Nobody would ever know why the sirens had sounded; all anybody would know was that life in Kobe had been disrupted yet again as the darkest clouds of war edged ever closer to the land and people of Nippon.

Stanley Camp

Topsy forced open her eyes against what felt like a heavy weight upon them. The hazy image of a face peered down at her, then slowly came into focus. She knew the face from somewhere but couldn't quite place it. That could wait. Right now it was sufficient relief to know that it had been a nightmare. There had been no Japanese firing squad, even though she had clearly seen the freshly dug trench and had knelt beside it. She could have sworn that she had felt the muzzle of the rifle thrust into the back of her head, just above the neck. That's what must have woken her.

'It's alright Topsy. It's me, Daisy. I heard you cry out and thought you might be awake.'

Daisy Turner had just come on duty at the camp hospital when they brought her roommate in. Topsy had blacked out whilst taking a class in the school. This was not the first time. Last year, she had collapsed whilst in their room but had soon recovered. The camp hospital was not equipped to enable any tests to be made, so the cause of her collapse had remained unknown. She had no previous history of blackouts. Come to that, Topsy couldn't remember any time before the war when she had been ill at all. She knew within herself that her health had never been the same after that traumatic evening when the Japanese soldiers had stormed through the University Relief Hospital, but she kept that to herself.

Daisy insisted that she remained in hospital overnight, just in case, and Topsy was content to comply. This second attack had knocked her back. For the first time since that very first night in the camp, she felt vulnerable. All last year the internees had lived off the hope that their second Christmas in the camp would be their last, but here they were still, with their third Christmas only two months away and no sign of an end to it all. They had little reliable knowledge of how the war was unfolding, but the rumours had become too consistent to ignore; they all pointed to the Japanese being on the run. But somehow the expectation of release made time drag by even more slowly and tediously.

Somebody had thought to fetch her handbag from the classroom where she had fallen ill. The bag had been a birthday present last year from Phyllis. She had had it made from scraps of material in one of the hobby classes. Topsy carried it with her everywhere. It contained the two letters she had received from Christopher. She took the second one out of the bag and read it for the umpteenth time. It had arrived in May and had been written only two months before that. The Japanese hadn't allowed him many words but at least she knew that in March he was safe and that he and Martin were together in the same camp. The bad news was that he hadn't received any of her letters. She had written the first of many as far back as June last year. How could it take so long to get to him? Come to that, it was now five months since she had received his second letter and there had been none since. It had occurred to her that he may not even know if she was alive. What if he had received no news of her? David knew she was alive and in Stanley, so Christopher's parents would know that, too. They were bound to have written to him, but what if he hadn't received their letters either? Time and again she had looked in the two letters she had received from Christopher for signs that he knew she was alive and well, but both could have been written merely in the hope that she would see them. Not for the first time, she cursed the Japanese for inflicting complete and utter separation on them. They were stealing what could have been the best years of their lives.

PART VI: 1945

Chapter 33

January

Kobe House

Christopher looked up from his task of loading cases of tinned food into the back of a lorry parked close to the edge of the quay in Kobe docks. He didn't speak German but recognised it when he heard it. Approaching from further down the quay, a group of German sailors were making their way towards the dock gates. The men in Christopher's working party paused in their work to watch them pass. The Japanese ganger who was supposed to be supervising them had left them to it while he had a smoke in the nearby rest hut, out of reach of the bitter north wind.

Christopher noted that the sailors wore the distinctive insignia of the U-boat service. They looked scruffy, even the three officers amongst them. Ten days ago, other working parties had reported seeing a German submarine leave the harbour, and yesterday it had been spotted being towed back in by tugs, clearly damaged.

A loud cockney voice amongst the Diehard working party made itself heard. 'Hi Fritz, fancy seeing you here.'

Christopher smiled to himself. Typical and entirely predictable, he thought. The Germans hesitated. They could easily have ignored the call, but instead, on the signal of one of the officers, they made a point of coming over to join the British prisoners of war. Christopher felt it was up to him to break the ice, but there was no need. Cockney soldiers and German submariners had already begun to mix, the language barrier seemingly no obstacle to men who had in common the experience of war at the sharp end.

One of the officers approached Christopher. 'It is strange. Meeting in this way, don't you think?' His English was impeccable, if heavily accented and deliberate.

'It is, indeed.' Christopher acknowledged. 'It's hard to think of ourselves as enemies, standing here on a Japanese quayside, thousands of miles from home.'

The German officer smiled ruefully. 'Perhaps we should think of ourselves as fellow survivors of war.'

Christopher hesitated before answering. 'Maybe it's a bit early to assume that. We've learned the hard way that we can't take survival at the hands of the Japanese for granted.'

One of the sailors interrupted them by asking a question in German.

The German officer explained. 'He wants to know if they can shake hands and give your soldiers their cigarettes. I said, go ahead. What about you?'

Christopher nodded his assent. Although a non-smoker, it was not lost on him that cigarettes were the common currency of men at war, whatever their uniform or allegiance. As he watched the shaking of hands and the German sailors emptying their pockets of their cigarettes, he reflected that war throws up experiences that seem unreal to those undergoing them, even at the time they play their part in them and before they have time to reflect on them. He turned to the German officer.

'This reminds me of the famous Christmas truce of 1914. If we had a football, we could have a game.'

Before the German could answer, the Japanese ganger emerged from his hut, shouting and waving the Germans on their way. As he watched the Germans head for the gate, Christopher felt no envy for their state of freedom. Ahead of them were futile battles followed by defeat – and they knew it. He was heading for freedom and knew it, too.

Later that evening, Private William Beningfield made his laboured way up to the second floor of Kobe House. It had been a long day, and even as a young man who had survived three years of captivity in better shape than most, he was breathing heavily. Eight hours of labour in the docks had left him aching from head to foot and the evening *tenko* had dragged on longer and more tediously than usual. But there was one last thing to do before he tried to get some sleep. He had been one of the working party who had engaged with the German sailors. He needed to debrief Christopher on what had been learned from them while it was still fresh in his memory. Unlike their officers, the sailors had wanted to talk about the way the war was going. They had been brutally frank: their morale was rock bottom, and they regarded defeat as being only a matter of time. They had confirmed some of the rumours that had been doing the rounds in Kobe House for months. The Italians were long since out of the war and Rome had fallen to the Allies back in June last year, then Paris a few weeks later. The German army was in retreat to the Russians in the east and to the Allies in the west. They were scared for their families if the Russians advanced into Germany ahead of the Allies. They just wanted the war to end so that they could go home.

Christopher was not surprised by what Beningfield told him. He had not overheard the chat between his men and the submarine crew, but the demeanour of the Germans had spoken for itself. That they were reconciled to imminent defeat was written all over them.

His message delivered, Beningfield was halfway out of the room when he turned back and handed Christopher a crumpled package. 'I almost forgot, Sir. One of the kraut sailors handed over some pipe baccy. We didn't want Captain Weedon to miss out.'

By now Christopher knew it with absolute certainty. They all did. They had spent their last Christmas as prisoners in Japan. The Japanese no longer had the wit or the means to keep news of the war from their captives. The prisoners on working parties were inevitably mingling with Japanese civilians, many of whom were disenchanted with the nation's military establishment and in no mood to keep quiet about it. In Kobe, barely a day or night passed without the warbling of the air raid sirens and the drone of American aircraft miles above announcing yet another disruption to the lives of citizens already bent double as they battled the cold-hearted wind of war. In their weary despondency, the Japanese people talked of defeat and dishonour, and the prisoners heard them.

Stanley Camp

'Bugger it.' Aileen Guerin looked up in surprise. Margaret Davies was normally a mild-mannered young woman. In all the three years that she had shared a room with her in Bungalow C, Aileen had never heard her swear. She gave Margaret an inquisitive look. 'What's set you off then?'

'Can't you hear them? It's the bloody air raid sirens going off again in Kowloon. They'll be starting up here in a minute.'

Aileen had heard the distant wail of the sirens, but like the rest of the internees, she was so used to the air attacks that she hardly noticed the warnings anymore. By now, the Japanese had given up forcing their prisoners to take cover; they left it to them. If they wanted to take their chances out in the open, then that was their look out. Not that there was any cover for them to take. Shelters had been dug for the camp headquarters staff and there were trenches along the camp perimeter for the guards, but that was it. The only measure that the camp guards insisted on enforcing was a blackout whenever a raid was threatened after dark. They were strict about that. When bombing of the island had begun, the internees had asked Yamashita to have white crosses painted on the roofs of their accommodation. When he had refused, they had remained relatively relaxed.

After all, the Americans knew that the camp held civilian prisoners because their own nationals had been repatriated from there two summers ago. Besides, the attacks were always directed elsewhere on Hong Kong and the closest they came to Stanley was when they hit Japanese ships in the coastal waters. If the internees were worried by the raids, it was because the Japanese had installed machine gun posts on the roof of the prison and an anti-aircraft gun only four hundred yards away on the road to Stanley village.

'It'll probably be just another raid that doesn't bother us,' ventured Aileen. 'Not worth you getting all steamed up about.'

Margaret allowed herself a smile. 'You're right. Don't get me wrong, I'm as glad as anybody to see the Japs getting a dose of their own medicine, but you know what it's like whenever there's been an air raid; there's bound to be a blackout that goes on for hours after the raid is all over. Just like it was after yesterday's attack on the lighthouse. That will mean three consecutive boring evenings spent in a blackout.'

As the sirens began to sound the alarm, Topsy was making her way from the hospital, where she had been on duty, back to her room in Block 15. Her instinct was to quicken her pace. She couldn't help it. Although the bombing of the Royal Naval Hospital was by now three years ago, the wail of the sirens was still enough to set her nerves on edge. Already she could hear aircraft approaching from the south-east. It wasn't the usual lofty rumble of the bombers she could hear. They hardly ever saw them. It was different for the fighter-bombers. The first the internees normally heard or saw of them was when they came screaming around the corner or over the top of the hills around the camp. They were gone in the blink of an eye unless they became engaged in a dogfight with Japanese fighters. What Topsy could hear now was more of a howl, full of menace and coming in low from out at sea. Out of sight beyond the hills to the north, the anti-aircraft guns protecting the harbour and the airport were filling the air above them with blast and shrapnel. Topsy strained her eyes as she peered out to sea beyond the southern tip of the Shek-O hills. That's where they were coming from. There they were. Just dots at first. She pressed herself against the wall of the nearest building, eyes fixed on the approaching aircraft. They were above her almost before she knew it. Four of them, fast sleek fighters, a bit different to the familiar Mustangs, soaring and screaming away over Shek O in a dash towards the harbour and the airfield. Behind them, four torpedo bombers growled their way over the camp, so low and ponderous that in the nearest one she could make out the helmeted heads of the pilot and behind him two crewmen, crouched one behind the other in the plane's long canopy. The anti-aircraft guns at Aberdeen harbour began to seek them out, sending up a barrier of shells and tracer that the first two bombers saw too late to avoid and flew straight through. The two rear aircraft had time to react but instead of veering to the left and keeping low above the sea, they both careered off to the right and began to climb, straining to clear the hills around Tai Tam Valley. It was a fatal mistake. Topsy watched horrified as the tragedy unfolded. She could see how it was going to happen. They were getting far too close. Like two giant birds of prey clashing on the wing, they collided and, still locked together, fell headlong onto the lower slopes of Mount Parker where they erupted in a ball of fire and black smoke. Topsy was about to drag her eyes from the scene when she spotted it. A lone parachute, silhouetted against the dark green of the hills, drifted serenely to earth until, with shocking suddenness, it was gone from her view. 'God help him if he's still alive,' she said to herself.

South China Sea

The USS *Langley* was making light of the mid-winter swell just over one hundred and fifty miles south-west of Hong Kong. She was one of the newest American aircraft carriers built in response to the national humiliation at Pearl Harbor, and at eleven thousand tons she scarcely noticed the six-foot waves driven by the Force 4 headwind. Conditions were good for the launch of the eight Hellcats that had been assigned to that afternoon's strike against Hong Kong. Lieutenant Frank Waters was feeling nervous as he sat in the cockpit and waited his turn to take off. Although only a junior grade in his rank, he already had more than twenty combat sorties behind him. He had no worries about getting airborne off the flight deck or about landing in one piece at the end of the mission. The Hellcat was ideal for both. The weather was favourable and there was plenty of time to complete the mission and get back to the carrier before last light. What worried him was some of the information they had received at the pre-mission briefing. Earlier that afternoon they had watched a strike force of four Avengers and four Hellcats take off from USS *Hancock*, one of fourteen carriers in a large task force of nearly one hundred ships and nine hundred warplanes. Waters and his fellow pilots had learned from the briefing that the target for the earlier mission had been Japanese ships in Hong Kong harbour and that only five of the eight aircraft had made it back to their mother ship. The surviving pilots had reported that the anti-aircraft fire over Hong Kong was the most intense and accurate they had encountered so far in the war.

Waters was typical of the young US Navy pilots who had signed up after Pearl Harbor. They were confident in themselves and in their warplanes and were keen to hit back at the Japanese. Their courage was beyond question; they wouldn't be in the dangerous business of piloting warplanes off carriers if they had wanted a safe war. But Waters was only human. The end of the war was in sight. The Japs were on the run, being defeated everywhere. It was only a matter of months, possibly even weeks, before the war would be over and he could get back to the farm in Virginia. He was twenty-one and had a girlfriend waiting for him. This wasn't the time to take unnecessary risks. Sure, he would get the job done, but he wouldn't be looking to make the mission any more dangerous than it was. The officer who briefed them on the sortie had made their mission clear. They were to destroy what remained of a Japanese tanker convoy that had dropped anchor in Victoria Harbour. These ships had been attacked by the Hellcats from USS *Hancock* but not all had been confirmed as hits. A second target was Kai Tak airfield, but only if there were aircraft out in the open on the field. Both the harbour and the airport had a prisoner of war camp close by, so there was little room for error. Apart from that they were free to select opportunity targets within Hong Kong Island. The Stanley Peninsula might offer rich pickings; there was a Japanese barracks somewhere on the peninsula and a small tanker had been reported as beached in Stanley Bay, alongside two lighters, close up against the eastern edge of the bay.

Waters watched as Lieutenant Mike Mosko's Hellcat lifted off at the far end of the flight deck. They had flown many sorties together and had an almost telepathic awareness of what the other was doing when in action. Waters was next to go. He felt the familiar tightness across the chest as he looked to his right for the signal. It was always the same for the take-off; no matter how many times you did it, the tension got to you.

Less than an hour later, they began their first circle of Hong Kong Island. Weather conditions were ideal with clear visibility out to fifteen miles. Victoria Harbour was a confused mess of flames and smoke but they could clearly identify that all five of the Japanese tankers were either on fire or part submerged. What remained was not worth the use of their bombs or of the 6-inch rockets carried by the other two Hellcats in the flight. Besides, the flak was intense immediately over the harbour and the airspace over the airfield at Kai Tak was no more welcoming, either. One pass was enough to confirm that there were no Japanese aircraft on the ground. This left them free to go hunting. They gained height and sheered away to the south-west. They would need the sun behind them when they hit the targets at Stanley.

Stanley Camp

Topsy was caught out in the open by the raid. Three hours earlier, after the crash of the two American warplanes, she had taken to her room and shared what she had seen with her roommates. Talking about it had helped to soften the shock, but it hadn't been enough to shake off the distressing images that invaded her head every time she closed her eyes. She kept seeing those three intense, young faces in the warplane's glass canopy, that single parachute falling to earth. She needed to get out. She had headed for her casuarina tree on the edge of the cemetery. It had become a bit of a daily ritual for her unless the weather intervened. It helped her cling on to a precious memory. As trees went, casuarinas weren't especially attractive, but they had their own distinctive scent and there was something special about the sound the breeze made when it eased through their branches. Scent and sound, two faithful guardians of memories.

As the air raid sirens sounded for the second time that afternoon, she reluctantly dragged herself away from her reminiscing and headed for her room. She made it to just beyond the camp headquarters, about halfway to Block 15, when the first Hellcat came screaming out of the western sky. Immediately above her head it pulled out from its shallow dive and soared in a tight right-hand turn over Tai Tam Bay. Behind her, from the direction of Stanley Bay, the muffled sound of an explosion hurried her on her way. She heard the second Hellcat coming and instinctively turned to face it. She was looking directly into the low sun and could see nothing. The hot blast wave of the exploding 500-pound bomb hit her and obliterated the din of the aircraft's frantic engine above her. She flung herself to the ground, her face pressed into the dirt of the path. The American planes just kept coming. There was no respite, no time to run for it. First were the bombs, perhaps three of them, she wasn't sure. Then came the rockets, some of them blasting targets out of sight in Stanley Bay, others fizzing their smoke-trailed path in the direction of the prison and the camp hospital. An anti-aircraft gun opened fire from somewhere close to Stanley village and a machine gun on the roof of the prison rattled belatedly into life, but still the Hellcats kept coming. Much lower now, their machine guns spraying the area of the prison.

It ended as abruptly as it had begun. An eerie silence settled over the camp as the sound of the departing Hellcats lingered awhile before fading to nothing when the last of them drifted out of sight high in the south-west sky. Topsy picked herself up as internees, in ones and twos, began to emerge from the accommodation blocks. Plumes of dark smoke were rising from the direction of

Stanley Bay and the cemetery. Topsy headed for them. That second explosion had felt very close; worryingly close.

When Topsy found her on the lawn of Bungalow C, Margaret Davies was lying on her side, half-curled up, childlike, for all the world as if she were asleep. There wasn't a mark on her. Not a sign of blood. Aileen Guerin was close by, sprawled on her back, arms flung out, like a discarded doll. It was the same with some of the others. It was the blast that had killed them. Others had been hit by shrapnel or by flying debris, and there were three bodies half-buried in the rubble that had once been the garage. Three years ago, during the battle for Hong Kong, death and disfigurement by bomb and bullet had confronted Topsy each of the days she had spent on duty in the two hospitals. She hadn't exactly become used to it at the time, but the need to just carry on had given her the strength to cope with it. Since then, life as a prisoner of the Japanese in Stanley Camp had been hard, at times almost insufferably hard, but at least the threat of violence had receded. Which was why its occasional, unpredictable return had been somehow more traumatic than when it had been a constant presence. That was how it had been when the Japanese had executed the seven men down near the jetty. A cold-blooded killing. And for what? For possessing a wireless. And so it was now for Topsy as she knelt and wept beside her lifeless friend amongst the carnage of Bungalow C.

South China Sea

The low sun had saved enough light for Frank Waters to pick out the ships of Task Force 38 from many miles distance. It was the mass of long, white wakes heading north towards Formosa that gave them away. His mother ship would be on her usual station close to the centre of the battle fleet. Plenty of time to get lined up. He would be the last in his flight to put down, after Mike Mosko. It had become a superstition. There would be a debrief, of course, before they could rest. He was sure that Mosko's bomb had hit the Jap ships close to the shoreline. He had followed his friend's run within seconds and had seen the impact for himself. But he wasn't so confident about his own first run. Had he got the timing right for release? He had tried to assess the damage as he strafed the target area on his second run, but there was too much smoke and dust to be sure. That was the way it was sometimes. That's why they called it the fog of war.

Chapter 34

Spring

Kobe House

The rumour had been doing the rounds for weeks: the officers would be moved to a new camp. Christopher warned Takahaka that if he wanted to avoid disorder when the end of the war came, he should not separate the officers from their men. He had made a further point. When the Allied bombing of Japan reached Kobe, the camp was so close to the docks and the railway network that it was certain to be hit. That being the case, all prisoners should be moved, not just the officers.

Takahaka was dismissive. He had his orders. All officers were to move camp soon. If the time came to move the remaining prisoners, they would be sent to a different camp. There was nothing to argue about.

Christopher shared his concern with Martin. 'Separating us, making a special case of us, will be so bad for morale. One of the things that's held us together is that we've shared everything. It was bad enough when they made us move out of Shamshuipo to Argyle Street, but I think it will be harder to take if we have to leave them here now after all we've been through together.'

Martin agreed. 'We'll have to handle this very carefully with the men. You need to speak to the RSM. The last thing we need at this stage is to allow the Nips to create a division between us.'

When the order to move came, they were given little notice. In mid-afternoon they were suddenly called in from digging air-raid shelters in the field opposite the camp. All officers were to be briefed by Takahaka. They assembled in his office, almost sure of what was to come. Takahaka looked as if he would rather be elsewhere. The responsibility of command was weighing heavily on him. It showed in his slumped shoulders and dull eyes that were reluctant to meet theirs. In the past week, Kobe had been devastated by repeated bombings. The docks were at a standstill, a scene of utter carnage, warehouses reduced to rubble, ships thrown together at grotesque angles. Just one railway station remained in operation. It was only a matter of time before the bombs fell even closer to the camp. Takahaka's message was brief. They would be leaving early tomorrow morning for another camp. There was no need for them to know where they were going.

The news went down badly with the Diehard prisoners when they returned from the working parties. From numerous canny hideouts, gifts of cigarettes, Japanese beer and tinned food appeared as if by magic and were carried up to the officers' room. They put on an impromptu concert that evening. All the regimental songs were played and sung with gusto, and each of the four Diehard officers had to endure wickedly funny and accurate impersonations of themselves.

Christopher didn't sleep much that night. He had often tried to picture for himself how their imprisonment at Kobe House would come to an end with a Japanese surrender. But it wasn't going to end like that. Much as he hated the place, it would be a wrench to leave the men here. And who was to say that where they were going would be any better?

As the first of the morning's light filtered into the room between the bars of the window, he took one last look out of the room that had been his home for the past two and a half years. There were the casuarinas guarding the crematorium up in the hills. Those trees had served him well as a daily reminder of Topsy. His thoughts turned to all those who had made their final journey up there, wedged into an apple barrel, unaccompanied by anyone they had known. When the war came to an end, they would need to be remembered. Their ashes would need to be retrieved and given some form of belated dignity.

The four officers walked together down to the camp gate. All the Diehards were lined up on the road outside to see them off. A Japanese coolie was waiting with a hand cart to take what few possessions they had to the station. They walked down the line, shaking each Diehard by the hand, all 131 of them. They were all that remained of the 358 who had boarded the *Lisbon Maru* at Shamshuipo three and a half years ago. There were no sentimental words exchanged. Soldiers didn't do that. Just an unspoken understanding that this was not the end; they would meet again.

It was the last day of March as they made their way to the station. Out of habit, they found themselves marching. They weren't made to. There were no words of command, no order to fall in. Not for the first time, Christopher found his mind drifting back to their arrival in Kobe. Then they had marched, half dead with fatigue and illness, still smothered in coal dust from their nightmare crossing of the East China Sea on that wreck of a ship. Many of them had marched barefoot, dressed in little more than underwear, but they had called on their last reserves of pride to march like soldiers. They had endured the screamed insults of their guards, prodded on at the point of a bayonet, accompanied by blows from rifle butts. The streets had been lined by curious civilians, anxious for a first glance of these disgraced enemies of their emperor. Now, there wasn't a civilian in sight on the rubble-strewn streets and the guard of two soldiers hadn't even bothered to fix bayonets to the rifles that they carried casually slung on their shoulders.

'I've been keeping count,' Ewan Graham announced. 'Today was our 903rd day in Kobe House.'

Martin Weedon was not in the mood to be nostalgic. 'And what a bloody waste of time it's been, every sodding one of them.'

Stanley Camp

There were no coffins, so the fourteen bodies had been sewn up in rice sacks, each one identified by a luggage label bearing a handwritten forename and surname. They had been buried in a communal grave the day after the raid that had killed them.

Looking at the three gravestones, Topsy thought they had got it just about right. It had taken three months, but it had needed to be done properly. She could see that in their own way the stones served as a metaphor for their life as internees in the camp; they had made do with what they had and had made a decent job of it. The stones were of different sizes and none of them was symmetrical. They had been hand-chiselled into a roughly rectangular shape, and the same hands had carved the crude lettering. They hadn't been the hands of skilled stonemasons. Most of the professions and trades were represented in the camp's population, but not stonemasonry. Yet they had made do. And it didn't matter that the finished gravestones weren't perfect; they stood where they belonged, at the edge of the cemetery, only a stone's throw from what remained of Bungalow C. The largest stone, in the middle, bore the Christian cross at its head, above a simple epitaph: 'KILLED DURING AN AIR RAID 16 JANUARY 1945'. It was flanked by two smaller stones, each bearing the name and age of seven victims. Topsy noticed that they weren't listed in alphabetical order. Come to think of it, there was no obvious order at all; it seemed to have been done at random, rather like they had been random victims of war. Margaret Davies was there on the left-hand stone, Aileen Guerin immediately below her.

Topsy and Margaret had shared teaching a class of children in the camp school. Topsy had taken to her straight away. Later, she had persuaded Margaret to join Phyllis's pool of bridge players. As a friend of Margaret, Topsy had been permitted to attend the burial. It had come close to crushing her. Violent death was no longer a stranger to her but somehow this had been of a different order, coming just when they were all thinking that the worst was over and the end of their captivity near. It just felt so unfair after all the hard times they had been through. And why them? Fate had been icily random in its choice of victim. It could so easily have been anyone, or nobody.

As she stood facing the fresh gravestones, she was prompted to think that if such accidents could happen there in Stanley, they were just as likely to happen in the prisoner of war camps in Japan. She wondered how the Japanese would react when their own homeland was threatened. Would they take it out on their prisoners? She was less worried about herself on that score. Things had changed for the better in the eighteen months since the execution down by the pier. There were signs that the Japanese recognised their days as victors were coming to an end. Colonel Tokunaga was still in command of all prison camps, but he was rarely seen in Stanley. That hideous interpreter, Niimori, the one who gave them all the creeps, had departed back in September, and Lieutenant Kadowaki was but a shadow of his former arrogant self.

But how safe was Christopher? It was already a whole year since she had received news of him, and that had been two months out of date when it had arrived. She took one last look at the gravestones before turning to make her way back to her room. Not for the first time, she found herself wondering how much more of this she would have to take.

Ikuno Camp

The train snaked its way up a long valley between densely wooded hills. It was the second train they had been herded into. Christopher had tried to keep track, checking their bearings whenever he could catch a glimpse of the sun through gaps in the shuttered windows. He couldn't be sure, but reckoned they were somewhere in the low mountains north-west of Kobe. There were forty of them on the train by now, the officers from Kobe House having been joined at the first stop by others from Osaka.

It was early afternoon when the train came to a halt at the edge of a small village. It wasn't a station, just a flat, open space suitable for allowing the prisoners to leave the train. Christopher stretched his arms and legs and filled his lungs with the fresh air. What a relief after being cooped up in overcrowded carriages for more than five hours. And what a welcome difference in the air up here. More invigorating than they were used to down in the city.

They set off through the village and left the main valley on a wide track bordered on one side by a stream that in early spring still ran strongly as the hills above emptied themselves of the late winter rains. They were now following a much narrower valley, the dark green of its steep sides interrupted at random by large patches of sakura in full bloom. They had marched for less than two miles when the track turned sharply and revealed a sturdy, wooden bridge over the stream. Their new camp lay along the far bank.

They paused to allow stragglers to catch up. First impressions from what they could see of the camp were favourable.

Martin Weedon was relieved. 'It's a rural version of Argyle Street. I think I'm going to be happy here.'

They crossed the bridge and followed their escort through the main gate of the camp. Christopher looked around him. Martin was right. These long, single-storey huts were reminiscent of those in Argyle Street Camp, but close up he could see that they were much more crudely built. They were constructed entirely of wood with a mud plaster covering. Christopher counted ten of them. The camp was surrounded by a boarded fence, about ten feet high and topped with sharp stakes.

He hadn't known what to expect. He had imagined a number of scenes, but none of them had included life within what amounted to a rural stockade.

There were nearly four hundred prisoners of war already in the camp. They had been there since the new camp had opened three days ago. They were allocated forty to a hut, four prisoners to each of a hut's ten small rooms, which meant that the Diehard officers kept together, as they had in Kobe. It was a typical Japanese wooden building with a raised floor. Their beds were rough wooden platforms covered in rattan mats that were filthy and smelt of rat urine. Ralph King took one look at his and hurried out of the room, reappearing five minutes later clutching four new mats that he had snatched from an unoccupied hut next door. He was just in time. The new arrivals were required to parade in front of the camp commander.

Lieutenant Hashimoto Shigeru was a veteran of Japan's war with China. A year ago he had been wounded and repatriated to Japan to recover. He was a tough soldier of the old school and, once recovered from his wounds, he had expected to rejoin his regiment on active service. Instead, he had been sent to command the new prisoner of war camp in Ikuno. He hated it. He hadn't joined the Imperial Nipponese Army to guard a bunch of prisoners. It was enough to drive a man to drink – as in his case it already had. If he had anything to do with it, he wouldn't be there for long. Standing close behind him, Corporal Minemoto Yoshinari had no such regrets about commanding the camp guard. He had spent the last two years indulging his brutal streak at another prisoner of war camp in

Tanagawa, near Osaka. When two American soldiers had escaped from there and been recaptured, he had beaten them so viciously with a club that one of them had died from his injuries. He loathed prisoners of war and relished having authority over them, whether in Tanagawa or from now on in Ikuno.

Hashimoto read out his message to the newcomers in a dull monotone which suggested that he was as anxious to get this done as were the prisoners themselves. A comically rotund interpreter in an ill-fitting safari suit read mechanically from his script. Christopher could barely suppress a laugh and dared not catch Martin's eye.

'I don't know why they bother with a translation. We had exactly the same script from Morimoto when we arrived in Kobe and we heard it again when Takahaka took over from him. We all know it by heart.'

It was the usual mixture: a reminder of their good fortune to be war prisoners of an emperor who insisted that they be treated fairly; a list of camp regulations and a warning of the punishments if they broke any of them. Not a hint that the war was drifting towards a close and they would soon be released. Instead, they had to sign yet again their pledge not to escape.

'Ridiculous,' commented Martin in weary acceptance of yet another irritating feature of camp life that had no logical purpose. 'Why would any of us make a run for it with the end of the war in sight? And anyway, where would we run to?'

The sole addition to the ritual message was an indication that the work required of them would be different to what they had been used to in Kobe. They would earn their keep by working for the Mitsubishi Copper Mining Company. The copper mine was within walking distance of the camp. They would be given work to suit their abilities. Hashimoto allowed himself a thin smile: officers would work further up in the hills, either carrying logs down to the local sawmill or clearing the trees and undergrowth and creating a camp garden to grow fresh food.

Back in their room, Christopher shared his thoughts with his brother officers.

'I'm glad that I won't be working in that mine. Did you see it when we passed it on the way in? It looked really grim. But I don't like the idea of the officers being treated differently. We had a bit of that in Kobe House, but our soldiers didn't allow it to become a them-and-us matter. Here, I'm not so sure.'

'You're right,' said Martin. 'In Kobe, we were all Diehards together. Here, the camp is a bunch of odds and sods with divided loyalties. It'll be much harder to make everybody pull together.'

*

While the people of Europe were singing and dancing in the streets to the music of victory and peace, for the prisoners of war in Ikuno Camp up in the hills of Honshu, life was just a series of pointless days in the interminable drift towards release from captivity.

For one thing, they knew little of what was happening beyond the camp and its environs. In the absence of hard news, they were left with interpreting the signs: the number of times they heard the waves of B29s droning far above them on the way to bomb Kobe, Osaka and Tokyo; the changing moods of the camp staff and guards, their ill-discipline and drunkenness; the shortage of food and fuel in the village of Ikuno; the absence of young men amongst the guards and the local population; and the degree to which the prisoners were being left to run the camp themselves, so long as they continued to labour in the mine and the forests.

It was six weeks since their move from Kobe and they had already made their mark on the camp. When they had arrived and had time to inspect their new home, they had been dismayed by what they had seen of the sanitation. Most of the latrines in the huts were not working and those outside were little more than deep ditches, with sump-pits completely open to sight and smell. Washing troughs, made of tin, had been installed close by. Far too close. Without drainage of any sort, the site was a quagmire. Within days, the prisoners had the hut latrines working and had drained the outside swamp. The four Diehard officers had gone to work on their room. They had scrounged enough timber to make a table and had put up shelves. They had even managed to give the walls a coat of whitewash which they produced by adding tooth powder to water.

They had also come to realise that their new daily routine, combined with a meagre diet, was bound to make for a harsh life in Ikuno. Reveille was at 5 a.m. followed by breakfast and the morning *tenko*. The day shift for the copper mine left the camp at 7 a.m. and arrived at the mine entrance in time to start work at 8 a.m. They had half an hour for lunch and then worked till 3 p.m. Back in the camp, supper was at 5 p.m. followed by the evening *tenko*. Those on the night shift worked from 3 p.m. till 11 p.m. Inside the mine, they operated drill machines, fixed timber supports, drove mine locomotives and shovelled ore into trailers. Outside the mine, they sorted the ore and graded it before loading it into trucks. It was back-breaking work six days a week and was made even harder by the imposition of a food ration that was only just above starvation level. Breakfast was a bowl of steamed rice and three quarters of a pint of soup that was little more than coloured water with soya paste to give it some flavour. If they were lucky, it contained a few leaves and potato tops. The bowls were small, no more than three and a half inches deep and four inches in diameter. Their lunch was either rice or a piece of bread provided by the mining company and washed down with foul-tasting tea that contained no leaves, only stalks and twigs the size of small pencils. Their evening meal was a repeat of breakfast.

For the officers who had come from Kobe House, the new regime was hard to take. In Kobe they had been sustained by food pilfered from the docks by the working parties and then shared out. Here in Ikuno, they awoke hungry every morning and went to bed hungry every evening. And already the inevitable results of a regime that combined hard labour with a poor diet could be seen in the camp hospital. Beriberi, dysentery and pellagra were back with a vengeance.

Their lives were now spent in an uneasy mixture of anticipation and apprehension. The anticipation was that they would be free within a few months, perhaps even just a few weeks. They were finding it hard to live with anticipation because it fired an insatiable excitement at the prospect of freedom only to dowse it with impatience as freedom remained stubbornly out of sight, day after day, week after week.

The apprehension was over how it would end. They had all seen what the Japanese were capable of when they were winning, and that was enough to make them wonder how they would behave when they were losing.

Minemoto had already left his mark on one of the American prisoners whose possession of a home-made cigarette lighter had been discovered during a snap search of his hut. Minemoto appeared to harbour a special hatred of anything American. He had lost all control of himself and had lashed the young American around the head with the buckle end of a leather belt until his face was unrecognisable.

But the danger didn't come from Minemoto alone. The entire management of the camp was in an ill-disciplined mess. Last night, Christopher had seen for himself that there was good reason to worry. He had been duty officer, responsible for providing the link between the Japanese guard and the prisoners. The previous day, Colonel Murata had visited the camp. He was still based in Osaka, and Ikuno was one of the camps under his authority. He had not been impressed by his inspection of the camp and he held Hashimoto responsible. Hashimoto's drunken bouts had become too frequent and outrageous to remain hidden from his superiors, and Murata had relieved him of his command on the spot. As soon as Murata had driven away from the camp to return to Osaka, the Japanese staff and guards had begun a farewell party for Hashimoto which had quickly turned into a drunken orgy. Christopher needed no reminding that alcohol and loaded weapons were a dangerous mix. He went to each of the huts to warn prisoners to lie low. Within two hours, not one of the camp's fifteen guards remained sober.

Four of them were supposed to be on guard duty and were armed. Two of these took to lurching around the camp, brandishing their rifles and hammering on the doors of the prisoners' huts. Christopher kept a close eye on Minemoto. He was dangerous enough when sober; fired up with drink and with a loaded pistol on his belt, there was no telling what he might do.

By midnight, the danger of a violent confrontation between armed guards and prisoners had passed. The guards, led by Minemoto, had broken into the camp stores and pilfered the Red Cross parcels that should have been distributed to the prisoners days ago. They had simply drunk and eaten themselves into a stupor so deep that they were all incapable of further menace, even Minemoto.

Hashimoto and all the guards were still asleep when the time for the morning *tenko* arrived. As duty officer, Christopher decided that the parade would go ahead as normal, and he would take it himself. It was in the best interests of everyone that the camp should not drift into chaos. At six o'clock that morning, Ikuno Camp offered a rare spectacle as four-hundred Allied prisoners paraded under the command of a British army captain and with not a single Japanese face in sight. The roll call had barely started when a half-dressed and unshaven Hashimoto emerged from the camp headquarters and weaved his unsteady way to take his place beside Christopher. He reeked of drink and could scarcely stand, but a voice from deep within his life as a soldier was telling him that there was a parade and it was his duty to take command of it. He smiled stupidly at Christopher and with a sigh sagged slowly to his knees.

They propped him up and walked him to the guardroom where they left him in the company of two of the night guards who were slumped face down on a table, noisily asleep, their loaded rifles leaning against a wall.

Hashimoto left later that day, still drunk, an unwitting allegory for the decline of the Imperial Nipponese Army from the heights of victory and glory to the depths of defeat and dishonour. The car that took him away to the station had brought his successor, Lieutenant Naruwa Hideo. Naruwa had been in command of a camp for American prisoners at Hirohata, near Osaka, for less than a year when Murata ordered him to relieve Hashimoto. He was older and more stable than his predecessor. He was more astute, too. He had seen enough to know that the end of the war was close at hand, and that the day of reckoning would arrive during his time as commandant at Ikuno. He would exercise command with that knowledge foremost in his mind. Ikuno Camp was now set to be a different place for the rest of its brief life, and the prisoners within it would soon feel the difference.

Chapter 35

Freedom: August–September

Return to Kobe

When freedom came, it was in a form that none of them, prisoners or their Japanese guards, could have predicted.

Up in the hills, Christopher and Martin and the rest of the work party prepared to begin the two-mile descent to Ikuno Camp. They had completed the day's quota of logs that had to be carried down from a clearing and then loaded onto the handcarts that would take them further down the valley to the sawmill in the village. The logs were from felled casuarina trees and the irony was not lost on Christopher. For him, the casuarina was a reminder of the best of his life that the Japanese had taken from him; for the Japanese, it would be the casuarina's oak-hard timber that would provide the pilings, beams and rafters needed to help rebuild the nation's devastated cities.

The work party had been escorted by one guard who had spent the day fishing in a stream further down the valley. As far as he was concerned, it didn't matter if the prisoners worked hard or not. If they completed the day's quota of logs by the time he returned, they would all march back to the camp. If not, they would carry on working till it had been.

When he reappeared in mid-afternoon, it was obvious that he had had a productive day, too. Smiling broadly, he made a big fuss of handing a fish to each pair of prisoners. Christopher was not alone in his cynicism. 'I'm not sure what it is that I dislike most about the Nips, their arrogance when they were winning the war or their grovelling now that they've lost it.'

Martin had no such doubts. 'Give me the grovelling, any time. I'm really enjoying it, especially from Minemoto. The other day he came up to me and said it was time that we were all friends together. I enjoyed telling him to get lost.'

Martin had reminded himself of something. 'You must add Minemoto to your list. He mustn't be allowed to get away with how he's behaved here. And I gather he was even more of a bastard in Tanagawa before he was posted here.'

Christopher didn't need reminding. Minemoto had been quick to test the tolerance of Naruwa when the new camp commandant had arrived. Hashimoto had allowed him full rein to treat the prisoners as he saw fit, but Christopher wasn't sure about Naruwa. The day after Naruwa's arrival, Minemoto had laid into an American prisoner during the evening *tenko*. Naruwa had done nothing to stop the assault, but the senior American officer in the camp had complained to Naruwa and left him in no doubt that when the war ended, the handover of the camp would not be peaceful unless Minemoto was reined in. It did the trick. Ever since, the guard commander had gone out of his way to ingratiate himself with the prisoners. None of them was fooled by this sudden conversion from brute to benefactor, but the following weeks of their captivity had been all the better for it.

Christopher concentrated on following in Martin's footsteps as the path meandered its way through the forest. Even though the way down to the camp sloped only gently, it was hard going for bodies drained of energy. The task given the work party that day would have been light work had they been fit, but they weren't. Christopher and Martin were both far weaker than they had been at any time since they had recovered from the diseases that had put them in hospital soon after their arrival in Kobe nearly three years ago. The food ration in Ikuno had dwindled to dangerously low levels over the past three months, and the prisoners had to resort to desperate measures in order to avoid starvation. They were caught in a vicious circle. They had to work to qualify for the full ration, but the full ration was not enough to keep them strong enough to work. If they didn't work, their ration was reduced, making them still weaker. The day's ration no longer included soup or tea; they simply drank hot water. There was not enough flour to make bread, so they added ground-up silkworms to give the dough sufficient body. The last time that Christopher had tasted meat or fish was when he had shared with Martin the one Red Cross parcel they had received last year in Kobe House. Yesterday, Christopher had been on fatigue duty in the camp and after the evening meal had swept the day's droppings off the cookhouse floor, washed them in the stream that bordered the camp and added them to the four Diehard officers' breakfast of steamed rice. And all the time, the Red Cross parcels, by now much reduced by the guards' pilfering, sat on the shelves of the camp stores.

It wasn't only the lack of food that made the work in the mines and up in the hills so exhausting. Dog tired as they were at the end of each working day, the prisoners couldn't get enough sleep. The summer's heat had brought out the bugs in the wooden ceilings and floors of their huts, and since May their sleeping mats had become so infested that each night had brought torment instead of sleep.

It didn't help that they now knew that the war in Europe had ended three months ago. In one way, it made matters worse because their frustration at having to endure their miserable existence whilst the inevitable Japanese surrender took its own infuriating time to arrive was all the more intense for knowing that the war was long since all over for everyone but themselves. They owed their knowledge to copies of newspapers stolen from the guardroom, often from under the noses of the guards. These had been translated by one of the prisoners and had provided the camp with reliable reports of events in Europe, but they gave no clue to what every prisoner in Ikuno wanted to know, when their war would end.

They knew something was up as soon as the camp came in sight. The camp gates were open and the guards, including Minemoto, were standing around on the bridge in subdued conversation amongst themselves, grim-faced, reluctant to look them in the eye as they made room for them to pass. Naruwa and the camp interpreter stood just inside the gates, waiting to greet each of the work parties on their return to camp. Naruwa's message was brief. There would be an early *tenko* that evening; he had some important news to announce.

They paraded at five o'clock that evening, around four hundred of them. They had been captives of the Japanese for three years and eight months and it showed. It showed in their gaunt faces, hollowed eyes and hair that had thinned before its time, some to no more than straggly tufts. It showed in their weary, emaciated bodies that were covered in dust from a day in the copper mine and in their skin, scarred by bites, scratches and bruises. And it showed in the assortment of shabby, ill-fitting clothes that they had managed to preserve and patch up since they were last issued with any. But for all that, as they stood there in their ranks and listened to Naruwa, they knew a happiness for which there would be no adequate words if ever they came to speak of it.

It was a parade and a day that each one of them would remember for the rest of their lives. Naruwa spoke slowly and quietly. The emperor wished to spare the Japanese people further suffering and had announced yesterday that Japan had surrendered with honour. The war in the east was over. In Ikuno Camp, they needed to wait for orders. In the meantime, there would be no more work parties. It would be for the prisoners' officers to set the routine for the days that followed. The Japanese camp staff and guards would keep themselves apart from the prisoners. It was time for the prisoners to be kind to all Japanese.

Later that evening, Christopher was summoned to Naruwa's office. Naruwa had received orders from Osaka. The officers who had come to Ikuno from Kobe would leave the next day. They were needed in Kobe where the prisoners were out of control. The commandant of the camp in Kobe urgently requested the officers to take over the camp and restore discipline.

Christopher could instantly picture the scene in Kobe. This was bad news. If the reports reaching Naruwa were accurate, there was a real danger that matters could get out of hand. It was the sort of end to captivity that he had dreaded. He headed back to the huts to brief the others.

There were only six of them heading back to Kobe. Just the four Diehard officers and two from the Royal Scots. They walked out of the camp, across the bridge and on down the rough road to Ikuno station with no hint of a sentimental backward glance as they left the past five months of their lives behind them. They were left to make their own way, accompanied only by the Japanese interpreter. There was no point in marching, but they had all agreed to look as soldierly as they could. They had raided the clothing store and kitted themselves out with new work shirts, trousers and boots. They needed to make a show for any Japanese watching.

There had been no celebrations to mark their last evening in the camp, although Christopher and Martin had treated themselves to a swim in the stream, something they had been itching to do since their arrival in Ikuno.

'My first swim since the *Lisbon Maru*,' Martin had observed drily.

The train was waiting for them at Ikuno where the station master bowed low to them and made a great performance of showing them to their carriage. It was a wildly different scene that greeted them when they changed trains in Himeji, a coastal town west of Kobe. The station and its surroundings had been flattened and burnt out by incendiary bombs. Demobilised Japanese soldiers, unarmed and with their badges of rank ripped from their uniform, pushed and shoved their way through hordes of civilians in a chaotic competition for space on every train. Within minutes of a train arriving at a platform, not an inch of space was left on it. Men, women and children clung to buffers, carriage door handles, carriage roofs. Others were packed tight into cattle trucks.

Christopher became aware of a woman stoically breast-feeding her baby as she sat on the roof of a carriage, patiently waiting for the train to get under way.

He turned to Martin. 'Look at her. This is the sort of scene that I have always imagined for the Russian revolution. What a mess!'

'More like Armageddon if you ask me,' was Martin's wry comment. 'How the hell are we supposed to get to Kobe with all this going on?'

'We'll do what we would do if we were on the platform at Canterbury East. We'll ask the station master.'

Christopher ordered the interpreter to find the station master and bring him to them. It had been a long, hard day for Hirate Isao. Yesterday had been the same.

Chaos from beginning to end. Running a station was not meant to be like this. In all his twenty years as station master at Himeji, he had known nothing like it. The last thing he needed was having to find six seats for British officers on a train that was already bursting at the seams. Hirate was in no mood to tread carefully and within minutes he had waded in and cleared half a compartment for them by liberal use of his baton. Christopher feared that this special treatment might trigger hostility from the civilians, but the Japanese around them were now a people cowed into deference.

*

It was late in the evening when the train slowed to a crawl and inched its cautious way through the suburbs of Kobe city. Never in their lives had the six officers seen such devastation. Nothing they had witnessed during the battle for Hong Kong compared with this. For mile after mile, the city was a burnt-out ruin. Virtually nothing above waist height remained. The houses, most of them wooden, were gone, and in their place the population was living in rough-and-ready, corrugated-iron shanties. Any wall left standing looked ridiculously out of place in this nightmarish scene from hell.

Kobe House, when they found it, was little more than heaps of bricks and rubble. RSM Bob Challis was there to meet them.

'Welcome back gentlemen. I trust you've enjoyed your life of luxury up in the mountains. It's been bloody awful down here, I can tell you. As you can see, we've been evicted by the Nips.'

He described how the street had taken a direct hit from an incendiary bomb just two months after the officers had been moved to Ikuno. Looking at the ruins of their former home, Christopher found it hard to understand how none of the prisoners had been killed. Some had been badly burned, but many had escaped unscathed. They had all been moved to nearby school buildings which was where Takahaka was waiting for them.

Christopher needed to know the situation before he confronted Takahaka. The days ahead could prove to be dangerous unless he and the camp commandant found a way of working together.

'What's the form RSM? We've been told that the men have been running wild since the surrender was announced. All sense of discipline lost. Looting the shops. That sort of thing.'

Challis shook his head. 'Nothing so bad. It's typical of the Nips. They've been panicking as always when they don't know what to do. They're just not used to having no control over our blokes. Admittedly, some of them have been carried away a bit. But there's been no violence. Mind you, I can see that it could easily get out of hand if we don't sit on it.'

'Sit on what exactly?' Christopher asked.

Challis shook his head. 'The Nips got it wrong when news of the surrender got out. They should've released more rations for us. By then, we were getting even less than when you left back in March. Instead, they carried on as if we were still prisoners. The blokes knew where the tinned food was in what remained of the warehouses, so they raided them. Before long, they were running a black market, trading food for cigarettes, beer, and some really rough *sake*. They were getting pissed, roaming the streets and losing their discipline in camp. The senior ranks are getting a grip of it, but it will help now that you're back. Takahaka will be pleased to see you. And so am I.'

It was well past midnight when they reached the makeshift camp. Takahaka and Morita were waiting for them. Christopher could see that they were nervous. Gone completely was the arrogance of the past three years, replaced now by exaggerated deference. They greeted Christopher with a low bow, their faces twisted into forced smiles. It was not lost on Christopher that Takahaka and Morita had just given him the full *saikeirei*. It had been deliberate. It came as close to being an apology as he would get. He knew the Japanese well enough by now to know that the likes of Takahaka and Morita would never bring themselves to say sorry. To apologise would amount to acknowledging that they had done something wrong, which in turn would mean losing face. More likely, their *saikeirei* was an act of ingratiation, a prelude to favours about to be begged.

Christopher didn't mince his words. The control of the camp was to be solely in the hands of the former prisoners. From this moment, he had authority as camp commandant. Captain Weedon was his deputy. They and their non-commissioned officers would ensure the good discipline of their men. There would be no mistreatment of the Japanese. He held Takahaka responsible for the conduct of all the Japanese camp staff. He had already noticed that the camp was in a filthy condition with poor sanitation.

Starting from tomorrow, Morita was to be responsible to Captain Weedon for making the camp fit to live in. Lieutenant Brownlow of the Royal Scots would be responsible for the administration of the camp, including the control of rations and stores. Takahaka was to report to the lieutenant each day for his orders.

Christopher watched closely as Takahaka and Morita listened to the interpreter translate his orders. Their faces gave nothing away, but they signalled their agreement with short nods of the head, point by point.

It was three o'clock in their morning by the time Christopher went to bed. He scarcely noticed that he was dog-tired. This was the moment that he had known would come one day. It was the expectation of this day that had kept him and hundreds of others alive. They were no longer prisoners of war. If they were prisoners of any sort it was in the sense that they were still trapped in Japan, and probably would be for days, even weeks.

His thoughts strayed to Hong Kong and Topsy. With luck, he would soon hear some news. In the meantime, he had a job of work to do. It should have been Monkey Stewart's, but that wasn't to be. He felt the weight of responsibility settling on his shoulders and was under no illusions about the dangers and frustrations that the next few days would bring. But already, freedom was feeling good.

Kobe: A strange sort of freedom

The next day, the Swiss Consul, Dr Robert Stunzi, called a conference in the camp to discuss how best to manage the new order in Kobe. Christopher attended as the camp commandant. The consul introduced him to a delegate of the Swedish government and a representative of the Red Cross. As he shook hands with them, Christopher kept his thoughts to himself. He didn't think much of the role played by the Red Cross during the past three years. On the few occasions they had visited the camp, they had never spoken to any of the prisoners. They seemed to have either been taken in by the window dressing which the Japanese had deployed on such occasions or had simply chosen to ignore it. Either way, Christopher concluded that long residence in the country had bred in them a relationship with the Japanese authorities that was too cosy. As far as he was concerned, the former prisoners had nothing to be grateful to them for. There would come a time when that needed to be said, but it wasn't now. For the time being, all that mattered was getting the men out of Kobe and Japan. That meant all interested parties working as a team.

A large group of Japanese officers and officials stood in one corner of the room. Christopher spotted Colonel Murata among them. The old fox was looking uneasy. He noticed Christopher looking his way and acknowledged him with a nervous bow of the head, clearly uncomfortable in meeting his eye.

Dr Stunzi revealed what had been agreed between the Americans and what remained of the Japanese government. A recovery team of Americans would arrive in Kobe to administer the city and organise the evacuation of all the men who had been held in the camps in the Osaka area previously commanded by Murata. The consul didn't know when the Americans would arrive; it could be days, it could be weeks. In the meantime, the former prisoners of war needed to be prepared to move at short notice.

Christopher nudged Norman Brownlow who sat beside him. 'That won't be a problem. I could pack everything I own in five minutes.'

When the conference broke up, Christopher became aware that Murata was making his way across the room towards him and Brownlow. Murata had not been invited to speak during the meeting. None of the Japanese had. It was a sign of the times. Stunzi had made it clear that the Japanese were there to listen. Before Murata could reach Christopher, one of the Japanese officials barked out an order. Murata stopped abruptly and rejoined the group of Japanese, looking sheepish.

Christopher gave Brownlow an inquiring look. 'I wonder what that was all about.'

Brownlow laughed. 'Perhaps he just wanted to talk about old times.'

Stanley Camp

Topsy and Phyllis walked side by side along the eastern perimeter of the camp that overlooked Tai Tam Bay. The beach below them was deep in the shadow cast by the cliffs as they walked in the last of the evening sun. Freedom was very close now but it would come with a sting.

It was a week since Phyllis had learned that Lance had been shot. He had been dead for twenty months. The Japanese had kept it from her. Such was their paranoia about enemy spies and agents that they hoped she might learn of Lance's death and present them with the opportunity to interrogate her and trace her informer.

Topsy still could scarcely believe how her friend had coped with the news.

Phyllis had asked but one question of Yamashita. 'Did my husband leave a message for me?' The same day that she was given the news, she had turned up as usual for her shift at the hospital. She had let it be known that she understood why everyone would want to offer her comfort, but she wanted no fuss. She wished to cope with it in her own way.

And she did. For a week. Then last evening, as she and Topsy were chatting after bridge, she had reached into a pocket and taken out her small diary for the year 1943.

'I wanted to show you this so that you would know that I'm ready to accept that I have lost Lance. I've been in denial. It was my way of dealing with it. Or not dealing with it. For some time I've known, deep down, that the Japs had killed him, but there was a part of me that clung on to the hope that they'd sent him to Japan.'

She opened the diary. 'See. It's there now. It's in the book. For the record. It's the nearest I can get to burying him.'

Topsy looked at the entry for 1 December. Over the faded original entry Phyllis had added, in bold pencil, the words 'Lance's court martial at 4.45'.

Phyllis turned the pages and pointed to a second entry. 'Dec 18th. Lance shot by Japanese in Stanley'.

She gave Topsy a pleading look. 'Just think, Topsy. They made him live for seventeen days with the knowledge that they were going to kill him in the end. And all the time he was there, so close I could almost have held his hand, and I didn't know a thing about it. I'll never forgive them.' And with that, all the grief that had been locked inside her for the past week poured out of her. The last of the day's light was fading fast when they reached the garden and cemetery on the far side of the camp. As they passed one of the new gravestones, Phyllis paused and ran her fingers over the stone's rough surface. Her eyes began to fill up again.

'I've been coming to this spot myself recently. It's peaceful and I like the view. More than that, it's where I want Lance to rest when this is all over. It needs to be somewhere that I can picture for myself. I can't bear not knowing where he's buried. You'd think that the Japs could at least tell me that. The rumour is that most of the executions took place on the far side of Shek O. I'll find him and get him moved to here. I'm really quite determined about that.'

Topsy said nothing. She sensed that Phyllis hadn't finished.

'If anything happened to me, would you do what you can to make sure they find Lance and bury him here? I hope it's not unfair to ask, but it would be such a relief to know that you would.'

Topsy hugged her. 'I promise. If Christopher has survived, we'll both come and visit Lance here.'

Kobe

Christopher directed Takahaka to summon the Chief of Police in Kobe for a meeting. Takahaka looked on the point of questioning the order, then thought better of it. Christopher detected the hesitation. 'Tell him it's urgent. I need to speak to him here – this morning.'

Five days had passed since Christopher's return to Kobe. He had not stopped working since then. Every day, from first light until late at night when he was close to dropping with fatigue, the demands on him just kept coming. Martin Weedon, Norman Brownlow and a handful of others shared the load, but Christopher had become recognised as the leader of the new order. Everybody wanted to see him.

Day by day, that new order established itself in Kobe. At first, Christopher felt it hard to accept as normal the sight of his men wandering the streets as free men. Some of the habits of three years still clung to them. They were used to looting from the docks and warehouses. For much of their captivity in Kobe House, looting and pilfering were all that had stood between them and starvation. So, they simply carried on looting until Christopher and his leadership team made it a punishable offence and made clear their determination to enforce it. Step by step, they took control of the black market in food and adapted it to provide food centres for the civilian population, with former prisoners working alongside missionaries. Within days, Christopher found himself in the dual role of local administrator and British Consul. Japanese mothers turned up at the camp, desperately pleading for food and money to support their families. Some of them thought he might have news of their husbands. It occurred to him that they were the first women he had spoken to in nearly four years: it felt weird. Civilian expatriates of many nations sought him out, seemingly thinking him able to recover property for them, find lost relatives or organise a flight for them out of the country.

The American bombers that had reduced Kobe to ruins had now switched their efforts to supplying the city and its people from the air. The air drops had begun yesterday. Plane after plane swooped in low, many of them too low to allow parachutes to open. For the men in the camp, these were exciting times. The planes were so low they could see the pilots waving to them as they waggled wings to celebrate victory. The streets of Kobe were once again dangerous places to be. These pilots were used to dropping their loads over jungle and open terrain, but a city of around one million people presented a different challenge. From all angles, heavy drums, crates and bales were crashing to the ground, leaving the streets strewn with a treacherous, foul-smelling mess of broken tins of fruit, tomato juice, cigarettes, flour and oil, all mixed together. Groups of men began to roam the streets, scrapping amongst themselves for a share of the spoils before the rats got at them.

Christopher and Martin had their own narrow escape on their way to one of the food centres when a B29 swept low over them, dropping a huge bale of clothing which thudded into the road beside them. Within seconds, several civilians appeared as if from nowhere and began to pull the bale apart, only to be scattered when a 90-gallon drum careered down the street, spraying out broken tins of peaches as it went.

Christopher and Martin had both seen the funny side of their near miss, but it was obvious that the American enthusiasm for supplying the city by air drop was getting out of hand in its delivery. Christopher was tempted to dismiss this as a problem for the Japanese to solve. Being in command of the camp was one thing, seeking authority over what was happening in Kobe was quite another. As far as he was concerned, only one thing mattered, and that was to look after the best interests of his men until the Americans arrived and evacuated them out of Japan. But he had to admit, it wasn't proving that simple because it was becoming clear that the best interests of his men were inextricably tied to establishing some sort of good order in Kobe. Chaos in the city was a danger to them all and if the Japanese weren't up to the job of sorting it out, then he and a few hundred British servicemen needed to help them. That was why he had summoned the Chief of Police.

Osakabe Saburo reported to Christopher two hours later. He had been promoted to Chief of Police only three months before the surrender, and he was beginning to regret it. He had coped when the military had been in charge, but by now they had all but disappeared from the scene, and the few who remained had become part of the problem. For the first time, maintaining law and order in Kobe was now down to him alone, and he found himself out of his depth. So when the British captain had sent for him, he was only too eager to respond.

When Osakabe arrived at the camp, RSM Challis greeted him and led him to the room where Christopher had set up his office. Osakabe bowed to Christopher who responded with a bow of his own and motioned to him to take a seat. This was no time to play the superior role of the victorious colonial administrator. It was important that he established an effective working relationship with what remained of the city's civil administration. From what he had learned of the Japanese, the most pragmatic way lay in not making them lose face.

His first impression of Osakabe didn't encourage him. It wasn't just his unkempt appearance: the dust and stains on his black uniform; the high, black leather boots that hadn't seen a brush since goodness knew when; the generous waist and fleshy neck which hinted that the general shortage of food had passed him by. More off-putting was his demeanour. Looking at him, Christopher saw a man who had lost confidence in himself and had settled for going through the motions. He could see it in the eyes that shifted this way and that, in the slumped shoulders, in the hands that refused to stay still. If Osakabe was going to be of any use, he needed a boost to make him feel an equal partner in a joint task. Christopher set about reassuring him. These were difficult times for everyone. Until the Americans arrived in numbers, it was important that the British soldiers and Kobe police worked together, helped each other. He had around three hundred former prisoners of war who could help. He could form them into squads to salvage as much as possible of the air drops. They would need to work closely with Osakabe's men to avoid confrontations between British soldiers and Japanese civilians. It would help if Osakabe could assign one of his officers as a liaison officer, based in the camp, working with RSM Challis.

Osakabe left the camp a happier man than when he had arrived. He no longer felt alone in facing the problems ahead. It dawned on him that he was more confident working with these British soldiers than he had ever been under the Japanese military authorities.

*

It was not long before Osakabe needed Christopher's support. Early the next morning he turned up unannounced in the camp and made straight for Christopher's office. Christopher was already deep into a thick pile of paperwork. He was dressed smartly in an American army shirt and trousers. An entire bale of them had fallen into the camp during yesterday's air drop, and all the men in the camp were now kitted out in them. He motioned Osakabe and his interpreter to take a seat.

'How can I help?'

The Chief of Police explained that he had a riot on his hands at a nearby camp for Chinese prisoners of war. There were around one hundred Chinese in the camp. They had armed themselves and taken some guards as hostage. They were demanding food and clothing which he didn't have. He had surrounded the camp with two hundred of his own men but was reluctant to order them into the camp.

Christopher could understand Osakabe's fears. There was no love lost between the Chinese and Japanese who had been at war for the past eight years. Now that the Japanese had surrendered, there would be lots of old scores to settle. Things could easily turn ugly in the Chinese camp.

Christopher called in Martin Weedon, Norman Brownlow and RSM Challis. They needed food and clothing for one hundred men. And they needed them quickly.

Two hours later, they drove out of the camp in a fully loaded lorry, having raided their own store for the tinned food and added what remained of the American army uniforms.

When they arrived at the gate to the block where the Chinese were held, Osakabe was already there. It was as he had described. The Chinese soldiers had armed themselves with whatever they could lay their hands on: iron crowbars, wooden poles, bricks. Christopher noticed a few of them had managed to grab long knives and Japanese bayonets from somewhere. They were lined up, obviously spoiling for a fight with the cordon of Japanese police.

Christopher took Osakabe aside. He wanted the cordon to hold off until he had spoken to the Chinese. He would go into the block and didn't need an escort. He needed assurance from Osakabe that he wouldn't take any action until he reported back. Osakabe nodded his agreement. He was just as anxious as Christopher to avoid a fight.

Christopher walked slowly through the gate and into the front courtyard of the block. A young Chinese, taller than most, detached himself from the line and came forward to meet him. Close up, Christopher noticed he was wearing a faded military shirt with a lieutenant's two stars on each red and yellow epaulette.

Christopher saluted him. 'Good morning. I am Captain Man. British Army. I want to help.'

The lieutenant half turned away and called out in Mandarin. A short, bent figure stepped forward. Christopher put him in his forties. Perhaps fifties. It was hard to tell. Thin as a rake and gaunt of face. One leg wrapped in a dirty bandage. Dressed only in a vest and shorts. No shoes. But he spoke fluent English.

The lieutenant began to speak. He and his men were some of the four thousand Chinese who had been captured when the ancient city of Loyang had fallen to the Japanese just over a year ago. He had been a student at the university when the Japanese had invaded in 1937, and the interpreter had been a teacher there. The Japanese had destroyed the city walls with their artillery and tanks, and he and his men had only surrendered when their ammunition ran out after a long siege. They had been badly treated as prisoners of war but they were lucky; many of their comrades had been butchered when they had surrendered.

Christopher wanted to know why they were still confined to their camp. The lieutenant pointed to the police cordon. He and his men knew that the Japanese had surrendered to the Americans, but the Japanese feared what the Chinese would do to them and intended to hold them until the Americans arrived in Kobe. His men remained as prisoners and were not given enough food to survive. Christopher could see the evidence all too clearly. The Chinese soldiers looked a tough lot, but they were painfully thin.

Christopher assured the lieutenant that they would not be attacked by the police. He asked to speak to the men. The lieutenant nodded his assent and gave a command. They gathered round Christopher, these homesick soldiers from one of China's most revered cities, much as the Diehards had done when Christopher had called a parade on his first morning back in Kobe.

He told them that he had food and new clothes waiting for them in a lorry just beyond the cordon. He would make sure they received more food in the coming days. He would order the Chief of Police to remove the cordon and release them from captivity. They would then be free to run their own camp and move outside it, the same freedom enjoyed by the British soldiers. In return, they must release their hostages and remain law-abiding under the orders of their own officer. They must promise to treat all Japanese with respect. There was to be no taking of revenge.

When Christopher spoke, the Chinese braced themselves to attention. Each time he paused to allow the interpreter to translate, they relaxed and then came to attention again as Christopher resumed speaking.

Martin Weedon looked on from outside the gate. He nudged Norman Brownlow. 'It's unbelievable. He's got them in the palm of his hands. It's as if he's the local commissioner for an army of occupation. A week ago, we were slave labour up in the hills. Monkey would have been proud of him.'

Osakabe was quick to agree to Christopher's terms. The hostages followed Christopher out through the gate, bowing to him before disappearing through the cordon. As soon as the police had withdrawn, RSM Challis drove the lorry into the courtyard and stood back to allow the Chinese to unload it. Christopher had feared there might be a free for all, but they had already organised themselves into unloaders and a chain of porters.

He exchanged looks with Challis. 'Very impressive eh! They've been given a hard time by the Nips poor buggers, but they're a hard bunch. Well disciplined, too.'

Challis thought the same. 'I'm glad they've been on our side.'

Christopher nodded. 'Me too, Mr Challis.' And then added enigmatically. 'Let's hope it stays that way.'

Stanley Camp

It was late afternoon when David Man stepped out of the front passenger seat of the Jeep onto the forecourt of the camp headquarters at Stanley, shook the worst of the dust off his battered Panama and looked about him. So this was where Topsy had been interned. He had tried to picture it to himself whenever Hong Kong matters came across his desk at the Colonial Office in London, but the image he had of it hadn't been anything like the place where he now found himself. He had already been shown round the camps at Shamshuipo and Argyle Street. They had made grim viewing. At first glance, this camp was not so forbidding.

He had been in Hong Kong since yesterday morning, but although he was certain that his sister-in-law had been interned at Stanley, he had not made straight for the camp there. The family connection partly explained why he was in Hong Kong in the first place, but once there, he resisted the temptation to let it influence his priorities.

He was there on duty for the Colonial Office where plans had been made with the Americans for the repatriation of British prisoners of war and internees once the war in the Far East was over. It had been agreed that the Americans would take responsibility for all Allied prisoners of war who had been held in Japan by flying them to the Philippines, but it would be up to the British to take them from there by sea. The British would repatriate those prisoners held by the Japanese in Hong Kong, Singapore and Burma, as well as the British families who had been evacuated to Australia in 1940. David had instantly volunteered to form a team to evacuate British nationals who had been captured in Hong Kong. It made sense. The three years he had spent working with Beryl Tidbury and the Hong Kong Fellowship made him a natural choice. They had compiled an impressive file of information so that by 1945 David knew more about the situation in Hong Kong than anyone else in the Colonial Office. They had flown him to Malta and then to Calcutta where he had made contact with the liaison officer to the American military mission in China. Within hours of his arrival, he was sitting beside the pilot of a Douglas C-47, 'flying over the Hump' as this route over the Himalayas had come to be known. At Kunming, he had thanked the young American pilot for a memorable flight. 'You're welcome,' was the first lieutenant's response. 'I've lost count of how many times I've flown it, but I never take it for granted. I tell you, in five years' time people will be paying a fortune for the privilege of seeing those mountains from above. And I've been paid for doing it for the past two years.' He had omitted to mention that it had been one of the most dangerous flight routes of the war in the Far East.

David had been given a lift from the Kunming airbase in one of the American B24s that had been bombing Hong Kong from there until a few weeks ago.

He had landed at Kai Tak in Kowloon soon after permission had been granted to begin flights to Hong Kong after the British naval task group had anchored off the island the day before. Admiral Cecil Harcourt had yet to formally receive the Japanese surrender at Government House, but already Hong Kong was once again a colony under British rule. It was the Union Flag and not the Rising Sun which now flew everywhere.

On arrival at Kai Tak, David had been driven to the supreme court building in Jackson Road where the British administration had re-established itself. He needed to brief the Colonial Secretary on the Colonial Office repatriation plan.

Later that day, he had been shown around the camps at Shamshuipo and Argyle Street. Those who had been imprisoned there had left him in no doubt about how damaging four years as prisoners of the Japanese had been. He had tracked down some of the Diehards in both those camps. He wanted to leave Hong Kong with a clear memory of where his brother had spent most of his first year in captivity and with an understanding of what life had been like for him there. The Diehards he met had willingly showed him around, but none of them was able to offer any news of Christopher. All they knew was that he was on the *Lisbon Maru* when it had sailed three years ago.

There wasn't a single Japanese face in sight that afternoon in Stanley Camp. The only remaining sign of the previous regime was a small group of Formosan guards, no longer in uniform, looking forlorn as they headed out of the camp in the back of an open-top truck. The Colonial Secretary had informed David that the offices in the camp headquarters were now manned temporarily by a handful of the internees who had been members of the camp council. He intended to relieve them as soon as he could spare some officials. David knocked on the first door he came to and poked his head into a poorly lit office containing a single desk and an upright, metal filing cabinet.

A middle-aged man looked up from the pile of papers on his desk. 'Hello, how can I help you?'

'I'm David Man. I'm in Hong Kong on Colonial Office business. I've come down to Stanley looking for my sister-in-law, Georgina Man. She may be better known here as Topsy Man.'

'You're in luck. I'm Charles Roberts. I was the billeting officer here on the camp council. I know where every single internee lives. You're right. We all know her as Topsy. She's in Block 15. I'll show you the way.'

Daisy Turner was alone in Room 33, writing up yesterday's diary. Those internees who had somewhere to go in Hong Kong had left the camp the previous week, leaving spare rooms in some of the best accommodation blocks. Daisy and her daughter Beryl had considered changing their room. Block 15 was generally considered to be amongst the worst of the blocks, and they were tempted by the chance to move to somewhere better and with more space for their last days in the camp. They had mentioned it to Topsy.

She hadn't hesitated. 'This has been my room since January 1942. I've become used to it. It's almost part of me. I'll leave it when I leave the camp and not before.' All three had stayed.

Daisy heard leather shoes on the stairs and then on the concrete floor of the corridor. Curious, she got up from the room's small table and took a look outside. A young man, slim, fair hair, wearing a shirt and tie under a loose-fitting linen jacket, was approaching from the far end of the corridor, pausing at each doorway.

He caught sight of her. 'I was beginning to think that nobody lives here anymore. It's so quiet. I'm David Man, I'm looking for room 33.'

Daisy smiled broadly. 'You've found it. I'm Daisy. I live here.'

When David explained the reason for his visit, Daisy couldn't disguise her excitement.

'Topsy's out. I think I know where she'll be. I'll take you there.'

When they reached just beyond the camp headquarters, Daisy stopped and pointed ahead of them. 'If you keep going straight, you'll come to the cemetery. You can't miss it. Topsy usually spends this time of day up there if the weather is kind.'

'I hope I recognise her,' joked David. 'We've never met. I only know her from photographs.'

Daisy hesitated before responding.

'You ought to know that Topsy had a tough time during the fighting and things have been very hard in the camp. Of course, it's been miserable for all of us, but she's had the additional worry about Christopher. She's had no news of him for ages and doesn't know if he's alive or dead in Japan. I think she's literally sick with worry. It hasn't helped that there's been a strong rumour running round the camp that prisoners of war in Japan have been killed during the American bombing raids. Do you have any news for her?'

'No, I don't. We know that a year ago he was alive and being held in a camp in Kobe. I'm afraid that Kobe is one of the cities that have been heavily bombed. Anyway, thanks for telling me about her. I'm glad I know before I meet her.'

Daisy watched him head up the rough path to the cemetery before making her way back to her room. There had been something unreal about meeting Topsy's brother-in-law. Unreal but comforting. Thinking about it, it occurred to her that he was the first person she had met who came from the world beyond Hong Kong's experience of Japanese rule. She wasn't used to seeing European men dressed smartly in jacket, shirt and tie. And another thing. He had shaken hands with her when he left. She hadn't shaken hands with anyone since… well, she couldn't remember when it would have been. It wasn't the sort of thing you did in the camp. It was like lots of other normal things that had been suspended for nearly four years. The afternoon had just brought getting back to normal life that little bit closer for Daisy Turner.

David easily recognised Topsy from the photographs he had seen of her and Christopher. She was sitting on the grass, back against a tree, looking out across the bay, lost in thought. She became aware of him approaching and pushed herself to her feet. She smiled and gave him a questioning look.

'Hello, you must be Topsy. I'm David, Christopher's young brother. I've come to take you home.'

Chapter 36

Going Home

Sayonara Kobe

The end came with a rush. Four days after the incident at the Chinese camp, Christopher was visited in his office by Dr Hertzog from the foreign affairs department of the Swiss Consulate. Hertzog was all smiles. He had good news. The American recovery team would arrive that evening and begin work tomorrow morning. It was hard to believe, but they intended to process the entire camp by the end of tomorrow. If all went well, the men would begin their journey home tomorrow evening.

Hertzog was buoyant. 'I'm very pleased for you all. It can't happen too soon after all that you've been through. Especially for you, Captain. You'll be able to hand over to them and relax at last. It's been good working with you these past two weeks.'

Christopher was momentarily taken aback. Had it really been two weeks since they marched out of the camp at Ikuno? Since then, he'd hardly had a moment to himself.

He gave Hertzog a rueful smile. 'I have to admit, there have been days when I missed the simple life as a prisoner of war.'

It was late that evening that at last Christopher was able to make his way back to his office in the camp. He was desperately tired but needed to clear as much paperwork as possible before handing it over to the Americans the next day. He and Martin had just returned from Kobe station where they had welcomed the arrival of the American recovery team. There were twenty-three of them under the command of a cheerful American colonel. Christopher had been impressed and relieved. It was clear to him that they fully understood what the men had been through and were keen to help. More than that, they obviously knew what they were doing. They were being put up for the night by the Swiss consulate and would arrive in the camp at seven o'clock the next morning, ready to get to work. They aimed to have all the men on the train to Yokohama by the end of the next day.

It was close to midnight when a knock on Christopher's office door made him look up. Murata and Takahaka were standing in the doorway, looking solemn. They were both dressed in full uniform: khaki cap, tunic buttoned to the neck, trousers tucked into knee-length, brown leather boots and a sword carried at their left side in a scabbard of polished wood.

Christopher beckoned them to come in. He felt awkward. They hadn't brought an interpreter with them. They had no English and Christopher's Japanese was limited to the words that were necessary to survive camp life as a prisoner of war. Murata stood before him, bowed and began to speak. Christopher listened, trying to make sense of it. The occasional word was familiar. Several times, Murata mentioned *bushido*, the Japanese warrior code. Christopher had heard it often enough these past three years to understand its significance to the Japanese military class, but he could only guess what Murata meant by speaking of it now. Murata didn't speak for long. When he stopped, he unhitched his sword from his belt and handed it to Christopher, long handle first, in its scabbard. As soon as he had done so, Takahaka did the same, without speaking, merely bowing his head.

Christopher placed both swords on his desk. He understood immediately the significance of what was taking place. It wasn't in any way an act of apology for any wrongdoing. That would be a loss of face too far. No, this was the two Japanese officers' way of acknowledging honourable defeat in battle. Japan had fought and lost a war with honour and at their level Christopher was the acceptable face of the victors; he was worthy of the surrender of their swords. With the handing over of their swords, their war was now over.

Without an interpreter, there was little point in Christopher saying much. He bowed and with just a suggestion of a smile said thank you. Morata and Takahaka turned and walked out of the room. It was the last Christopher ever saw of them.

Left alone with his thoughts, Christopher felt part of a bigger history unfolding. The world was changing. Not only here in this battered Japanese city but everywhere. Thousands of miles to the west, the new world order was already four months old. Would it have left them behind? They would soon know. Meanwhile, here in Kobe, these swords belonged to all those who with him had survived Shamshuipo, Argyle Street, Kobe House and Ikuno. And they belonged to those who hadn't made it, to those whose corpses had been left to rot among Hong Kong's streets and hillsides, and to those whose ashes now rested impatiently in the temporary keeping of a Buddhist temple here in Japan.

Martin was still awake when Christopher made it back to their room. It was well past midnight, but the prospect of leaving Kobe during the coming day was keeping most of the camp awake.

Christopher told Martin of his final meeting with Murata and Takahaka.

Martin shook his head in disbelief. 'How extraordinary. But then they are an extraordinary race. Mind you, they probably think the same of us. That's where most of our problems have come from, we and the Nips simply can't understand each other.'

Christopher handed him Takahaka's sword.

'I want you to have this. We've been through a lot together and it's only right that we both have one.'

Martin was happy beyond words. He had set his heart on leaving Japan with an officer's sword and had begun to give up hope of securing one.

They took the swords from their scabbards. Both were in excellent condition with beautifully engraved hilts.

Christopher ran his finger along the gently curved steel blade of Murata's sword. 'Of course, it should have been Monkey who took possession of these. I so wish he could have made it. He would have been in his element here now.'

Martin chuckled. 'Mind you, there might have been some sore Nip heads around. Monkey's idea of diplomacy was not the same as yours.'

Reveille that morning was at five o'clock. Two hours later, the entire camp was on parade. When RSM Challis reported to Christopher that all were present, he slammed the heels of his new boots into the school playground, his back ramrod straight, his right hand quivering at the salute, much as he had regularly done four years ago when reporting the battalion present to Monkey Stewart on the parade ground in Shamshuipo.

The American colonel addressed the parade by going straight to the point. 'I know you boys have had a tough time. A really tough time.' He turned and pointed to his team. 'And we are here to look after you and send you home.' To a man, the parade cheered. For some of them, it was only now that they dared believe it. After nearly three years of captivity in Kobe, the inevitability with which rumour and hope had always come to nothing had taught them to be wary of hope itself. The colonel spoke about the plan to get them home. They would all be processed by the team during the day: their particulars would be recorded; they would be medically examined and graded; they could fill in forms to send a cable home. That evening they would leave Kobe by train for Yokohama where they would see more aircrafts than they had ever seen before. From there they would be flown out of Japan to Manila in the Philippines. He paused while the parade cheered again. They would wait in Manila to board a troop ship that would be evacuating those who had been prisoners of war in Hong Kong. This was the first mention of Hong Kong that Christopher had heard. His first thought was that if Topsy had survived, she could well be on that ship.

By six o'clock that evening, they were on parade again, ready to leave camp life for the last time. As they marched out of the camp gates, they soon passed the Chinese contingent from the nearby camp, stood at attention, their colours proudly held by their young lieutenant. Christopher was moved close to tears by this simple expression of thanks and solidarity. He acknowledged the officer with a salute. Their paths had crossed only briefly, these two men who knew what it was to lead others in war and during the hard times that had followed the humiliation of defeat in battle, but that was enough to share a fleeting bond. The sight of the Chinese in their new uniforms brought a smile to his face. The American shirts and shorts were ridiculously too big for them and hung loosely from their emaciated limbs, but it didn't matter, they looked smart and could go home looking like the disciplined soldiers he knew them to be.

With Christopher and RSM Challis at their head, the Diehards marched, arms swinging, through the ruins of Kobe only one month short of three years since they had first arrived in the city. Christopher was proud of them. Many faces were missing, of course. Too many. Christopher took one last look up into the hills. He couldn't see the crematorium or the two casuarinas that guarded it. Those trees might be needed when the people of Kobe came to rebuild their city.

It was not long before the marching column fell into chaos. The Royal Artillery contingent at the front of the column stopped a passing tram and piled into it. Within minutes, the Royal Scots had done the same with the next tram. Challis caught Christopher's eye. RSMs didn't approve of chaos. Christopher didn't hesitate. 'We're going for a ride, Mr Challis. We'll need two trams. Let's stop the next two.'

They crammed themselves in, 130 Diehards, all that remained in Kobe of the 358 who had climbed aboard the *Lisbon Maru* in Hong Kong three years before. It was not long before the streets leading to the station echoed to the sound of soldiers singing at the top of their voices, happy beyond words to be going home. All the old war songs came out, and so did the Diehard versions with verses that would have made their mothers blush. The people of Kobe watched them go, uncomprehending. If they had anything to celebrate it was that there would be no more bombs, no more fire storms racing through the city, consuming everything in their path. And perhaps some of their fathers, husbands, brothers and sons would come home, too.

They left Kobe as darkness fell. Once on the train, each man was given an American five-man ration pack. They ate and ate until they could simply eat no more, no matter that it would mean leaving behind tins and packets of food that they would have given anything for until a few days ago. Christopher was unable to sleep. His mind kept turning to the prospect of Topsy being on the troop ship bringing former prisoners from Hong Kong. He had asked the American colonel if the civilian internees would be included, but he hadn't known and wasn't able to find out. It wasn't only thoughts of Topsy that kept Christopher awake. This journey was history being made and needed to be savoured and not lost in sleep.

As dawn broke, Mount Fuji came into view, its peak tantalisingly shrouded in cloud. They were taken in open trucks from Yokohama station to the docks. Christopher took in the view of the harbour. What a sight. Everywhere he looked, warships were at anchor. There were hundreds of them. The men were greeted on the quayside by an American swing band playing Glen Miller. Young American women in Red Cross uniform and carrying trays of cigarettes, sweets, magazines and toilet kit, descended on the new arrivals who scarcely dared believe their eyes and ears. They were led into a warehouse on the quay where they were to wait until called forward for the road journey out to the airfield. When the swing band took a break, the members of the Kobe House concert party joined them, borrowed some of their instruments and gave an impromptu performance of their own, much to the delight and amusement of the Americans.

The airfield was fifteen miles outside Yokohama. They were called out in batches of twenty and taken there in open trucks that roared through village after village, dust swirling everywhere. Close to the airfield, the woods and fields were littered with the remains of Japanese warplanes that had either crashed or been destroyed.

The trucks drew up outside a huge hangar. Christopher and Martin, covered in dark dust from the journey, stood in amazement as they looked around them. Christopher had to shout to be heard above the din. 'I've never seen anything like it. You have to see this to believe it.'

Everywhere they looked, aircraft were either landing, taking off or taxiing, with lorries dodging in and out beneath and between them. They watched as a truck full of Diehards dashed across the landing strip as a B-29 flew just a few feet above them.

They were greeted inside the hangar by the sound of New Orleans jazz being played by another big band. A long canteen had been set up along one side of the hangar, tables groaning with the weight of yet more Red Cross gifts and food.

'This is unreal,' shouted Martin. 'It's just like in the films. Pure Hollywood. I'm half expecting Errol Flyn to appear any moment.'

Christopher was helping himself to some fresh fruit from the canteen tables when a hand touched him on the shoulder, accompanied by a familiar voice. 'Hello Chris. Somehow, I knew you would make it.'

Christopher turned. It was Harry Badger. Graham Hill stood beside him, grinning broadly. Christopher had last seen them just before they and the so-called hard men of Shamshuipo Camp had left Kowloon for Japan, three weeks before the *Lisbon Maru* had sailed.

They shook hands and swapped news. Badger related how they had made it safely to Japan. They had been bombed on the way but had escaped with some near misses. They had been held in a camp on the outskirts of Tokyo. Life had been hard, and they had come close to being bombed out of the camp when the Americans had begun to hit the city. They had lost many of the Diehards who had been part of that first draft from Shamshuipo, among them Private 'The Major' Cullen who had uttered his last 'old boy' just over a year ago, and his fellow troublemaker Private Middleton, the Cockney who couldn't resist disrupting *tenko* parades with his rhyming slang. Middleton had almost made it to the end but had died just a few months ago. Predictably, Private 'Mickey' Head, who had survived the mock execution in Hong Kong for refusing to sign away his right to escape, had survived all that the Japanese had thrown at him in Tokyo and had been as defiant as ever right up to the last days of captivity.

Badger and Hill had already learned that Monkey Stewart had died. His absence was a rare cloud over the joy they felt to be going home themselves.

Lorries took them to the far side of the airfield where Douglas Skymasters were lined up waiting for them. They took off into a sun that was low in the early evening sky, four engines labouring hard as each Skymaster struggled to escape the ground and then slowly gained height. Suddenly, they were in cloud and their last sight of Japan had gone.

Sitting beside Christopher, Martin wrote briefly on a scruffy sheet of paper before rolling it up and inserting it into a length of hollowed out bamboo.

He looked satisfied. 'That's it then.'

Christopher gave him a questioning look.

'My diary. I began it that first day we arrived in Japan. Now that we've just left the bloody country, I've closed the book.'

Christopher said nothing. He wished he could close his book, but he couldn't.

The Skymaster reached its cruising height, flattened out and headed south-west towards Okinawa. Far ahead, the eye of Typhoon Ursula began to creep its way northwards across the Philippine Sea.

Farewell to Hong Kong

As David Man sat beside his sister-in-law close to the cemetery in Stanley Camp, he was hiding his frustration with her well. It wasn't proving easy to persuade her to accept his offer. He had explained to her that he had to get to Colombo as soon as his work in Hong Kong was complete. Colombo was set to serve as a staging post for the repatriation of former prisoners of war and internees, as well as the families who had been evacuated to Australia. Ships heading for England from Australia and the Far East usually stopped over in Colombo at the southern tip of Asia, so it would make sense if Topsy headed there, too. Instead of staying in Hong Kong for a couple of weeks, waiting for a ship, she could come with him as far as Calcutta. He told her of his work with Beryl Tidbury in London. Beryl had spent her childhood in Calcutta where she still had close family friends, the Hendersons. She had sent them a cable and they had offered to put Topsy up so that she could begin to recover from her ordeal before facing the long sea journey home.

Topsy wasn't too keen on flying, but that didn't fully explain her reluctance. She instinctively felt bad about the prospect of receiving privileged treatment and leaving others behind. It didn't feel right, especially when she thought of Phyllis. That wasn't all. She hung on to the hope that Christopher was alive and might be brought back to Hong Kong on the way home from Japan. She could imagine how he would feel if he came ashore looking for her and found that she had gone.

She needed time to think. 'Do I have to decide right now?'

David hesitated, feeling torn between twin loyalties. 'My work here should be finished by the end of tomorrow. I couldn't justify staying much longer after that. Think about it overnight. I'll come back first thing tomorrow for your answer.'

When he returned to Stanley the next morning, it was with fresh news. Overnight, he had received a cable informing him that all former prisoners of war in Japan were being flown by the Americans to the Philippines. They wouldn't be coming anywhere near Hong Kong. Topsy hesitated only briefly before making her decision. 'I'll come with you if we can take Phyllis Newnham with us. We're the only Diehard wives in the camp and we should stick together.'

They found Phyllis clearing out her room in Block 10. When Topsy put the offer to her, Phyllis wouldn't hear of it. 'You won't catch me going up in one of those. I can't stand the thought of flying. You should go. I'll be fine. Besides, I'm not leaving Hong Kong until I find out what happened to Lance. Where he's buried. I've somewhere to stay until I do.'

David turned to Topsy. 'That's settled then. I need to go to Kai Tak to find out about flights to Kunming. With a bit of luck, you've only one more night to spend in Stanley Camp.'

The next morning, there were tearful farewells with Daisy and her daughter Beryl. They were on the move, too, now that their husbands had been released from Shamshuipo. Apparently, their homes in Hong Kong were in a mess, but at least they had somewhere to go. It proved harder saying goodbye to Phyllis. Topsy had never forgotten that it was Phyllis who had influenced Monkey Stewart to change his mind and give Christopher permission to get married. Since then, the two women had shared so many ups and downs. For both of them, Hong Kong would always offer the best and worst of memories, but what made the farewell even more painful for Topsy was her awareness that while her future rested on the hope of finding her husband, for Phyllis, hope lay in finding her husband's grave.

Topsy wanted to make one last visit to her two places of retreat in the camp. For just a few moments, she sat once more on that rocky outcrop close to the east perimeter from where she had often watched the sun rise above the hills of the Shek O Peninsula on the far side of Tai Tam Bay. She would always associate the beach below with the English girl who in those early days had come to the wire and watched over the remains of her brother.

From there, Topsy walked to the other side of the camp, past the remains of Bungalow C, and paused at the fresh gravestones that marked the resting place of the fourteen victims of the bombing, already more than six months in the past. She sat awhile with her back against the familiar casuarina. If ever a place offered contrasting memories, it was here. She could still picture the dreadful execution of the seven men down there, just across the road close to the jetty. It had happened nearly two years ago, but the image of it had never left her. But this was also the place where she had come to close her eyes and inhale the memories of her life with Christopher.

She watched as the jeep carrying David Man turned off the road from Stanley village into the camp and climbed up towards camp headquarters. All that she owned was there, in a small Red Cross box. She had left it there so that she wouldn't have to return to an empty room.

She pushed herself to her feet and took one last look across Stanley Bay. Almost four years of her life had been wasted here. It was time to go.

Calcutta

The Dakota hit the runway with a thump and careered on for a few breath-taking seconds, barely under control, before slowing down and sloshing its way in a cloud of spray towards the nearest taxiway. Topsy breathed deeply, allowing the tension to seep out of her. David had said that a few days of rest in Calcutta in mid-September would be just what she needed to recover her strength. It would be cooler than the intense heat of high summer and the monsoon season would be all but over. She looked out of the window at the curtain of rain that swept across the airfield, driven by a fierce wind from the Bay of Bengal. She gave David a look of mock disapproval.

'I didn't enjoy that. I thought you said we'd miss the worst of the monsoons. If this is the best of them, I'm glad we didn't make it here when it was really wet.'

David was not a bit chastened. 'Don't worry. It'll pass. Take my word for it, in a couple of hours we'll be sitting on the verandah at the club, sipping our chota pegs in the sun.'

Topsy grinned. 'You can keep your whisky and soda. Mine's a gin and tonic.'

David was right. By the time the battered Ford taxi had driven them from the airfield to the Tollygunge Club, the storm had passed. They intended to stay at the club overnight until the Hendersons came to collect Topsy the next day. As for him, he was needed on duty in Colombo and would leave on the first flight out. He would call for her when he had news.

Okinawa

Christopher looked around him at the edge of the low plateau on Okinawa's west coast. He had needed to stretch his legs. These last few days he had spent too long being crammed into a train or lorry or plane. It was good to have space and time to himself. Immediately below was one of the beaches where the Americans had first landed when invading the island. Not that it was obvious now. The beach had been cleared of the debris of war and some American marines were having an early morning swim there. Nonetheless, he was aware that one of the most savage battles of the war had been fought on this island, and it had begun here. It was not yet three months since the battle for Okinawa had ended. The Japanese had not surrendered the island; they had simply fought until there were none of them left to fight and their generals had committed ritual suicide.

As far as Christopher could see, the plateau above the beaches was a sea of tents and prefabricated huts. Former prisoners of war in their hundreds were pouring into the camp, most of them from camps in Japan. Teams of bulldozers scurried like beetles along the camp perimeter, flattening out yet more ground in the frantic struggle to keep pace with the inflow.

Christopher was impatient to move on to the Philippines. They all were. They had been told to expect a wait of two days and to a man they resented every single hour of it. Christopher told himself it was ridiculous; after nearly four years of harsh captivity there was no point in getting worked up about two days. There might be nothing to do in Okinawa except wash, eat, sleep and wait for your name to be called, but a month ago they would have settled for that and counted their blessings.

It was late on the second day when the call came. They were told that they would be called forward in groups of twenty. That was all that a B-24 Liberator would take, and that was pushing it. They were heading for the main airbase in the Philippines and from there they would be taken into a camp just outside Manila.

The flight of eleven Liberators took off at first light the next morning. Christopher had been relieved to learn that nearly all the Diehards from Kobe and Tokyo had been allocated to the first eight aircraft. It was important to him that they kept together till the end, whenever and wherever that proved to be.

Sergeant Sid Gilham, Lance Corporal John Burke, and Privates Tom King and Ernie Pargeter were the only Diehards who found themselves in the ninth aircraft, separated from their mates. They had all fought together in Hong Kong. Burke had been part of the first group to be transported to Tokyo under the command of Harry Badger. The other three had survived the sinking of the *Lisbon Maru* and had endured the misery of imprisonment in Kobe. Now that they were on their way home, they didn't like being separated from the rest of the Diehards one bit. Gilham had been quick to reassure them. 'Don't worry. I'll make sure we rejoin the others when we get to the other end.'

Christopher shivered and drew a blanket round his shoulders as he looked about him. There wasn't much room for twenty passengers. They had to sit on wooden planks fitted above the bomb bay and couldn't lean back for fear of interfering with a network of wires and cables. The Liberator lumbered up to 8,000 feet and levelled out. At that height, the air temperature was just below freezing point. Beneath their feet, the wind whistled through the gaps between the folded shutters of the bomb racks.

Martin leant into Christopher's ear to make himself heard above the din of the Liberator's four Pratt and Whitney engines that were working hard against a strong headwind.

'Sod this for a game of soldiers, Chris. It's bloody freezing up here. And I can't even light my pipe.'

Christopher grinned. 'Just wait till it gets bumpy. You won't care how cold it is then.'

The co-pilot had warned them when he had given them their pre-flight briefing. A typhoon lay ahead of them, close to the Philippines. Once past Formosa, they could expect a rough ride.

Philippines

Christopher braced himself for the landing. All around him the others were doing the same, except for Ewan Graham. He was sprawled flat out on the wooden boards covering the bomb racks, too ill to care how rough the landing might be. All that mattered was feeling solid ground under him again. They had been in the air for six hours and Ewan was not the only one showing signs of having undergone a nightmare of a journey. Christopher was weak with airsickness and beside him, unusually quiet, eyes closed, Martin Weedon was looking decidedly green.

The B-24 Liberator hadn't escaped the typhoon unscathed, either. One of the port engines had shut down when they were still more than one hour's flying range from Nielson Field, their intended destination. The flight engineer had advised the pilot to get them on the ground as soon as possible, which meant diverting to Clark Field airbase.

The relief that the passengers felt after a tense landing was short-lived. They were driven to the airbase reception centre where an American staff-sergeant waited to brief them.

'Welcome to Clark Field, gentlemen. I'll give you the bad news first. You're still fifty miles from your new camp at Cavite, just outside Manila. We're gonna have to ferry you to Nielson Field airbase. You're going by air.'

He greeted their groans of protest with a broad smile and a raised hand.

'I know you've had a rough ride here. I won't bullshit you; it'll be bumpy up there again. But there's good news. You're going in one of Clark Field Airline's very best aircraft. It even has seats. And it'll take only forty minutes.'

Within an hour of landing, they were airborne again, having been fortified with a hasty black coffee and doughnut. It was not long before it became obvious that the turbulence was as bad as ever. The worst of the typhoon had moved to the north of Luzon by now, but what remained of it treated the Dakota with undiminished malevolence. Christopher and Martin sat side by side, their hands gripping the edge of their seats, willing the minutes to pass. Three times the pilot circled the Nielsen Field base, each time a bit lower, getting a feel for the gusts and air currents until at last he committed himself and put the wheels of his Dakota onto the runway. Twenty Diehards cheered and clapped their relief.

Christopher gave Martin a grin. 'I really do not want to do that again. I never thought that freedom would be like that.'

Martin was just as unimpressed. 'I tell you this Chris. There were times when I wished we were still lugging logs up in the hills of Ikuno.'

On arrival at the camp near Manila, the officers were allocated to three-man tents. Christopher and Martin found themselves sharing with Norman Brownlow. It was a fitting arrangement. Together, the three of them had been the key leaders of the temporary camp in Kobe during those hazardous days immediately after Japan's surrender.

That night, Christopher slept on a camp bed between clean sheets. It was the first time he had slept in a bed since Corporal Hughes had woken him and Topsy to announce that war had arrived in Hong Kong nearly four years ago. By all rights, sleep should have come easily. Reveille that day had been at two o'clock in the morning, and the two flights through the typhoon had drained him of energy. But sleep wouldn't come. The closer he came to finding news of Topsy, the more nervous he was of what that news might be. That wasn't all that was on his mind. Four Diehards couldn't be accounted for. Ever since they had arrived in the new camp close to Manila, rumours had begun to reach them that not all the aircraft in the flight from Okinawa had made it. There was talk that the ninth aircraft, 'Ginny', and two others were missing, but there was hope that they had been diverted elsewhere by the typhoon. Christopher sensed the presence of Monkey Stewart's legacy. Somehow, he felt responsible for bringing all the Diehards from Kobe home. He couldn't bear the thought that, after all that they had gone through, any of them should fail to make it home because of some freak storm. Back in Kobe, in those exhilarating days after the Japanese surrender, he had arranged for many of them to send cables home, confirming they were safe and giving news of their imminent return. There would be many families counting the days to promised reunions.

As Christopher struggled to find sleep, seven hundred miles to the north, the *Empress of Australia* weighed anchor in Hong Kong's Junk Bay. Aboard, several hundred former prisoners and internees from Shamshuipo, Argyle Street and Stanley had been ferried out to the ship and were settling down to their first night at sea on their journey home. Their first port of call would be Manila in the Philippines.

Christopher ignored the teeming rain and joined the queue to be issued with new clothing and kit. It was their third morning in the camp. They had been given notice that they would remain there for at least a week and had better get used to the rain. It was the wet season in Luzon. They would have to acclimatise in other ways, too. The process of adjusting to life as free men was not straightforward. They could now send their first letters home as free men but, unused to being free to write what they wanted, many of them struggled, scarcely knowing how to start. It was the same with food. For several days now, they had been offered all the food they could eat, but Christopher, like many others, simply couldn't cope with it. When he had been medically examined during their first day in the camp, he still weighed the same as when he was a thirteen-year-old.

They also had to learn to deal with their own impatience. They understood why they needed to wait their turn for a ship, but that scarcely reduced the sheer tedium of their existence. Just as they had been doing as prisoners of war, they were once more killing time.

But the worst of this wait was that they now knew that some of those who had fought with them in Hong Kong and then survived the nightmare of prison life under the Japanese would not be going home with them. For two days there had been nothing more than rumours, but last evening a notice had been posted on the board at camp headquarters. Three Liberators, 'Ginny', 'Les Miserables' and 'Liquidator', had crashed into the sea close to Formosa. The five crew members and eight of the twenty passengers from 'Les Miserables' had been picked up by a British cruiser, but there had been no survivors from 'Ginny' and 'Liquidator'. The news had hit them all hard, not least Christopher. Four more Diehard families were now destined to open their door to be given one of those cruel telegrams.

*

When Christopher returned to his tent, Martin had news for him. He had to report to camp headquarters where he would be interrogated. The Americans were wasting no time; they had already begun the process of investigating Japanese war crimes and tracking down those who needed to be brought to account in the courts. Christopher was relieved at the news. He had prepared well for this moment. It would be good to get this out of the way so that he could put it to one side and move on.

At the camp headquarters he was shown into a small room where Captain James Gardiner of the United States Judge Advocate General's Corps stood up from behind a plain wooden table and extended his hand in greeting. Gardiner had just graduated from law school when the Japanese bombed Pearl Harbor. He hadn't hesitated. He had put his planned legal career on hold and enlisted into the US Army. Still only twenty-five, he was now on the front line of the Allied hunt for Japanese war criminals.

He was crystal clear in explaining what he needed from Christopher. Any evidence given by him needed to stand up to being challenged in the courts. There would be proper trials in the form of international tribunals specifically set up for the task of bringing war criminals to justice. The normal rules of evidence would apply. Vague allegations about what may or may not have happened were of no use to him. If Christopher had not witnessed criminal conduct himself, Gardiner was not interested unless he could give him the details of someone who had.

Christopher took him through the log of events he had prepared. Gardiner was impressed. It was all there: hard details of the conduct; precise or approximate dates; names and rank of offenders; names of witnesses. Christopher hadn't witnessed the killing of wounded prisoners in Hong Kong but he was able to give Gardiner the names of those who had. Those who had fired the shots or stabbed with the bayonet were unlikely to be brought to justice, but the commanders who had allowed – even encouraged – the killing should be. It was the same for the Japanese refusal to allow the bodies of the dead to be recovered and treated with even basic dignity. Christopher didn't know who the senior Japanese commanders were and where the lines of guilt should be drawn. That was for the courts. He just wanted it to be recorded as having been part of the Japanese military culture against which individuals should be judged. For the rest, he gave chapter and verse of what he had witnessed. He did so as dispassionately as he could. The Japanese had indulged in a special form of cruelty. It had given them pleasure. It had gone far beyond what could be reasonably explained, let alone condoned, by the most perverse interpretation of the code of *bushido*.

By the time Christopher gave Gardiner the last names from his time in Ikuno Camp, his interrogation had lasted three hours. It left him drained, but had served a cathartic purpose. It was as if a burden he had carried for more than three years had finally been lifted from him and he could now safely leave it to be carried on by others. As he made his way back to his tent, he knew that he could now draw a line under his life at the hands of the Japanese. He had resolved, long ago, that once he was free, he would not live his future through his past. One more duty did remain though. He would do all he could to make sure that those who hadn't made it to freedom would not be forgotten.

*

The *Empress of Australia* eased her way through the wide entrance to Manila Bay and headed towards the port immediately ahead. The ship's captain had a lot on his mind. It had been smooth sailing so far, and they had avoided the worst of the typhoon by keeping well south of Formosa. But he was worried. Although the ship was already overcrowded, he was now expected to pick up hundreds of former prisoners of war from Japan. The ship had left Hong Kong four days ago with so many former prisoners of war and civilian internees that it had taken five days to ferry them out to the ship and embark them. There weren't enough bunks for them all, so hundreds of them had been sleeping on the ship's decks or in hammocks slung wherever space for them could be found.

Despite the overcrowding, morale had been high when the ship sailed from Hong Kong. It wasn't as if the passengers were unaccustomed to a lack of comfort and privacy. After nearly four years of it, what were a few more days? All that mattered was that they were going home. The mood had changed when they learned that the ship would be putting into Manila and would be at anchor there for six days. Manila was in ruins and was still recovering from the shock of Japanese occupation. Six days was an awfully long time to be stuck there with nothing to do.

*

It was two days after his debriefing by Captain Gardiner when Christopher learned that a troop ship carrying former prisoners of war and internees from Hong Kong was due to arrive that afternoon. He and other leaders were summoned to camp headquarters for a briefing. Captain Charles Monroe had been running the distribution centre of his family's international logistics business back home in West Virginia when the war had broken out and he had signed up to join the new US Army Transportation Corps. Just over three years later, here he was in the resettlement camp just outside Manila, responsible for arranging repatriation of all former prisoners of the Japanese, whatever their nationality and wherever they were heading. It was as if his previous life had prepared him for this task. Christopher immediately sensed that they were in the hands of someone who knew what he was doing. Monroe had some good news. The *Empress of Australia* would be at anchor in Manila for a few days. She was carrying former British prisoners and internees from Hong Kong. Some of them were due to disembark in Singapore, but the bulk of them were heading for England, calling in at Colombo and Aden on the way home. There wasn't room on her for all those British prisoners now in the camp. As an alternative, he could arrange flights to the United States from where they could travel home by sea. He needed to know who were volunteering to leave on the troopship and who were willing to either fly or sail to the United States. And he needed to know by the end of tomorrow.

Some of the Hong Kong prisoners of war were allowed ashore the next day. For the Diehards who had been held in Japan, their reunion with comrades they had left behind in Kowloon was hugely emotional. Stories, news and gossip were all shared over a plentiful supply of free beer. Not all the news was good. The new arrivals brought news that Lance Newnham had been executed, and in their turn, they were devastated to hear that Monkey Stewart had died in Osaka. Much of Christopher's mind was elsewhere. He asked around after Topsy. None of them brought news of her. Even worse, they told him that Stanley Camp had been bombed by mistake and there had been fatal casualties. Christopher went cold at the news. He fired questions at them. All they could tell him was that the loss of life had been limited to no more than a dozen or so. No, they hadn't come across any Diehard wives on the ship during their days at sea. That didn't necessarily mean they weren't on board. There were several thousand passengers of all sorts, and there wasn't the space on the ship to wander around looking for someone. All they knew was that there were hundreds of Stanley internees on board. Any of them left behind in Hong Kong, for whatever reason, were being offered passage on an aircraft carrier that was due to leave Hong Kong in ten days' time, but they would be sailing direct to Colombo and would not be calling into Manila.

Christopher felt crushed. He had dared to hope that someone would have known about Topsy. Then it occurred to him; Monroe might have access to the passenger list for the *Empress of Australia*. He made his way to camp headquarters. Monroe was up to his neck in aircraft serviceability reports when Christopher tracked him down, but he was happy to listen. He had not yet received the ship's passenger list, but he could arrange for the ship to be called up on the radio and asked to check for specific names. Were there any other names to look for? Christopher had to check his memory. As far as he knew, he and Lance Newnham had been the only Diehards whose wives had remained in Hong Kong after the evacuation in 1940.

Monroe advised Christopher to come back in a couple of hours. That would give him time to get a call through to the ship and for the list to be checked.

To kill time, Christopher went for a walk by himself. He wasn't the best of company for the reunion that was in full flow. He needed to clear his own thoughts. If Topsy was on the ship, there was nothing to decide. But if she wasn't? What then? He wouldn't know why she wasn't on board. Nor would he know if she would be on the warship that was scheduled to sail direct to Colombo from Hong Kong.

When Christopher returned to camp headquarters, Monroe was not in his office, but he had left a message for him. Georgina Man and Phyllis Newnham were not on board the Empress.

Chapter 37

Reunions

Calcutta

The telegram from David Man could not have arrived at a better time for Topsy. She had been in Calcutta for nearly three weeks. David had been right; it had been just the rest she needed before making the long journey home. Each day she had felt her strength returning so that by now she was feeling almost like her old self. Not that she had a clear sense of what her old self had been before the Japanese had interned her. It hadn't been easy to adjust to something approaching normal life. Even now, she hadn't quite shaken off her years of camp life. She still felt it the height of luxury to sleep between clean sheets in a bed, to wash her hair with shampoo and clean her hands with soap. She knew that she would never allow herself to take such things for granted again. She had needed to learn once more what it was to take her time over a meal, to enjoy the occasion of it. Meals in Stanley Camp had rarely been more than a joyless, rushed intake of sufficient fuel to give her the strength to get through another day. Pleasure and conversation hadn't come into it.

The Hendersons had gone out of their way to make her feel at home in their colonial-style bungalow in Alipore on the southern fringe of the city. They had insisted on kitting her out with new clothes. On Topsy's second day in the house, a dressmaker had appeared and taken her measurements. Within a week she had returned with a silk jacket, three dresses, four blouses and a small pile of underwear.

Topsy's life as the guest of an established colonial family had quickly settled into a comfortable routine. Morning walks taken before the sun rose too high, a tiffin lunch served on one of the bungalow's verandahs, a swim at the Tollygunge Club in the afternoon followed by an early evening film or game of bridge at the club before returning home for a dinner served with style by the Henderson's butler.

She had read the telegram several times. FLIGHT 10 A.M. SAT 29 SEP TO COLOMBO. WILL COLLECT FROM AIRPORT. SEA PASSAGE HOME FIRST WEEK OCT.

She was ready to move on. She still had no news of Christopher and felt out of touch up here in Calcutta. David had established himself in Colombo which had become a key hub for repatriation. She would feel more at ease down there. The Hendersons had been generous hosts without smothering her with attention. Thanks to them, she was now better prepared for what lay ahead of her. Their own lifestyle was itself about to change and they knew it. India would never be the same. The war may have ended in victory, but it had unleashed forces that were unstoppable.

Colombo

Far to the south in Colombo, David Man had requisitioned a complete floor of rooms at the Galle Face Hotel. The hotel had escaped unscathed from the few bombing raids mounted against the city by the Japanese. Close to the port and sitting at the very edge of the Indian Ocean, it provided ideal short-term accommodation for those passing through the city on their way home in the aftermath of war.

As promised, David was at the airport to meet Topsy. He looked at her anxiously as she waited to collect her new suitcase. The Dakotas were a splendid, reliable workhorse but they were not known for their quiet and comfort. A seven-hour flight from Calcutta was not for the faint-hearted. He needn't have worried; Topsy looked a whole lot better than when he had left her in Calcutta. From the airport, it was a twenty-mile drive that closely followed the line of the waterfront to the Galle Face. The two of them had plenty to talk about, but Topsy had only one thing on her mind.

'Any news of Christopher?'

David shook his head. 'I'm afraid not. Things are still very confused. What I do know is that there's an aircraft carrier, HMS *Smiter*, due to arrive in Colombo tomorrow or the day after. She's carrying some of the former prisoners from Shamshuipo and Argyle Street and internees from Stanley. I've checked the passenger list and Phyllis Newnham is on board.'

Topsy let out a sigh of relief. 'So she made it. I was worried that looking for Lance's grave might leave her stranded in Hong Kong. But what do you know about the prisoners from Japan?'

'I know that some of them are on the *Empress of Australia*. They embarked at Manila in the Philippines but I don't know how many of them or what unit they are. They left Manila a week ago and are due into Colombo on the second of October, that's next Tuesday.'

Topsy's face lit up. 'I hope that's an omen. It's my fifth wedding anniversary.'

David made a show of crossing his fingers.

'I'll book you onto the *Empress of Australia*. She'll be in port here for a couple of days. I promise you, as soon as she arrives, I'll get a copy of her passenger list and let you know straight away. There's no point in your hanging on here if Christopher isn't on board.'

Topsy thought about that for moment.

'Tell me straight David, what are the chances of Christopher being on the *Empress*? I've got to the point where I don't know what to think.'

David felt uncomfortable. He was aware that he wasn't just a Colonial Office representative doing his job; he was a brother-in-law, too. He looked straight ahead, concentrating on his driving.

'I really don't know. There are thousands of former Allied prisoners being repatriated from Japan and most of them are being channelled through the Philippines. Some are being offered flights and sailings to America. The trouble is, I can communicate with the authorities in Hong Kong, but I'm not yet in direct touch with the Americans in Manila.'

Topsy didn't know why, but she sensed that David was holding something back from her. She gave him a long, hard look.

'There's something you're not telling me. I need to know everything. If there's bad news, I deserve to know it.'

David pulled over and stopped the car. He looked Topsy directly in the eye.

'I'm sorry. I didn't want to worry you unnecessarily. But I suppose there are bound to be rumours going the rounds soon. We learned yesterday from the Americans at the airbase here that three aircraft were lost on flights bringing Allied prisoners from Okinawa to Manila. There's a rumour that there may have been a fourth. They went down in one of the worst typhoons the region has experienced in years. There were around twenty former prisoners on each of those aircraft, but we don't yet know who they were. I'm afraid they are missing, presumed dead.'

October 2nd

Christopher leaned against the port rail on the top deck of the *Empress of Australia* and took in the view of the Colombo waterfront. He had last seen the city eight years ago when he was on his way to join the Diehards in Hong Kong. Those had been exciting times for a young officer joining his battalion on his first posting overseas. That time, he'd been able go ashore during the ship's two days there.

He recalled how struck he had been by the blazing kaleidoscope of colour wherever you looked, whether from the ship across the glistening surface of the harbour or from a trishaw threading its perilous way through the chaos of the city's streets. This time, there would be no shore leave, and although the colour remained as dazzling as before, the excitement had been replaced by anxiety. Today was his fifth wedding anniversary. He had spent only one anniversary with Topsy, their first. He had marked the second by escaping from the hell of Hold 2 on the *Lisbon Maru* and swimming to Qingbang Island. The third and fourth anniversaries had been spent whilst they were both unwilling guests of Emperor Hirohito, separated by the breadth of the East China Sea. He'd had high hopes that the fifth would see them reunited, but those hopes had just been dealt a cruel blow.

The *Empress of Australia* had anchored in Colombo harbour soon after first light that morning. Closer to the shore, almost within hailing distance, the auxiliary aircraft carrier HMS *Smiter* had been at anchor since the day before. Passengers on the *Empress* had been briefed that some of the warship's passengers were being disembarked at Colombo while others would be transferred onto the *Empress*. The *Empress* had disembarked several passengers in Singapore and now had space to take on a few more. Not that there was much of it. When they had boarded the ship in Manila, Christopher had opted to set himself up on one of the upper decks where they slept on camp beds, so tightly packed that the beds and all their kit had to be packed up each morning at reveille so that the passengers could move about. Martin had opted for a hammock on a lower deck and had quickly regretted it.

As soon as Christopher had learned about the intended transfer of passengers between the two ships, he had hurried to the purser's office and asked if he had a copy of *Smiter*'s passenger list. He had. Christopher had run his finger down the list. Phyllis Newnham was listed but there was no Georgina Man. Christopher had been left numb. If both Phyllis and Topsy had been missing from the list, he would have been less worried. It could have meant that other arrangements had been made for some of the internees from Stanley, although the purser wasn't aware of any.

Christopher's mind was still racing as he watched the comings and goings in the harbour from the ship's rail. Why had Topsy not travelled on either the warship or the *Empress*? He couldn't think of an explanation that offered him any comfort. He couldn't even ask Phyllis. He had checked with the purser; she wasn't listed as one of the *Smiter*'s passengers being transferred to the *Empress*.

He watched as a launch made its way out from the harbour quay. He had seen it leave HMS *Smiter*, presumably ferrying some of the passengers ashore.

He assumed it was now returning to the warship to collect more of them, but instead it held its course towards the Empress. The launch drew alongside and paused just long enough for a man to step nimbly across to the small platform at the bottom of the ship's gangway. It then pulled away and headed for the warship. There was something vaguely familiar about the way the young man carried himself, but Christopher couldn't place him. Looking down from the upper deck, he couldn't make out the face beneath the Panama hat. Not that he was all that interested. His mind was elsewhere.

*

Topsy watched as the *Empress of Australia* edged her way towards her anchorage in the harbour some two miles to the north. Yesterday she had watched HMS *Smiter* follow the same course. Seen from her deck chair on the first-floor verandah of the Galle Face Hotel, the deep blue of the Indian Ocean was framed by a succession of palm trees that rose tall and spindly in the foreground from amongst the lawns and low shrubs of the hotel's neat gardens. At this distance, the *Empress* seemed to be scarcely moving at all but Topsy was able to measure the ship's progress as she nudged her bow level with one tree and then, painfully slowly, with the next.

She had shared last evening's dinner with two of her former colleagues from the University Relief Hospital in Hong Kong. Margaret and Anne had arrived on the warship and were being treated to two nights ashore before boarding the *Empress of Australia*.

Topsy had arranged to share a bottle of champagne with them at lunchtime to celebrate her fifth wedding anniversary. She was determined to mark it in some way or other. She knew Christopher would want her to.

By now, she was weary beyond words with running the possibilities through her mind. She had only ever received two brief letters from him during the entire length of their separation. The last had been written in March of the previous year. She had hoped that David might have more up-to-date news of him by now, but he hadn't. For months, she had been haunted by the fear that Christopher had been killed by the American bombing of Japan. There had been disturbing rumours about prison camps being hit by accident. Then, two days ago, David had broken the news about the loss of the aircraft in the typhoon on the way from Japan to the Philippines. She couldn't help but fear the worst.

*

Christopher was on his second lap of the upper deck when the call came for him over the ship's tannoy. He was to report to the purser's office immediately.

As soon as he spotted the slim figure standing at the door to the purser's office, Christopher recognised his younger brother. He'd last seen David when he was in his final year at boarding school, eight years ago, but now that the Panama hat had been removed, there was no mistaking that mop of hair, the slightest tilt of the head, the way he stood, hands in the small of his back.

As they hugged, David gave him the news. 'Topsy's here in Colombo. She's fine.'

Christopher held on to him and allowed the tears to come. It was as if all the stored-up hurt of the past four years – all the grieving for lost comrades, all those hopes raised and then dashed, all that anger never satisfied, those countless humiliations never avenged and the ever-present fear for Topsy's safety – had at last found a way out of him.

An hour later, a harbour launch brought the two brothers ashore, Christopher having been given special shore leave after David had had a word with the ship's captain. David's duties in Colombo were due to end when the *Empress of Australia* sailed. He would then be headed for Australia to help repatriate the British families who had been evacuated there back in 1940. He didn't expect to be back home in England until just before Christmas.

They said their goodbyes in the port's passenger terminal. Christopher was still feeling overwhelmed by their chance meeting. He was conscious that they had a lot of catching up to do and was reluctant to go their separate ways again so soon.

'Let's promise that we won't let another eight years pass before we see each other again.'

'Promise.'

'And thanks for everything you've done to make sure Topsy was safe. I can't tell you what it means to me.'

'I'm just happy that I was able to. I'll always be able to say that I first met my sister-in-law when I got her out of prison.'

And with that, David turned and made his way back along the quayside to take the next launch out to HMS *Smiter*. He still had many names to track down over the next two days.

Christopher watched him go until he reached the far door of the terminal where he turned and waved before being lost from view. Christopher looked around for a taxi. He had a choice between a trishaw and a solitary four-door Ford that had seen better days. He chose the car: he'd had enough of being crammed into tight spaces.

The Tamil driver saw him approaching and leapt out to open the door.

'Where to, Sir?'

Christopher gave him a broad smile. 'I'd very much like you to take me to the Galle Face please. And on the way, I want to stop and buy some flowers.'

*

Two miles to the south, Topsy relaxed in the shade of the verandah that ran along the west face of the hotel's first floor. She was immersed in the pages of *Brideshead Revisited* which had been published earlier in the year. The Henderson's had bought a copy for her as a farewell gift, promising her that once she started reading it, she wouldn't be able to put it down. They were mistaken. Books had been a rare treat in Stanley Camp and time to read them had been endless. Topsy had learned to savour the reading of them at a gentle pace.

In half an hour, a hotel waiter would bring the bottle of champagne she had ordered, and Margaret and Anne would join her to toast her fifth wedding anniversary. Four glasses were already on the table. The fourth was for her brother-in-law. David had promised to make it if his duties allowed. With luck, he might bring news of Christopher.

Epilogue

Two days after their reunion in Colombo, Christopher and Topsy Man sailed together on the *Empress of Australia* and arrived in England three weeks later.

Christopher was awarded the Military Cross for his part in the battle for Hong Kong. He rose to the rank of Major General and would have risen higher but for those four lost years as a prisoner of war. Like many others who were imprisoned by the Japanese, his subsequent career prospects suffered because his contemporaries had meanwhile been earning their spurs and coming to prominence in the defeat of Germany in Europe. To his great disappointment, he never commanded the Diehards, but as a Major General he was appointed Colonel of the Regiment, an honorary role of which he was immensely proud. Christopher made a return visit to Hong Kong in 1949. He was determined that the kindness and courage of the Chinese fishermen who had saved so many lives after the sinking of the *Lisbon Maru* should not be forgotten. He organised a fund amongst the survivors and was present when the governor of Hong Kong presented a motor fishing launch and funds to Qingbang's island elder.

Like many of his contemporaries, he rarely spoke of his war and harboured no hatred of post-war Japan and its people. He visited Kobe in 1963 on a diplomatic mission, after which he reflected as follows. 'It is no good keeping hate alive, but it is not, I think, a bad thing to take one's memories out from time to time, and dust them off. To remember the comradeship and courage of those days in Kobe, and most of all those who were not lucky enough to be able to make, like me, the pilgrimage back.'

He did, however, live for many years with a quiet anger that those returning from captivity in the Far East did not receive the respect and attention they deserved. When at last they finally arrived home in late autumn 1945, it seemed to him, and to many of those who had suffered similar experience, as if the nation, the army and even the hierarchy of his own regiment had basked for six months in the joys of victory in Europe and were so intent on moving on that the return of the former prisoners of war was regarded by some almost as an inconvenient intrusion.

Topsy never fully recovered her health. To her and Christopher's great sadness, her treatment at the hands of the Japanese left her unable to have children. She never spoke about what had happened to her when the Japanese captured the hospital in which she was serving; even amongst those closest to her it was a strictly taboo subject. I have chosen to respect her wish by not speculating about it when writing this story. Like Christopher, she didn't allow her subsequent life to be defined by what had happened to her during the war; despite her fragile health, she never lost her sense of fun and zest for life.

In retirement, the couple lived in Perthshire where they died within a few months of each other in their mid-seventies. They lie together in Kilmaveonaig Church cemetery, Blair Atholl.

Martin Weedon left the Army within a year of his return to England and trained as a barrister at Gray's Inn. He was awarded the Military Cross for his part in the battle on the Stanley Peninsula. He never fully recovered from the war and his imprisonment by the Japanese, and it was a changed man who returned home. He and Elizabeth were divorced and they both remarried. He died in his early sixties in a tragic shooting accident. I am most grateful to his son Mark who kindly entrusted me with the impressive diary which his father wrote in Kobe and which was published under the title *Guest of an Emperor*.

Tony Hewitt, Eddy Crossley and Douglas Scriven made it to the safety of the Chinese Nationalist lines and on to the British military mission in Kukong. On the way they had to fight for their lives, surviving several attacks by armed bandit gangs and pirates and coming close to recapture by the Japanese. Their extraordinary story is recorded in Hewitt's book 'Bridge with Three Men'. All three were awarded the Military Cross. Tony Hewitt made his way back to England via India in time to join the Diehards' second battalion and take part in the Normandy landings and the defeat of Germany. He married Martin Weedon's former wife Elizabeth in 1948 and went on to follow a successful military career. He died in 2004, aged 89.

Eddy Crossley returned to flying duties in North Africa, Sicily and Italy until the end of the war, finishing as a Squadron Leader. Back home in Wellington, New Zealand, he began a business career but died in an accident in 1958, aged 39.

Douglas Scriven rejoined the war against the Japanese, commanding a field ambulance in Burma and Java, and finishing the war in the rank of Colonel. In time, he returned to Hong Kong where he took up private practice until his death in 1989, aged 79.

Frank Waldron returned to Hong Kong when the Diehards were posted there in 1949 and remained with the regiment until he retired from the Army, having been granted a Quartermaster Commission and reaching the rank of Major.

William Beningfield outlived all other Diehards who had survived the sinking of the *Lisbon Maru*. He emigrated to Canada where he died in 2020, aged 100.

Lance Newnham's body was recovered from the beach at Shek O and was reinterred in the cemetery at Stanley, as Phyllis had wished. She stayed for several days in Colombo with a member of the family before sailing home to England. A year later, King George VI presented her with Lance's George Cross, awarded to him posthumously for his courage in resisting interrogation under torture.

Monkey Stewart was posthumously awarded the Distinguished Service Order for his gallant leadership of the Diehards during the battle for Hong Kong. His ashes lie in the Yokohama War Cemetery administered by the Commonwealth War Graves Commission.

Willard Johnson's original drawing of the doomed *Lisbon Maru* is in the care of the National Army Museum and is reproduced on a memorial stone at the National Memorial Arboretum.

Of the six men who crewed the two Avenger torpedo bombers involved in the mid-air collision witnessed by Topsy in January 1945, only one survived. Pilot Lieutenant Richard Hunt parachuted clear of his stricken aircraft but was badly burned and broke his leg. He was captured by the Japanese and transported to a prisoner-of-war camp in Japan where he died, aged 21.

Lin Agen was the last survivor of those fisherman who took part in the epic rescue of 2 October 1942. He died in 2020, aged 96. His ashes were carried to the pier at the edge of the beach where all those years ago he and his fellow fishermen had brought survivors ashore. After a simple farewell ceremony, his ashes were cast into the sea, not far from where the wreck of the *Lisbon Maru* and the remains of several hundred prisoners of war still lie in thirty metres of water. Over the years, several survivors of the tragedy visited Qingbang and its neighbouring islands to thank in person these brave communities who had come to their aid.

The war crimes trials conducted in Hong Kong and Yokohama soon after the end of the war brought several of the Japanese who are mentioned in this book to justice.

In Hong Kong, Colonel Tokunaga, who commanded all the prison camps in the colony, and Captain Saito, his medical officer, were sentenced to death by hanging. Tokunaga's sentence was subsequently commuted to imprisonment for life, Saito's to twenty years imprisonment. If either of them lived out their sentence with a conscience, it would have needed room for the ghosts of many hundreds of prisoners. Colonel Noma and Sergeant Major Yamada of the Kempeitai were both hanged, ironically in the same Stanley Prison in which they had subjected Lance Newnham and others to a regime of torture. Tokunaga's ubiquitous and sadistic interpreter Niimori was sentenced to fifteen years imprisonment. Many would judge him to have been fortunate. His accomplice in malice, Lieutenant Wada, was killed during the defence of Japan's Pacific islands, thereby escaping the justice of the courts. Kyoda Shigeru, the master of the *Lisbon Maru*, was also tried in Hong Kong and was sentenced to seven years imprisonment. All prison sentences were served in Stanley Prison.

In Yokohama, justice caught up with Colonel Murata, who had been responsible for all the camps in the Osaka area. He was sentenced to imprisonment for life. Captain Morimoto was sentenced to forty years imprisonment for the cruel and neglectful regime he had imposed at Kobe House, a regime which had allowed Sergeant Morita to indulge his own brand of sadistic brutality. Morita was sentenced to fifteen years imprisonment.

Another sadist, Corporal Minemoto, was brought to account for his killing of the American prisoner in Tanagawa Camp before his redeployment to Ikuno Camp. He was sentenced to ten years imprisonment. All prison sentences were served with hard labour. The 'mad doctor', who had habitually run amok in Kobe House, was not identified and it is not known if he was ever brought to justice.

The Diehards' Colours that had been buried in the grounds of Government House were never found, but the regimental silver survived the Japanese occupation of Singapore and was recovered intact. The site of the camp at Stanley has changed little over the decades that followed the end of the war, but nothing now remains of the other camps at Shamshuipo and Argyle Street in Hong Kong and at Kobe and Ikuno in Japan. Memories of the horrors that took place within them have now been taken to the graves of those who experienced them. If they live on at all, it is in stories such as this.

Author's Acknowledgements

In recording Christopher and Topsy Man's remarkable story, I have kept as much faith with historical accuracy as is possible at a distance of 80 years from the troubled times in which it unfolded.

I am grateful to those who entrusted me with access to personal letters, diaries and family records of Christopher and Topsy Man, Martin Weedon, Monkey Stewart and Phyllis Newnham, and to the dwindling band of fellow Diehards who assisted and encouraged me along the way. I hope that the completed story does justice to the memory of those who inspired the writing of it.

Bibliography

Banham, T., *The Sinking of the Lisbon Maru* (2006).
Carew, T., *Hostages to Fortune* (1971).
Carew, T., *The Fall of Hong Kong* (*1960*).
Dew, G., *Prisoner of the Japs* (1943).
Finch, B., *A Faithful Record of the Lisbon Maru Incident* (2007).
Hewitt, A., *Bridge With Three Men* (1986).
Kemp, P., *The Middlesex Regiment (Duke of Cambridge's Own)* (1956).
Lindsay, O., *The Lasting Honour* (1978).
Salmon, A., and C. Henderson, *Remember My Face* (1997).
Weedon, M., *Guest of an Emperor* (1948).